INFORMATION SYSTEMS

Video training courses are available on the subjects of these books in the
James Martin ADVANCED TECHNOLOGY LIBRARY of over 300 tapes and disks,
from ALI INC., 1751 West Diehl Road, Naperville, IL 60566 (tel: 312-369-3000).

Database	Telecommunications	Networks and Data Communications	Society
AN END USER'S GUIDE TO DATABASE	TELECOMMUNICATIONS AND THE COMPUTER (third edition)	PRINCIPLES OF DATA COMMUNICATION	THE COMPUTERIZED SOCIETY
PRINCIPLES OF DATABASE MANAGEMENT (second edition)	FUTURE DEVELOPMENTS IN TELECOMMUNICATIONS (third edition)	TELEPROCESSING NETWORK ORGANIZATION	TELEMATIC SOCIETY: A CHALLENGE FOR TOMORROW
COMPUTER DATABASE ORGANIZATION (third edition)	COMMUNICATIONS SATELLITE SYSTEMS	SYSTEMS ANALYSIS FOR DATA TRANSMISSION	TECHNOLOGY'S CRUCIBLE
MANAGING THE DATABASE ENVIRONMENT (second edition)	ISDN	DATA COMMUNICATION TECHNOLOGY	VIEWDATA AND THE INFORMATION SOCIETY
DATABASE ANALYSIS AND DESIGN	**Distributed Processing**	DATA COMMUNICATION DESIGN TECHNIQUES	TELEVISION AND THE COMPUTER
VSAM: ACCESS METHOD SERVICES AND PROGRAMMING TECHNIQUES	COMPUTER NETWORKS AND DISTRIBUTED PROCESSING	SNA: IBM's NETWORKING SOLUTION	THE WORLD INFORMATION ECONOMY
DB2: CONCEPTS, DESIGN, AND PROGRAMMING	DESIGN AND STRATEGY FOR DISTRIBUTED DATA PROCESSING	ISDN	**Systems In General**
IDMS/R: CONCEPTS, DESIGN, AND PROGRAMMING	**Office Automation**	LOCAL AREA NETWORKS: ARCHITECTURES AND IMPLEMENTATIONS	A BREAKTHROUGH IN MAKING COMPUTERS FRIENDLY: THE MACINTOSH COMPUTER
SQL	IBM's OFFICE AUTOMATION ARCHITECTURE	OFFICE AUTOMATION STANDARDS	SAA: IBM's SYSTEMS APPLICATION ARCHITECTURE
Security	OFFICE AUTOMATION STANDARDS	DATA COMMUNICATION STANDARDS	
SECURITY, ACCURACY, AND PRIVACY IN COMPUTER SYSTEMS		CORPORATE COMMUNICATIONS STRATEGY	
SECURITY AND PRIVACY IN COMPUTER SYSTEMS		COMPUTER NETWORKS AND DISTRIBUTED PROCESSING: SOFTWARE, TECHNIQUES, AND ARCHITECTURE	

DB2

A _James Martin_ **BOOK**

THE JAMES MARTIN BOOKS
currently available from Prentice Hall

- Application Development Without Programmers
- Communications Satellite Systems
- Computer Data-Base Organization, Second Edition
- Computer Networks and Distributed Processing: Software, Techniques, and Architecture
- Design and Strategy of Distributed Data Processing
- Design of Man-Computer Dialogues
- Design of Real-Time Computer Systems
- An End User's Guide to Data Base
- Fourth-Generation Languages, Volume I: Principles
- Future Developments in Telecommunications, Second Edition
- Information Engineering, Book I: Introduction and Principles
- Information Engineering, Book II: Strategy and Analysis
- An Information Systems Manifesto
- Introduction to Teleprocessing
- Managing the Data-Base Environment
- Principles of Data-Base Management
- Recommended Diagramming Standards for Analysts and Programmers
- Security, Accuracy, and Privacy in Computer Systems
- Strategic Data-Planning Methodologies
- Systems Analysis for Data Transmission
- System Design from Provably Correct Constructs
- Technology's Crucible
- Telecommunications and the Computer, Second Edition
- Telematic Society: A Challenge for Tomorrow
- Teleprocessing Network Organization

with Carma McClure
- Action Diagrams: Clearly Structured Specifications, Programs, and Procedures, Second Edition
- Diagramming Techniques for Analysts and Programmers
- Software Maintenance: The Problem and Its Solutions
- Structured Techniques: The Basis for CASE, Revised Edition

with The ARBEN Group, Inc.
- A Breakthrough in Making Computers Friendly: The Macintosh Computer
- Data Communication Technology
- Fourth-Generation Languages, Volume II: Representative 4GLs
- Fourth-Generation Languages, Volume III: 4GLs from IBM
- Local Area Networks: Architectures and Implementations
- Principles of Data Communication
- SNA: IBM's Networking Solution
- Strategic Information Planning Methodologies, Second Edition
- VSAM: Access Method Services and Programming Techniques

with Kathleen Kavanagh Chapman and Joe Leben
- DB2: Concepts, Design, and Programming

with Adrian Norman
- The Computerized Society

with Steven Oxman
- Building Expert Systems

DB2:
Concepts, Design, and Programming

JAMES MARTIN

with
Kathleen Kavanagh Chapman
Joe Leben

PRENTICE HALL, Englewood Cliffs, New Jersey 07632

Library of Congress Cataloging-in-Publication Data

```
Martin, James
    DB2, concepts, design, and programming.

    "A James Martin book."
    Includes index.
    1. Data base management.  2. IBM Database 2
(Computer system)  I. Chapman, Kathleen Kavanagh.
II. Leben, Joe.  III. Title.
QA76.9.D3M363  1989    005.75'65        88-30727
ISBN 0-13-198581-7
```

Editorial/production supervision: *Kathryn Gollin Marshak and Karen Skrable Fortgang*
Jacket design: *Bruce Kenselaar*
Manufacturing buyer: *Mary Ann Gloriande*

Printed in the United States of America

10 9 8 7 6 5 4 3 2 1

ISBN   0-13-198581-7

PRENTICE-HALL INTERNATIONAL (UK) LIMITED, *London*
PRENTICE-HALL OF AUSTRALIA PTY. LIMITED, *Sydney*
PRENTICE-HALL CANADA INC., *Toronto*
PRENTICE-HALL HISPANOAMERICANA, S.A., *Mexico*
PRENTICE-HALL OF INDIA PRIVATE LIMITED, *New Delhi*
PRENTICE-HALL OF JAPAN, INC., *Tokyo*
SIMON & SCHUSTER ASIA PTE. LTD., *Singapore*
EDITORA PRENTICE-HALL DO BRASIL, LTDA., *Rio de Janeiro*

CONTENTS

PART III

QUERY MANAGEMENT FACILITY (QMF)

PART V DB2 SYSTEM ADMINISTRATION

PART **VII** **APPENDIXES**

PREFACE

Databases are playing an increasingly important role in supporting an enterprise's information processing requirements. The development of corporate databases will continue to be an extremely important data processing activity for many years to come. Data will be regarded as a vital corporate resource that must be managed so as to maximize its value. Both the quantity of data stored and the complexity of its organization are increasing by leaps and bounds.

The pointer-structured databases of an earlier era are giving way to *relational* database technology because relational databases are more flexible, are based on formal mathematics, and support a wide diversity of user languages. SQL is now an international standard, and many different user tools produce SQL code that can execute with DB2 or other relational databases.

DB2 is a *relational* database management system (DBMS) and is IBM's primary strategic product in the database area. Much other IBM software is being designed to link to DB2, and this represents a major part of IBM's strategic thrust in software. DB2, along with associated products such as Query Management Facility (QMF) and Data Extract (DXT), provides a wide range of capabilities, suitable for both ad hoc access by end users and the development of production applications by professional programmers.

ACKNOWLEDGMENTS The authors would like to thank Peter Tierney, Vice President of Marketing for Oracle Corporation, who supplied us with a copy of the very fine Oracle relational DBMS. We were able to use Oracle, running on an IBM Personal Computer AT, to initially develop the SQL examples and to validate the content of tables in Chapter 2 and in Appendix I. Two people at IBM contributed to the writing of this book: John Gridley made it possible for us to develop the QBE examples on an IBM mainframe in Chicago, and Bill Kellow provided the technical information needed to write the parts of the book that deal with the referential integrity features of DB2.

James Martin
Kathleen K. Chapman
Joe Leben

DB2

PART █ **INTRODUCTION**

Part I of this book examines key concepts underlying DB2, IBM's large-system relational database management system. Chapter 1 examines the characteristics generally associated with a *database management system* (DBMS) and the functions and facilities provided by the DB2 program product and related products such as *Query Management Facility* (QMF) and *Data Extract* (DXT). Chapter 2 then introduces the *relational model,* examines key concepts associated with it, and shows how DB2 implements relational DBMS facilities. Chapter 3 looks at the three views of data that are used with database management systems and examines how these views are implemented by DB2.

1 THE DB2 ENVIRONMENT

THE DB2 PRODUCT FAMILY
DATABASE 2, or DB2 as it is more commonly called, is one of several database products offered by IBM. DB2 is a relational database management system designed for the large-system (MVS) environment.* IBM offers another relational database management system, called SQL/DS, for midrange systems running DOS/VS or VM. The first database management system offered by IBM was Information Management System (IMS), which also runs in the MVS environment. A product called DL/I is the counterpart to IMS for midrange systems running the DOS/VS operating system.

In addition to DB2 itself, there are two other important program products that are widely used in the DB2 environment to extend the capabilities of DB2. These two products are closely associated with DB2, and we will be making numerous references to them throughout the book:

- **Query Management Facility (QMF).** QMF is a product that serves as an easy-to-use front end to DB2. It allows end users to retrieve data interactively, to format data into reports, and to display the data graphically.

- **Data Extract (DXT).** DXT is used to extract data from IMS, SQL/DS, or DB2 databases, from VSAM files, or from physical sequential files in order to make the data available to DB2.

---

*Many terms used in data processing literature begin as two or more words, such as *real-time* or *offline*. It is quite common in the computer industry for a widely accepted, often-used term to evolve into a new single word. The term *database* is now widely used and generally accepted as one word. In this book, we use the term *database* except when we are referring to an IBM product or manual name that uses the older two-word form. It is interesting to note that at the time of this writing, IBM uses the one-word form in naming the DB2 product—DATABASE 2—but continues to use the two-word form in the text of the DB2 reference manuals.

BOX 1.1   IBM products that can be used with DB2.

- **DB2 Performance Monitor.** This product is used to collect and format information about DB2 system and application activity.
- **Data Base Relational Application Directory.** This product provides directory support for application development in the DB2 environment.
- **Host Data Base View.** This product can be used to extract DB2 data and make it available to an IBM Personal Computer.
- **Data Base Migration Aid Utility.** This product helps migrate data and catalog information from one DB2 system to another.
- **Data Base Edit Facility.** This product provides a simple-to-use interface for DB2 data manipulation.
- **Cross System Product (CSP).** This product is a fourth-generation language (4GL), primarily intended for professional application developers, that can be used to generate applications that access DB2 databases.
- **Application Development Facility (ADF).** This is another 4GL, also primarily intended to be used by information systems professionals, to generate IMS and DB2 applications.
- **Application System (AS).** This product is a 4GL, primarily intended for end users, that can be used to access DB2 databases.

We will not discuss the many other IBM program products that can be used with DB2. Some of these are briefly described in Box 1.1. Also, many products from other vendors can also be used to access DB2 databases.

THE DB2 OPERATING ENVIRONMENT

Describing the operating system and telecommunications environment in which the DB2 software runs requires generating a little IBM "alphabet soup." If you are not well acquainted with the software that is used in the IBM large-system environment, this section can safely be skipped over and the alphabet soup ignored. Having said that, DB2 runs under any of the currently supported versions of the MVS operating systems and can be used in conjunction with either IMS, CICS, or TSO. When run with TSO, DB2 data can be accessed from a TSO terminal running in foreground or by a batch job running in background. When using DB2 with TSO, DB2 provides the database services and TSO provides data communication services. When DB2 is run in the IMS environment, an application program can access data in both DB2 and IMS databases; IMS-DC provides data communication services in the IMS environment. When DB2 is run in the CICS environment, CICS provides the data communication services. CICS also provides an interface to IMS databases so that a single CICS application program can access both DB2 and IMS data. When an application program uses the data communication services of IMS or CICS, DB2 provides the facilities needed to be able to access both DB2 and IMS databases with full data integrity and recoverability; the user need not know the physical locations of the data in either environment.

IBM has stated that DB2 is an important part of its *Systems Application Architecture* (SAA). SAA is IBM's long-range plan for integrating its diverse computing system lines and providing common user and programming interfaces for all of its large, medium, and small systems.

DB2 provides services that are used to access data either interactively using a terminal or via an application program. DB2 application programs can be written in a variety of programming languages, including COBOL, PL/I, FORTRAN, BASIC, APL2, Assembler, C, and many fourth-generation languages.

THE SQL DATA LANGUAGE

The primary language used by both application programmers and end users in accessing a DB2 database is the *Structured Query Language* (SQL). SQL (often pronounced "sequel") is the standard language interface to DB2 and supports facilities that allow it to be used as both a *data definition language* (DDL) and a *data manipulation language* (DML). Many products other than DB2, such as IBM's Application System (AS), support interfaces to SQL and thus to DB2. SQL statements can be used to define, retrieve, and update data in DB2 databases. In addition to the basic data definition and data manipulation statements, there are also SQL statements that provide for processing related to security, integrity, and recovery and for the physical administration of DB2 databases. SQL statements can be executed interactively from a terminal, or they can be embedded in an application program.

Having a single data language that encompasses all functions needed to both support and use databases helps make DB2 easy to use while still providing a powerful set of facilities. All SQL statements use the same syntax. This allows a person to perform a full range of functions, from simple retrieval of data at a terminal through application system development to complete administration of a DB2 system, without having to learn several languages.

THE DB2 CATALOG

DB2 maintains information about the data that it manages in a set of tables known as the *DB2 catalog*. Since the DB2 catalog consists of DB2 databases, authorized users can access and manipulate data in the catalog using SQL statements in the same manner as they manipulate data in application databases. Data in the catalog can be used to determine what data items exist in the DB2 databases and how they are related. Also, data definitions stored in the catalog can be included in application programs, thus eliminating the need for individual users to each enter their own data descriptions.

DB2 UTILITIES

DB2 contains a set of utility functions. Each utility performs a specific task related to overall DB2 management and administration. Utilities can be used to perform the following functions:

- Back up and recover data
- Load and reorganize data
- Check and repair data
- Monitor performance and perform system-tuning functions

DBMS CHARACTERISTICS

DB2 is a member of a large category of products known as *database management systems* (DBMS). The general purpose of a DBMS is to provide for the definition, storage, and management of data in a centralized pool that can be shared by many users.

A database management system generally conforms to one of three major database structures: *hierarchical, network,* or *relational.* In a hierarchical DBMS, illustrated in Fig. 1.1, data records are typically connected with embedded pointers to form a tree structure. IMS is an example of a hierarchical database management system. With a network database management system, a mesh structure such as that shown in Fig. 1.2, in which dependent records can have more than one parent, is used. Cullinet Software's IDMS/R is an example of a DBMS that uses a network-structured database. With a relational DBMS, data is represented in the form of tables, as shown in Fig. 1.3, and no embedded pointers are required to represent associations between records. DB2 is a relational DBMS.

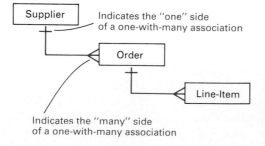

Figure 1.1   A hierarchically structured database typically uses embedded pointers to create a tree configuration in which a dependent record type has one and only one parent.

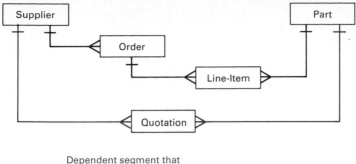

Dependent segment that
has more than one parent

Figure 1.2   A network-structured database typically uses embedded pointers to create a mesh configuration in which a dependent record type can have more than one parent.

Figure 1.3   A relational database maintains data in the form of tables in which all associations are expressed using the stored data rather than with embedded pointers.

DATABASE OBJECTIVES

Database management systems have the potential for allowing application systems to be built that have many advantages over conventional file-oriented systems. The objectives of modern database management systems fall into the following key areas:

- Data redundancy
- Data independence

- Security
- Recovery
- Concurrency

We end this introductory chapter by seeing how DB2 achieves its objectives in these five areas.

DATA REDUNDANCY

Prior to the availability of database management systems, data processing operations were typically characterized by a multiplicity of files and application systems. The same data elements were often stored in multiple files and were processed by multiple application programs. For example, a file used by the marketing department for promotional mailings might contain the names and addresses of customers and prospects, while a file used in an order processing application might also contain customer names and addresses. This *data redundancy* often led to problems with the consistency of data, since it was difficult to ensure that the same changes were made to all the copies of a particular piece of data. For example, the order processing department might make a change to a customer's address but might not communicate this change to the marketing department. Thus the mailing system might work with out-of-date data. As we have already mentioned, a database management system provides for the centralized storage and management of data. Data can be accessed by a variety of applications without requiring multiple copies of the data to be maintained. Thus the use of a database management system has the effect of reducing data redundancy. When a change is made to the database, applications that use the shared database will all access the changed data.

DB2 allows data to be stored and managed centrally and permits it to be accessed by multiple end users and application programs. With properly defined databases, DB2 facilities allow data redundancy to be minimized.

DATA INDEPENDENCE

A second problem associated with file systems is that of *data dependence* in application programs. A particular file might be used by many application programs. Each program contains a description of the logical and physical characteristics of the file. If the file needs to be changed, perhaps to change the size of a field, every program that accesses that file has to be changed.

DB2 provides for data independence in two ways. First, DB2 separates the logical structure of the data from the way in which it is physically stored. End users and application programs need describe only the logical structure of the data they use and are not affected by changes made to its physical structure. Second, DB2 provides a mechanism, called a *view,* that allows a user or program to define its own limited logical data structure that is based on the underlying database. The program's or user's view of the data is then mapped to the database by DB2. Views allow changes to be made to the underlying logical data structures without affecting programs or user procedures.

SECURITY

The centralized storage of data in databases, and the accessing of this data by multiple end users and application programs, brings with it a need for *security*. There must be mechanisms that will allow users to access the data they need but will prevent them from accessing data that they are not authorized to see. In addition to controlling the data a particular user has access to, a database management system may also control the type of access the user has—whether the user is allowed only to retrieve the data or may also make changes to it or add data to the database.

To provide for security facilities, DB2 provides an *authorization* mechanism that permits different users to be allowed or denied access to different parts of a database and controls the operations a user can perform on data that can be accessed. The authorization mechanism can also be used by one user to control the authorizations given to other users. Authorization, and other security facilities, are discussed in detail in Chapter 18.

RECOVERY

Part of managing the centralized store of data includes being able to recover the data in the event of software or hardware failures. A common approach to recovery is periodically to make copies of the database and to maintain a log of all changes made to the database following the copy operation. The database can then be restored by using the copy and reapplying all the changes recorded in the log.

DB2 provides for recovery by automatically maintaining a dual logging system that records all changes made to a database. DB2 also provides utility programs that assist in making backup copies of databases and in restoring a database following a failure. DB2 also performs an automatic recovery operation when the DB2 system is restarted.

CONCURRENCY

As we have seen, one of the goals of a database management system is to allow multiple end users and application programs access to the same shared data. For a DBMS that runs in a large-system environment, as DB2 does, this includes allowing multiple users or programs to access the same database at the same time, or providing *concurrent* access. Providing concurrency, however, brings with it some potential problems. If two programs are permitted to make changes to the same row of a database table at the same time, the two programs may interfere with one another in a variety of ways.

DB2 supports concurrent access and allows more than one user or program to access the same data at the same time. In order to prevent the problems associated with concurrent access, DB2 provides a system of locks. Locks control whether and in what way other programs or users can access data a particular user or program is currently using. The DB2 locking system ensures that no program accesses data that has been changed by another program before the changes are completed. DB2 uses a commitment process for determining when changes made to a database are considered permanent. An application program or user can determine that particular changes are to be committed or rolled back. DB2 will also automatically roll back uncommitted changes when certain types of failures occur.

2   DB2 AND THE RELATIONAL DATA MODEL

DB2 is a database management system that is patterned on the *relational data model,* first described in an article published in 1970 by Dr. E. F. Codd, then of IBM. The relational data model presents a generalized way of thinking about data and is described in terms of *objects, operators that can be applied to these objects,* and a set of *integrity rules.* DB2 is an implementation of the relational model and embodies most of its characteristics; however, at the time of writing, DB2 does not implement quite all the aspects of the relational data model described by Codd.

In this chapter, we will introduce the concepts associated with the relational data model and show which relational concepts are implemented by DB2. The formal definition of the relational data model was stated by Codd using precise mathematical terminology, but we will not attempt to describe it here in a rigorous mathematical fashion. Instead, we will rely on informal explanations and examples of the important relational concepts. We will begin by examining the objects that are part of the relational data model.

TABLES

With the relational data model, and with DB2, a database is represented by, and perceived by its users in the form of, a set of *tables* that contain *rows* and *columns.* A table represents an *entity type*—the type of person, object, or concept about which we are storing information. A column represents an *attribute* of the entity type—one type of information that we are storing about the entity. A row represents a particular *entity occurrence,* or *entity instance.* A particular row contains a set of *data items,* one for each column in the table. Here is an example of a possible table:

Employee

Employee-Name	Sex	Birth-Date	Employee-Number	Department-Number	Skill-Code	Job-Title	Salary
Jones	M	100335	373	04	73	Accountant	2000
Blanagan	M	101019	871	17	43	Plumber	1800
Lawrence	F	090932	355	04	02	Clerk	1100
Rockefeller	M	011132	963	09	11	Consultant	5000
Ropley	M	021242	597	17	43	Plumber	1700
Smith	M	091130	188	04	73	Accountant	2000
Ralner	M	110941	645	04	02	Clerk	1200
Horace	F	071235	161	17	07	Engineer	2500
Hall	M	011030	190	17	21	Architect	3700
Fair	F	020442	292	09	93	Programmer	2100

This table represents the *Employee* entity type. The columns in the table represent the kinds of information that we are storing about employees. Each row in the table stores a set of data items that describe a particular employee.

ALTERNATIVE TERMINOLOGY

In this book, we will use the terms *table, column, row,* and *data item* to describe the data stored in a DB2 database. In the more formal terminology used to define the relational data model, a table is called a *relation,* a column is called an *attribute,* and a row is called a *tuple* (rhymes with *couple*). A relation is considered to be a *set of tuples.* If a relation has *n* columns, it is said to be of *degree n,* and the tuples are called *n-tuples.* A table is also sometimes referred to in the literature as a *flat file.*

When discussing the way in which a table might be stored in a conventional computer file, the column structure of the table might describe a particular *record type,* with each column being one of the record type's *fields.* Each row can be thought of as a particular *record occurrence* in the file.

TABLE PROPERTIES

The relations, or tables, that make up a relational database have certain properties. DB2 tables have most, but not all, of the properties associated with the relations of the relational data model. The properties of the relations of the relational data model and of DB2 tables are as follows:

- Each row-column entry in a table consists of a single, or *atomic,* data item; repeating groups are not allowed. A data structure from which repeating groups have been removed in order to place the data into tabular form is called a *normalized data structure.* Removing repeating groups is only the first step in a further normalization process that can be performed on the data. This first level of normalization, in which the data has been placed into *first normal form,* is the only level of normalization that is addressed by the relational data model itself. Normalization is discussed in more detail in Appendix I.

- All the data items in a given column are of the same type. The relational data model specifies that for each column, a *domain* must be defined that describes the set of values that are allowed for the data items in that column. For example, we might define the domain for the *Birth-Date* column in the *Employee* table as the set of all possible calendar dates. Or we might define a certain range of dates, or a particular set of dates, as being valid. The definition of a DB2 table specifies a particular data type for each column, but DB2 does not support the concept of a domain. DB2 allows a data item to take on any value of its specified type. If the concept of a domain is important to an application, for example, for data value validation, this feature must be implemented by the application itself.

- Each column in a table has a unique name within that table.

- The relational data model specifies that all the rows in a table must be unique. Although it is possible with DB2 to impose this condition on a table, uniqueness is not required. DB2 allows tables to contain duplicate rows.

- In the relational data model, the sequence of the rows and columns in a table is not meaningful; we can view the rows and the columns in any sequence without affecting either the information content or the semantics of any function that uses the table. It is possible with DB2 to impose a sequence on the rows or columns of a table if this is necessary for processing. However, the basic definition of a DB2 table does not assume any particular sequence.

KEYS

One of the properties of a table, as defined by the relational data model, is that each row must be unique. This means there must be a column, or a set of columns, that uniquely identifies each row. This column, or set of columns, is called the table's *key*. In many cases, an individual column can be found that uniquely identifies each row. For example, in the *Employee* table, the *Employee-Number* column has a unique data item value in each row and can serve as the table's key. We will indicate the key of a table by underlining its column name and placing it on the left in the table:

Employee

Employee-Number	Employee-Name	Sex	Birth-Date	Department-Number	Skill-Code	Job-Title	Salary
373	Jones	M	100335	04	73	Accountant	2000
871	Blanagan	M	101019	17	43	Plumber	1800
355	Lawrence	F	090932	04	02	Clerk	1100
963	Rockefeller	M	011132	09	11	Consultant	5000
597	Ropley	M	021242	17	43	Plumber	1700
188	Smith	M	091130	04	73	Accountant	2000
645	Ralner	M	110941	04	02	Clerk	1200
161	Horace	F	071235	17	07	Engineer	2500
190	Hall	M	011030	17	21	Architect	3700
292	Fair	F	020442	09	93	Programmer	2100

With many tables, two or more columns must be combined to provide unique identification. In the worst case, all the columns must be combined to identify each row uniquely, thus forming an *all-key table*. Two or more columns that are combined to serve as a key are called a *concatenated key*, as in the following example:

Hours

Employee-Number	Project-Number	Hours-Worked
120	01	37
120	08	12
121	01	45
121	08	21
121	12	107
270	08	10
270	12	78
273	01	22
274	12	41
279	01	27
279	08	20
279	12	51
301	01	16
301	12	85
306	12	67

The key of a table has two important properties:

- **Unique identification.** The value of the key in each row must be different from the value of the key in any other row.
- **Nonredundancy.** If a key consists of more than one column, none of the columns that make up the key can be discarded without destroying the property of unique identification.

As mentioned earlier, DB2 departs from the relational model with respect to keys. Since DB2 allows duplicate rows to exist in a table, it is not necessary to identify a key for a table if the application does not require one. However, in practice, most DB2 tables do have keys.

PRIMARY KEY

In many cases, a table has more than one possible key. For example, in this particular *Employee* table, the *Employee-Name* column also happens to have unique data item values:

Employee

Employee-Number	Employee-Name	Sex	Birth-Date	Department-Number	Skill-Code	Job-Title	Salary
373	Jones	M	100335	04	73	Accountant	2000
871	Blanagan	M	101019	17	43	Plumber	1800
355	Lawrence	F	090932	04	02	Clerk	1100
963	Rockefeller	M	011132	09	11	Consultant	5000
597	Ropley	M	021242	17	43	Plumber	1700
188	Smith	M	091130	04	73	Accountant	2000
645	Ralner	M	110941	04	02	Clerk	1200
161	Horace	F	071235	17	07	Engineer	2500
190	Hall	M	011030	17	21	Architect	3700
292	Fair	F	020442	09	93	Programmer	2100

The different possible keys for a table are called *candidate keys*. One of the candidate keys must be chosen as the key for the table and is called the *primary key;* the other candidate keys are called *alternate keys*. Some judgment must be applied in identifying candidate keys. In our *Employee* table example, *Employee-name* data item values are unique. However, in an actual *Employee* database, it would be possible for two employees to have the same name; thus we would not consider *Employee-Name* to be a candidate key.

DB2 allows a primary key to be explicitly defined for a table. As we will see in Chapter 3, DB2 uses separate objects called *indexes* to ensure that each row has a unique primary key value when a primary key is defined for the table. A particular form of index, called a *unique index*, is used for this purpose.

REPRESENTING RELATIONSHIPS
Another characteristic of the relational data model is that all relationships between entity types are expressed in the form of data stored in the tables. In the following example, we can express the relationship between an employee and a department by using data item values in the *Department-Number* column of the *Employee* table and data item values in the *Dept* column of the *Department* table:

Employee

Employee-Number	Employee-Name	Sex	Birth-Date	Department-Number	Skill-Code	Job-Title	Salary
373	Jones	M	100335	04	73	Accountant	2000
871	Blanagan	M	101019	17	43	Plumber	1800
355	Lawrence	F	090932	04	02	Clerk	1100
963	Rockefeller	M	011132	09	11	Consultant	5000
597	Ropley	M	021242	17	43	Plumber	1700
188	Smith	M	091130	04	73	Accountant	2000
645	Ralner	M	110941	04	02	Clerk	1200
161	Horace	F	071235	17	07	Engineer	2500
190	Hall	M	011030	17	21	Architect	3700
292	Fair	F	020442	09	93	Programmer	2100

Department

Dept	Location
02	Detroit
01	New York
04	Chicago
03	Miami
17	Houston
09	Denver

Although column names must be unique within a single table, there is no requirement that they be unique among the various tables that make up a database. So we often make relationships between tables more clear by using the same column name in two related tables:

Employee

Employee-Number	Employee-Name	Sex	Birth-Date	Department-Number	Skill-Code	Job-Title	Salary
373	Jones	M	100335	04	73	Accountant	2000
871	Blanagan	M	101019	17	43	Plumber	1800
355	Lawrence	F	090932	04	02	Clerk	1100
963	Rockefeller	M	011132	09	11	Consultant	5000
597	Ropley	M	021242	17	43	Plumber	1700
188	Smith	M	091130	04	73	Accountant	2000
645	Ralner	M	110941	04	02	Clerk	1200
161	Horace	F	071235	17	07	Engineer	2500
190	Hall	M	011030	17	21	Architect	3700
292	Fair	F	020442	09	93	Programmer	2100

Department

Department-Number	Location
02	Detroit
01	New York
04	Chicago
03	Miami
17	Houston
09	Denver

As we will see later when we discuss relational operators, we can perform operations on tables that make use of the relationships that exist between tables.

With database management systems that use hierarchical or network structures, relationships between entities are represented by defining explicit relationships between different record types. These relationships are often implemented in the form of pointers that are stored apart from the data in a record. For example, the following example of a hierarchical database structure shows that *Employee* records are logically related to *Department* records.

Employee

Employee-Number	Employee-Name	Sex	Birth-Date	Skill-Code	Job-Title	Salary

Department

Dept	Location

Notice in this example that there is no department number value stored in the *Employee* record. The relationship is implemented apart from the data stored in the records.

When relationships are defined apart from the data, a user or application program that accesses the database must be aware of the structural relationships that exist. The user or program must then employ a process called *navigation* in order to locate the desired records in the database. With a relational database, all accessing of the database can be performed by referencing data stored in the database; no separate navigation process is necessary.

Representing all relationships through stored data has two advantages. First, it makes a relational database easy to use, since the user or application program does not have to be aware of structural relationships. Second, it contributes to data independence. Where application programs are dependent on structural relationships and explicitly refer to them in navigating the database, changes made to the database structure may require that changes be made to application programs. With a relational database, changes in relationships are made simply by changing data, and such changes are less likely to require changes in application programs.

DB2 conforms fully to the relational data model with respect to the way in which relationships are represented. DB2 represents relationships only by the data that is stored in the tables that make up the database. No structural relationships can be defined in any other manner.

RELATIONAL OPERATORS

The *operators* that are defined as part of the relational data model make up a *relational algebra* that is used to specify operations that can be performed on data. The operators that form the relational algebra share certain common characteristics. The first is that they operate on an entire *table;* they do not operate on individual *rows* of a table. The second is that when a relational operator is applied to one or more tables, the operation always results in another table. This is important for two reasons:

- All data in a relational database, including that derived as a result of relational operations, takes the form of tables.

- Operations can be nested; a second relational operator can always be applied to the result of a previous operation.

Statements coded using the SQL language are generally used with DB2 to perform relational operations on tables. To provide some background for the chapters on SQL in Part II of this book, we will next describe the general operations that can be performed on tables as they are described by the relational data model. Keep in mind as you read the following sections that the SQL language does not use the same verbs or operators as those of the relational data model to perform the relational operations that we describe here.

SET OPERATORS

Relational theory draws heavily on the branch of mathematics called *set theory,* and four of the relational operators correspond to operators that are used to perform operations on sets. These are the *union, intersection, difference,* and *Cartesian product* operators.

THE UNION OPERATOR

The *union* operator combines the rows from two similar tables to form a new table, usually having more rows than either of the two tables being combined. The new table consists of all rows that are in *either* or *both* of the original tables. In the following example of a union operation, the resulting table contains all the rows that are in the *Welders* table, the *Programmers* table, or both tables:

```
Welders                                          Programmers
```

Employee-Number	Employee-Name	Department-Number
301	Hansen	01
185	Donatelli	02
079	Smith	02
482	Michaels	01

Employee-Number	Employee-Name	Department-Number
079	Smith	02
127	Robinson	01
301	Hansen	01
246	Chapman	02

```
                         ─────── UNION ───────
```

```
Result
```

Employee-Number	Employee-Name	Department-Number
301	Hansen	01
185	Donatelli	02
079	Smith	02
482	Michaels	01
127	Robinson	01
246	Chapman	02

Suppose the *Welders* table represents employees who can weld and the *Programmers* table describes employees who can program. This union operation might then be used to obtain a list of all employees who are either welders, programmers, or both.

The Venn diagrams used in set theory can help make clear the set operations that can be performed on tables. The Venn diagram in Fig. 2.1 illustrates the union operation. If the two tables each contain a different set of unique rows, the union of the two tables consists of all the rows from both tables. If some of the rows are duplicated in the two tables, as in the previous example, the duplicates are removed from the resulting table as part of the union operation.

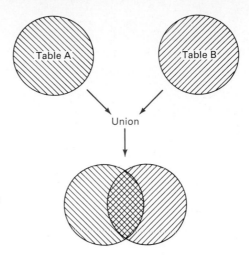

Figure 2.1 The union of Table A and Table B is a table whose rows are those that are in Table A, in Table B, or in both Table A and Table B.

THE INTERSECTION OPERATOR

The *intersection* operator combines the rows from two similar tables to form a third table that is typically smaller than either of the tables being combined. The new table consists of only rows that are in *both* original tables. The following example of an intersection operation produces a table that contains only the rows that exist in both the *Welders* table and the *Programmers* table:

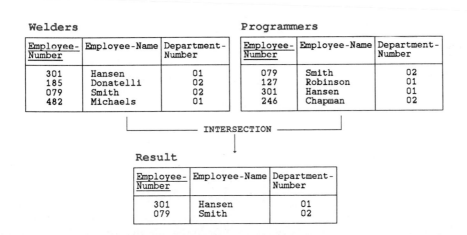

We might use the intersection of the *Welders* table and the *Programmers* table to obtain a list of employees who can both weld and program. Figure 2.2 shows a Venn diagram that illustrates the intersection operation.

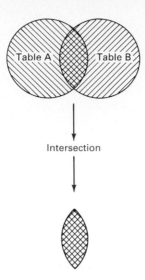

Intersection

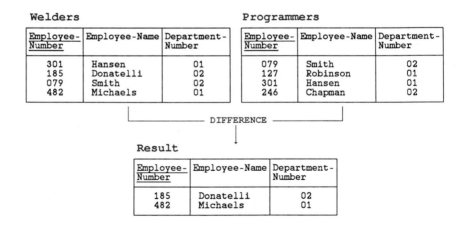

Figure 2.2   The intersection of Table A and Table B is a table whose rows are those that are in both Table A and Table B.

THE DIFFERENCE OPERATOR

The *difference* operator combines two tables to produce a third table that contains all rows that are in the first table but not in the second table. In the following example of a difference operation, the two rows of the resulting table are those that are in the *Welders* table but not in the *Programmers* table:

Welders

Employee-Number	Employee-Name	Department-Number
301	Hansen	01
185	Donatelli	02
079	Smith	02
482	Michaels	01

Programmers

Employee-Number	Employee-Name	Department-Number
079	Smith	02
127	Robinson	01
301	Hansen	01
246	Chapman	02

DIFFERENCE

Result

Employee-Number	Employee-Name	Department-Number
185	Donatelli	02
482	Michaels	01

Figure 2.3 shows a Venn diagram that illustrates the difference operation.

Notice that the union and intersection operators are associative but the difference operator is not. The difference between the *Welders* table and the *Programmers* table could be used to obtain a list of employees who can only weld but not program. The difference between the *Programmers* table and the

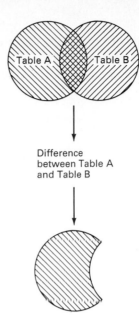

Difference
between Table A
and Table B

Figure 2.3 The difference between Table A and Table B is a
table whose rows are those that are in Table A and are not in
Table B.

Welders table gives the opposite result—a list of employees who can program
but not weld:

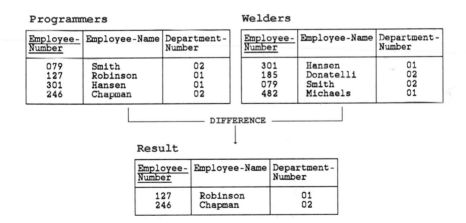

Programmers

Employee-Number	Employee-Name	Department-Number
079	Smith	02
127	Robinson	01
301	Hansen	01
246	Chapman	02

Welders

Employee-Number	Employee-Name	Department-Number
301	Hansen	01
185	Donatelli	02
079	Smith	02
482	Michaels	01

DIFFERENCE

Result

Employee-Number	Employee-Name	Department-Number
127	Robinson	01
246	Chapman	02

THE CARTESIAN PRODUCT OPERATOR

The previous three set operators work with tables that
are essentially similar in that they have the same column structure. Tables having the same column structure are called *union-compatible* tables. The final set
operator—the *Cartesian product* operator—works with two tables whose column structures are different. To form the Cartesian product of two tables, we
concatenate each row of the first table with each row of the second table. Thus

the number of rows in the resulting table is the product of the number of rows in the first table and the number of rows in the second table. In the following Cartesian product operation, the resulting table is the Cartesian product of the *Employee* table and the *Room* table:

Employee

Employee-Number	Employee-Name	Department-Number
301	Hansen	01
482	Michaels	01
127	Robinson	01
147	Bono	01

Room

Room-Number	Lock-ID
010	1246
020	3472
030	1873

CARTESIAN PRODUCT

Result

Employee-Number	Employee-Name	Department-Number	Room-Number	Lock-ID
301	Hansen	01	010	1246
301	Hansen	01	020	3472
301	Hansen	01	030	1873
482	Michaels	01	010	1246
482	Michaels	01	020	3472
482	Michaels	01	030	1873
127	Robinson	01	010	1246
127	Robinson	01	020	3472
127	Robinson	01	030	1873
147	Bono	01	010	1246
147	Bono	01	020	3472
147	Bono	01	030	1873

Notice that each row from the *Employee* table is repeated three times, once for each of the rows in the *Room* table. Suppose that the *Employee* table represents employees in department *01* and that the *Room* table represents room numbers and lock identifiers for the rooms in department *01*. The Cartesian product of the *Employee* table and the *Room* table might then be used to obtain a list of the room numbers and lock identifiers that can be accessed by each of the employees in department *01*.

OTHER RELATIONAL OPERATORS

In addition to the operators that apply to conventional sets, four more relational operators are defined by the relational data model. These are the *select, project, join,* and *divide* operators.

THE SELECT OPERATOR

The *select* operator (not to be confused with the SQL SELECT statement) allows a table to be formed that contains all the columns from *selected rows* in the original table. In the following example of a select operation, the resulting table contains only rows from the *Employee* table that have a data item value of *02* in the *Department-Number* column:

Employee

Employee-Number	Employee-Name	Department-Number	Salary
301	Hansen	01	2000
482	Michaels	02	1800
127	Robinson	04	1100
185	Donatelli	02	5000
079	Smith	01	1700
246	Chapman	03	2000

|

SELECT (Department-Number = '02')

↓

Result

Employee-Number	Employee-Name	Department-Number	Salary
482	Michaels	02	1800
185	Donatelli	02	5000

This select operation might be used to obtain a list of all employees who are in department *02*. Use of the select operator can make a database easier to use by providing access to only the part of the database that is of interest to the user. A select operation could also be used to restrict access to only those rows that a given user is allowed to access.

THE PROJECT OPERATOR

The *project* operator is used to produce a new table that contains all the rows from the original table but only a subset of the columns. The following project operation produces a new table that contains all the columns from the *Employee* table except the *Salary* column:

Employee

Employee-Number	Employee-Name	Department-Number	Salary
301	Hansen	01	2000
482	Michaels	02	1800
127	Robinson	04	1100
185	Donatelli	02	5000
079	Smith	01	1700
246	Chapman	03	2000

PROJECT (Employee-Number, Employee-Name, Department-Number)

Result

Employee-Number	Employee-Name	Department-Number
301	Hansen	01
482	Michaels	02
127	Robinson	04
185	Donatelli	02
079	Smith	01
246	Chapman	03

As with selection, projection can be used to make a database easier to use by presenting only pertinent information, or it can be used to restrict access to only those columns that the user is authorized to access.

Depending on the columns chosen in the project operation, the initial table that results from the project operation might be one that contains duplicate rows:

Employee

Employee-Number	Employee-Name	Sex	Birth-Date	Department-Number	Skill-Code	Job-Title	Salary
373	Jones	M	100335	04	73	Accountant	2000
871	Blanagan	M	101019	17	43	Plumber	1800
355	Lawrence	F	090932	04	02	Clerk	1100
963	Rockefeller	M	011132	09	11	Consultant	5000
597	Ropley	M	021242	17	43	Plumber	1700
188	Smith	M	091130	04	73	Accountant	2000
645	Ralner	M	110941	04	02	Clerk	1200
161	Horace	F	071235	17	07	Engineer	2500
190	Hall	M	011030	17	21	Architect	3700
292	Fair	F	020442	09	93	Programmer	2100

PROJECT (Department-Number, Skill-Code)

Department-Number	Skill-Code
04	73
17	43
04	02
09	11
17	43
04	73
04	02
17	07
17	21
09	93

Notice that this table contains rows with duplicate department/skill combinations and thus violates the uniqueness rule. In such a situation, the project operation goes a step further and eliminates duplicates from the final result:

Result

Department-Number	Skill-Code		Department-Number	Skill-Code
04	73		04	73
17	43		17	43
04	02		04	02
09	11	→	09	11
17	43		17	07
04	73		17	21
04	02		09	93
17	07			
17	21			
09	93			

THE JOIN OPERATOR

The *join* operator combines the rows from two tables, resulting in a third, wider table. The join operation must be based on one or more columns from each of the two tables whose data values share a common domain. The resulting table is formed in such a way that in each row, the data values from the two columns (or sets of columns) on which the join is based have the same data item values. In the following example of a join, we are joining the *Employee* table and the *Department* table on the *Dept-A* and *Dept-B* columns:

Employee

Employee-Number	Employee-Name	Dept-A
301	Hansen	01
482	Michaels	02
127	Robinson	04
185	Donatelli	02
079	Smith	01
246	Chapman	03

Department

Dept-B	Location
01	New York
02	Detroit
03	Miami
04	Chicago

JOIN on Dept-A and Dept-B

Result

Employee-Number	Employee-Name	Dept-A	Dept-B	Location
301	Hansen	01	01	New York
482	Michaels	02	02	Detroit
127	Robinson	04	04	Chicago
185	Donatelli	02	02	Detroit
079	Smith	01	01	New York
246	Chapman	03	03	Miami

In performing this join, each *Dept-A* value is compared against *all* the *Dept-B* values. Where the values are equal, the row from the *Employee* table is combined with the row from the *Department* table to form a row in the resulting table. This particular join operation could be used to obtain a list of the locations at which each employee works.

Because we made an *equal* comparison in performing the join, the operation is known, formally, as an *equijoin*. We can also perform joins using other types of comparisons. For example, we might perform a *greater-than* join, or a *less-than-or-equal-to* join. In such cases, the columns on which the join is performed will not have equal values; instead, the values in each row will be related according to the type of comparison made. The most common type of join operation in practice, however, is the equijoin.

Because of the way the equijoin operation is defined, the resulting table from an equijoin contains two columns that have identical data item values. In the previous example, these were columns *Dept-A* and *Dept-B*. We can, if we like, eliminate one of the two columns:

Employee

Employee-Number	Employee-Name	Dept-A
301	Hansen	01
482	Michaels	02
127	Robinson	04
185	Donatelli	02
079	Smith	01
246	Chapman	03

Department

Dept-B	Location
01	New York
02	Detroit
03	Miami
04	Chicago

JOIN on Dept-A and Dept-B

Result

Employee-Number	Employee-Name	Dept-A	Location
301	Hansen	01	New York
482	Michaels	02	Detroit
127	Robinson	04	Chicago
185	Donatelli	02	Detroit
079	Smith	01	New York
246	Chapman	03	Miami

An equijoin with one of the identical columns eliminated is called a *natural join*. When we use the term *join* without qualification, we generally mean an equijoin that is also a natural join.

In the foregoing join example, we explicitly named the columns from each table on which the join operation is based. In some cases, we can specify a join operation without naming the joining columns. When this is done, the two tables being joined generally have columns that share a common name:

Employee

Employee-Number	Employee-Name	Department
301	Hansen	01
482	Michaels	02
127	Robinson	04
185	Donatelli	02
079	Smith	01
246	Chapman	03

Department

Department	Location
01	New York
02	Detroit
03	Miami
04	Chicago

— JOIN —

Result

Employee-Number	Employee-Name	Department	Location
301	Hansen	01	New York
482	Michaels	02	Detroit
127	Robinson	04	Chicago
185	Donatelli	02	Detroit
079	Smith	01	New York
246	Chapman	03	Miami

The column on which the join is performed is implied, and the two tables are joined on the basis of the data item values in the *Department* column.

INNER JOINS

The join operations that we have discussed so far are all examples of joins that are more accurately called *inner join* operations. With all types of inner joins, there is a possibility that some of the rows from either or both of the tables being joined will not be represented in the table that results from the join operation. For example, examine the following *inner* equijoin operation using different table contents from earlier examples:

Employee

Employee-Number	Employee-Name	Department
301	Hansen	01
482	Michaels	02
127	Robinson	04
185	Donatelli	02
079	Smith	01
246	Chapman	03
128	Leben	09
248	Martin	08

Department

Department	Location
01	New York
02	Detroit
03	Miami
04	Chicago
05	Los Angeles
06	Houston

— INNER EQUIJOIN on Department —

(Continued)

(Continued from page 27.)

Result

Employee-Number	Employee-Name	Department	Location
301	Hansen	01	New York
482	Michaels	02	Detroit
127	Robinson	04	Chicago
185	Donatelli	02	Detroit
079	Smith	01	New York
246	Chapman	03	Miami

Notice that there are no corresponding rows in the *Department* table for the *Leben* and *Martin* entries in the *Employee* table. Also, there are no corresponding rows in the *Employee* table for the *Los Angeles* and *Houston* entries in the *Department* table. By the rules of the inner equijoin operation, information for *Leben, Martin, Los Angeles,* and *Houston* is not included in the resulting table. In many applications, this would be the result that is required. However, there are some applications in which we would like to perform a join operation in which no data is lost in the resulting table when data values do not match. An *outer join* operation can be used to produce such a result.

OUTER JOINS

With an outer join, all rows in the tables being joined are represented in the resulting table, even if no matching values are found for one or more rows. Here is an example of an *outer* equijoin based on *Department* data values:

Employee

Employee-Number	Employee-Name	Department
301	Hansen	01
482	Michaels	02
127	Robinson	04
185	Donatelli	02
079	Smith	01
246	Chapman	03
128	Leben	09
248	Martin	08

Department

Department	Location
01	New York
02	Detroit
03	Miami
04	Chicago
05	Los Angeles
06	Houston

OUTER EQUIJOIN on Department

Result

Employee-Number	Employee-Name	Department	Location
301	Hansen	01	New York
482	Michaels	02	Detroit
127	Robinson	04	Chicago
185	Donatelli	02	Detroit
079	Smith	01	New York
246	Chapman	03	Miami
128	Leben	09	-
248	Martin	08	-
-	-	05	Los Angeles
-	-	06	Houston

28

Notice that the resulting table contains null values in the rows for which department values do not match in both tables. We can interpret the null values as
representing information that is *missing* or that is *not known*.

Keep in mind that our discussion represents something of an oversimplifi-
cation of the outer join concept. Outer joins are relatively straightforward when
only two tables are being joined, but they become more complex when we
attempt to perform an outer join on three or more tables. The table that results
from such an operation may depend on the sequence in which the tables are
joined. Discussions of complex outer join operations are beyond the scope of
this book.

One of the shortcomings of the SQL language is that it is incapable of
directly expressing outer join operations. An outer join can be simulated by
using multiple SELECT statements connected with UNION operators; this technique is described in Chapter 5. Many vendors other than IBM have added
extensions to SQL that allow outer joins to be specified directly and it is possible that IBM will also extend the language to allow outer joins.

THE DIVIDE OPERATOR

The *divide* operation is also based on a comparison
of data item values contained in columns from the
two tables. The following example of a divide oper-
ation is based on the *Employee-Number* and *Skill* columns in the *Employee-Skill*
table and the *Skill* column in the *Skill* table.

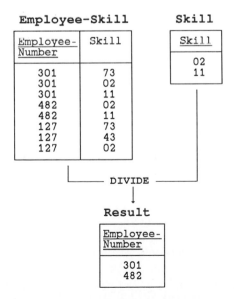

The *Skill* data item value for each *Employee-Number* value in the *Employee-Skill* table is compared with all the *Skill* data items in the *Skill* table. The result of the divide operation is a new table that contains only *Employee-Number* values where there are *Employee-Number/Skill* pairs in the *Employee-Skill* table that match *all* the *Skill* values in the *Skill* table. Thus the result of the divide operation is a table with *Employee-Number* values *301* and *482,* since these are the only two *Employee-Number/Skill* pairs in the *Employee-Skill* table that have *Skill* values of both *02* and *11.* We might use this divide operation to produce a list of employees who have skills *02* and *11.*

THE SQL LANGUAGE

As mentioned earlier, relational operations are specified on DB2 tables by issuing SQL statements. SQL does not perform relational operations using verbs that have the same names as the relational operators we have been discussing. All relational operations on data are performed by issuing various forms of the SQL SELECT statement. It is possible, using an SQL SELECT statement, to perform any of the operations defined by the eight relational operators (with the possible exception of outer joins, as discussed previously). However, it is sometimes awkward to express certain relational operations using the syntax of the SQL SELECT statement.

INTEGRITY CONSTRAINTS

In addition to defining objects and operations that can be performed on those objects, the relational data model also defines two *integrity constraints* that concern the data item values that can be placed in tables. These two integrity constraints are called *entity integrity* and *referential integrity*. DB2 supports both the entity integrity rule and the referential integrity rule.

ENTITY INTEGRITY

The *entity integrity* rule states that no column that is part of a primary key can have a null value. This rule is necessary if the primary key is to fulfill its role of uniquely identifying the rows in a table. If we allowed a particular primary key value to be completely null, we would be saying that there is some particular entity occurrence that could not be distinguished from other entity occurrences. This is a contradiction, since two entity occurrences that cannot be distinguished from one another must be the same occurrence. Similar arguments can be made for disallowing partial null key values.

DB2 implements primary keys by means of unique indexes. DB2 ensures entity integrity for a given table only if a unique index is defined for that table. If a table is defined with no unique index associated with it, the entity integrity rule does not apply for that table.

REFERENTIAL INTEGRITY

It is possible for one table to contain a column, or set of columns, that contains data item values drawn from the same domain as the column or columns that form the primary key in some other table. This column or set of columns is called a *foreign key*. In the following example, the *Manager-Number* in the *Department* table is a foreign key because each *Manager-Number* is drawn from the same domain as the *Employee-Number* values in the *Employee* table, the set of valid employee numbers:

Department

Department-Number	Location	Manager-Number
04	Chicago	127
05	Chicago	null
01	New York	301

Employee

Employee-Number	Employee-Name	Salary
301	Hansen	2000
482	Michaels	1800
127	Robinson	1100
185	Donatelli	5000
079	Smith	1700
246	Chapman	2000

The referential integrity rule states that every foreign key value in the first table must either match a primary key value in the second table or must be wholly null. In other words, any value of *Manager-Number* in the *Department* table must either be null or match an *Employee-Number* value in the *Employee* table. The referential integrity rule guarantees that the *Department* table will not reference a manager who is not also an employee. Allowing a null value in the foreign key, however, does allow the *Department* table to contain a row for a department that currently has no manager.

Early versions of the DB2 software did not support the referential integrity rule of the relational data model. However, comprehensive facilities for referential integrity are now supported.

CODD'S RELATIONAL RULES

In the 1980s the relational approach to database management became extremely popular. Because of this popularity, vendors of all types of database management systems loudly proclaimed the latest releases of their database offerings now to include relational facilities. E. F. Codd, the first to describe the relational approach, became concerned that it was becoming difficult to determine just how "relational" a particular database management system package actually was. To help clarify the situation, Codd published two articles in Computerworld [1,2] that clearly described what features a database management system should have to be considered "fully relational." These features are described in terms of 12 rules preceded by a general principle called rule 0. Individual vendors will continually debate whether all of these principles are, in fact, valid, and vendors will disagree over just how closely a particular offering conforms to Codd's principles. However, we feel that it is interesting to list Codd's rules using informal language.

0. *Relational Database Management.* A relational database management system must use only its relational capabilities to manage the information stored in the database.

1. *Information Representation.* All information stored in a relational database must be represented only by data item values that are stored in the tables that make up the database. Associations between data items must not be logically represented in any other way, such as by using pointers from one table to another.

2. *Logical Accessibility.* Every data item value stored in a relational database must be accessible by stating the name of the table it is stored in, the name of the column under which it is stored, and the value of the primary key that defines the row in which it is stored.

3. *Representation of Null Values.* The database management system must have a consistent method for representing null values. For example, null values for numeric values must be distinct from zero or any other numeric value, and null character strings must be distinct from strings of blanks or any other character values.

4. *Catalog Facilities.* The logical description of a relational database must be represented in the same manner as ordinary data so that the facilities of the relational database management system can be used to maintain database descriptions.

5. *Data Languages.* A relational database management system may support many different types of languages for describing data and accessing the database. However, there must be at least one language that uses ordinary character strings to support the definition of data, the definition of views, the manipulation of data, constraints on data integrity, information concerning authorization, and the boundaries of recovery units.

6. *View Updatability.* Any view that can be defined using combinations of base tables that are in theory updatable must be capable of being updated by the database management system.

7. *Insert, Update, and Delete.* Any operand that describes the results of a single retrieval operation must be capable of being applied to a single insert, update, or delete operation as well.

8. *Physical Data Independence.* Changes that are made to physical storage representations or access methods must not require that changes be made to application programs.

9. *Logical Data Independence.* Changes that are made to tables that do not modify any of the data already stored in the tables must not require that changes be made to application programs.

10. *Integrity Constraints.* Constraints that apply to entity integrity and referential integrity must be specifiable by the data language implemented by the database management system and not by statements coded into application programs.

11. *Database Distribution.* The data language implemented by the database management system must support the ability to distribute the database without requiring changes to be made to application programs. This facility must be provided in the data language whether or not the DBMS itself supports distributed databases.

12. *Nonsubversion.* If the database management system supports facilities that allow application programs to operate on tables a row at a time, an application program using this type of database access must be prevented from bypassing entity integrity or referential integrity constraints that are defined for the database.

CONCLUSION

We will leave it as an exercise for you to determine just how closely DB2 conforms to Codd's relational principles and how important this conformance (or lack of it) is to your own information system environment. We feel that DB2 conforms quite closely to Codd's rules in all but a few areas.

REFERENCES

1. Codd, E. F. "Is Your DBMS Really Relational?" *Computerworld,* October 14, 1985.

2. Codd, E. F. "Does Your DBMS Run by the Rules?" *Computerworld,* October 21, 1985.

3 LOGICAL AND PHYSICAL DATA STRUCTURES

As we saw in Chapter 1, a database management system provides for the centralized definition and description of the data in the database. Most database management systems allow for a separation between different levels of data definition. In this chapter, we look at the three views of data that are most commonly used and show how DB2 implements them.

In talking about the data stored in a database, it is common to look at the data in at least three different ways. The following are descriptions of these three different views of the database:

- **User Views.** This is the collection of data items, and their relationships, as perceived by an individual application program or group of related application programs. A user view generally encompasses only a small subset of the data items stored in the database.

- **Logical Data Model.** This is the entire collection of data items, and their relationships, that will be stored in one database. The logical data model documents the enterprise's overall view of the database. It is a logical map that identifies *all* the data stored in a database and combines all the individual user views into one integrated structure. It is not likely that any application program would ever require access to all the data items documented by the logical data model.

- **Physical Data Structures.** These are the data sets, indexes, and other storage structures that are used to physically implement the logical data model on the physical storage medium.

A key benefit to the multiple-view approach to data definition is an increase in data independence at the application program level. Generally, an application program is not concerned with any physical storage issues. These are handled directly by the database management system. If changes are made to physical storage structures, perhaps to improve performance, application programs are not affected and can continue to be used without change. Changes can also be made at the logical level without affecting application programs. Data items and rows can be added to and deleted from the database and data item formats changed, and only programs that directly process the data items in question are affected.

The three terms defined above are used to describe the *logical* nature of the data and are independent of any software implementation. We will use three different terms to describe the way the data is physically implemented using a specific database management system, such as DB2.

ANSI/SPARC ARCHITECTURE

In 1975, a study group was formed within the American National Standards Institute (ANSI) to investigate database management. This study group was called ANSI/Systems Planning and Requirements Committee (ANSI/SPARC). The ANSI/SPARC committee published a report that, among other things, defines three views of data that are generally in agreement with the three views we have described. The ANSI/SPARC views of data have become widely accepted in today's database environment, and much of the literature refer to ANSI/SPARC's *three-schema approach* to database management. Each of the data views is described separately, and, ideally, a database management system should be capable of making the necessary transformations from one data view to another. In ANSI/SPARC terminology, each of the data views is called a *schema*. Each of the ANSI/SPARC schemas describes the way one of the logical views of data that we defined earlier is implemented using a specific database management system.

The ANSI/SPARC committee defined the following schemas:

- **External Schema.** A given database will generally have many *external schemas*, each of which describes a single user view. An external schema defines a specific software implementation of a user view.

- **Conceptual Schema or Software Schema.** The *conceptual schema* defines a software implementation of the logical data model, from which all the external schemas are derivable. Most of today's full-function database management systems, including DB2, are capable of representing any conceivable logical data model. However, each database management system supports its own internal language, which is used to define the conceptual schema. The term *conceptual model* is often used in the database literature instead of *logical data model*. To avoid confusion, the authors prefer the term *software schema* to describe a software implementation of a logical data model instead of *conceptual schema*.

- **Internal Schema.** The *internal schema* defines the physical data structures that are used to physically implement the software schema. The internal schema defines the actual data that is stored in the database. Computerized descriptions of the physical data structures define the data files that make up the database to both the DBMS and the operating system software.

A database management system that implements the three-schema approach to database management generally provides a data description language that allow each of the three schemas to be described independently. The database management system software then performs the transformations that are necessary to convert from one schema to the others.

DB2 implements data independence in a way that is similar to ANSI/ SPARC's three-schema approach. End users and application programs do not reference or specify anything about DB2 physical data structures or the way they are described to DB2 in the internal schema. End users and application programs reference the data on a logical level, and changes can be made to the underlying physical data structures without requiring changes to application programs or user procedures.

DB2 also provides a mechanism, called a *view*, that corresponds to ANSI/ SPARC's external schema. A view allows a particular program's description of a particular user view to differ from the logical structure of the underlying database. DB2 then maps an individual program's or user's view of the data first to the logical data model and then to the underlying physical data structures. This can allow changes to be made to the underlying logical data model without affecting programs or user procedures.

The form of data independence provided by the DB2 view is not complete, however, and there may be times when a change to the underlying logical data model will require certain views to be changed, thus potentially affecting end-user or application program processing. We will now look at the way in which DB2 implements the three-schema approach.

DB2 LOGICAL DATA MODEL

In DB2, the logical structure of data is defined and represented in the form of tables, consisting of rows and columns. Relationships between tables are based on the values of data items stored in the tables. The overall logical data model, or conceptual schema, for a given DB2 database consists of the definitions of the set of tables that make up that database.

DB2 USER VIEWS

As we saw in Chapter 2, the result of any relational operation is a new table. This fact allows us to define a new table in terms of an operator that is applied to one or more existing tables. In DB2, a table that is defined in this manner is called a *virtual table*, or a *view*. A table that is not derived from other tables is called a *base table*. A view corresponds to what we have described as a user view, or an external schema in ANSI/SPARC terminology. The following example of a view is the result of a project operation that is applied to the *Employee* table:

Employee

Employee-Number	Employee-Name	Department-Number	Salary
301	Hansen	01	2000
482	Michaels	02	1800
127	Robinson	04	1100
185	Donatelli	02	5000
079	Smith	01	1700
246	Chapman	03	2000

PROJECT (Employee-Number, Employee-Name, Department-Number)

Result   (a view derived from Table A)

Employee-Number	Employee-Name	Department-Number
301	Hansen	01
482	Michaels	02
127	Robinson	04
185	Donatelli	02
079	Smith	01
246	Chapman	03

The values in the resulting table are derived from the values in the *Employee* table. Views are useful for simplifying a particular user's perception of the database. For example, we might use a view to provide a user with only information that is of interest to that user. Or we might use a view to provide only the information that a user has the authority to access. Through the use of views, data can be made accessible in a variety of ways without requiring that it be stored redundantly.

DB2 PHYSICAL DATA STRUCTURES

DB2 defines physical data structures, or the internal schema, using several different types of objects, including indexes, table spaces, index spaces, databases, and storage groups. These objects define both how data is accessed and how it is stored.

Indexes

An index is an optional DB2 object that controls the way in which a table is accessed or stored. Indexes are separate objects defined apart from the tables to which they refer. Indexes are the mechanisms that DB2 uses to implement table keys. The table column or columns that form the table's key are the columns that are used to generate the index. For a table's key, we specify that the index is unique. DB2 then ensures that there are no duplicate key values in the table. An index can also be used to access a table using nonkey values, where there may be multiple rows for a given index entry. In this case, the index is not defined as unique. For example, consider this *Employee* table:

Employee

Employee-Number	Employee-Name	Department-Number	Salary
301	Hansen	01	2000
482	Michaels	02	1800
127	Robinson	04	1100
185	Donatelli	02	5000
079	Smith	01	1700
246	Chapman	03	2000

Defining a unique index on *Employee-Number* ensures a unique key for this table. A non-unique index on *Department-Number* allows direct access to all employees in a given department. An index can also be used to control the physical sequence in which rows in a table are stored. This type of index can be used to divide a table into partitions.

DB2, rather than the end user or the application program, determines whether an index is used to access a table. This means that indexes can be used to improve performance without causing an application to be dependent on the existence of the index.

Table Spaces and Index Spaces

A *table space* represents the physical storage area in which certain tables are stored. Physically, a table space consists of a set of one or more data sets that contain data from one or more tables. An *index space* represents the physical storage area used for an index. Each index is stored in a separate index space.

Databases

A DB2 *database* consists logically of a collection of tables and their associated indexes. It consists physically of the table spaces and index spaces that contain those tables and indexes. The physical makeup of a DB2 database is illustrated in Fig. 3.1.

Storage Groups

A table space or index space can be associated with a particular *storage group*. A storage group consists of one or more direct-access storage device (DASD)

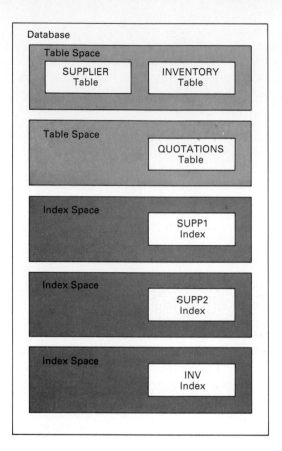

Figure 3.1 DB2 physical database structure.

volumes. When storage space is required for a table in a table space or for an index in an index space, the space is allocated from one of the volumes in the storage group. Figure 3.2 shows the use of storage groups. A table space or index space can also be assigned to specific VSAM data sets.

Partitions

Ordinarily, database recovery facilities operate on table spaces. Each table space can be recovered separately, meaning that an entire database does not necessarily have to be restored in recovering from a failure. A table space can also be divided into *partitions,* where each partition contains a portion of a table. The data in the table space is divided up on the basis of data item values, with a specified range of values associated with each partition. When partitions are used, each partition can be assigned to a separate storage group and can be recovered separately. This is illustrated in Fig. 3.3.

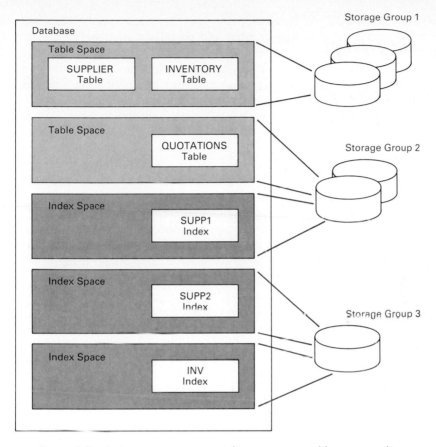

Figure 3.2   A storage group can contain one or more table spaces and/or index spaces.

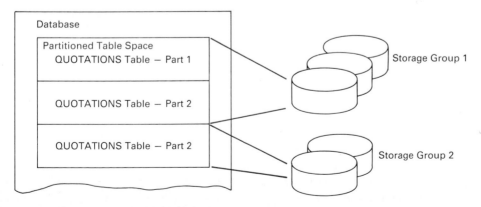

Figure 3.3   A partitioned table space can be stored on one or more storage groups.

LOGICAL VERSUS PHYSICAL REPRESENTATION   Indexes, table spaces, index spaces, databases, storage groups, and partitions all concern the way DB2 data is physically stored and accessed. Because of the separation that DB2 provides between the logical and the physical representation of data, an end user or application program is not aware of DB2 physical storage structures. Physical storage structures are the concern only of those involved with DB2 system administration.

DATA VIEWS AND SQL   As we stated earlier, SQL is the main language that DB2 supports for describing tables and other DB2 objects and for retrieving and manipulating the data stored in tables. SQL includes statements that can be used to define user views, logical data models, and physical storage structures. It also includes statements that can be used to retrieve and manipulate data and to handle the special processing requirements associated with database management systems, including security, integrity, recovery, and dynamic SQL execution.

DATA DEFINITION   SQL statements associated with logical data definition are used to define and describe tables and views and are concerned with the way data is logically represented to and accessed by end users and application programs. SQL statements associated with physical data definition are used to create and drop databases, indexes, storage groups, and table spaces and to alter these objects. Box 3.1 lists the SQL statements used for data definition.

BOX 3.1   SQL data definition statements

Logical Data Definition

The following statements are used to define and describe tables and views:

- ALTER TABLE
- COMMENT ON
- CREATE TABLE
- CREATE SYNONYM
- CREATE VIEW

BOX 3.1   *(Continued)*

- DECLARE TABLE
- DESCRIBE
- DROP TABLE
- DROP SYNONYM
- DROP VIEW
- INCLUDE
- LABEL ON

Physical Data Definition

The following statements are used to define and describe databases, indexes, storage groups, and table spaces:

- ALTER INDEX
- ALTER STOGROUP
- ALTER TABLESPACE
- CREATE DATABASE
- CREATE INDEX
- CREATE STOGROUP
- CREATE TABLESPACE
- DROP DATABASE
- DROP INDEX
- DROP STOGROUP
- DROP TABLESPACE

DATA RETRIEVAL AND MANIPULATION   SQL statements associated with retrieving and manipulating data are used to perform relational operations on tables, to delete rows, to insert rows, and to modify existing rows. The statement used to retrieve data and to perform all types of relational operations on tables is the SELECT statement. The result of a SELECT statement is another table that often contains multiple rows. The conventional programming languages used to develop SQL applications are typically not designed to operate on a set of rows, or records, as a unit. To accom-

BOX 3.2   SQL data manipulation statements

Data Retrieval and Manipulation

The following statements are used for basic data manipulation:

- SELECT
- DELETE
- INSERT
- UPDATE
- EXPLAIN
- WHENEVER

Cursor Manipulation

The following statements are used to define and manipulate cursors to do row-at-a-time processing:

- DECLARE
- OPEN
- FETCH
- CLOSE

modate these languages, SQL uses a cursor to process rows one at a time. Box 3.2 lists the SQL statements used for data retrieval, data manipulation, and cursor processing.

PROCESSING SUPPORT SQL includes statements that can be used to control authorization to access various DB2 objects and to perform certain types of operations on them, to control data integrity by placing locks on table data, and to control whether and when changes are committed, or made permanent.

There are also statements that allow SQL statements to be dynamically constructed and executed during program execution, rather than requiring the SQL statements to be compiled into the program. Box 3.3 lists the SQL statements used to support DB2 processing.

BOX 3.3   SQL processing support statements

Security, Integrity, and Recovery

The following statements are used to provide for security, data integrity, and recovery in DB2 processing:

- GRANT
- REVOKE
- LOCK TABLE
- COMMIT
- ROLLBACK

Dynamic Processing

The following statements are used to dynamically construct and execute SQL statements:

- DECLARE STATEMENT
- EXECUTE
- EXECUTE IMMEDIATE
- PREPARE

SUMMARY OF PART I

DB2 runs under any currently supported version of the MVS operating system in conjunction with either TSO, CICS, or IMS. DB2 data can be accessed either in foreground or in background and either interactively or in batch mode. With CICS and IMS, an application program can access both DB2 and IMS data.

A database management system provides for the centralized definition, storage, and management of data. Centralized storage and management help to reduce data redundancy. Data can be accessed by multiple applications without storing multiple copies of the data. Centralized definition and description of data also increase data independence. There can be a separation between logical and physical data definition, allowing applications to be independent of the physical storage structures that are used to implement the database. Each program can have its own logical view of the data and be less affected by changes to the structure of the database. Since multiple applications and users can access the data, security features must be provided to prevent unauthorized database access. A database management system also provides for recovery of data in the event of hardware or software failures. Recovery capabilities are implemented by periodically making copies of databases and logging changes to databases as the changes are made. A system of resource locks is used to control concurrent access to data so that the information in the database remains accurate and consistent.

The relational model consists of a set of objects, a set of operators, and a set of integrity rules. Data is represented in the form of tables consisting of rows and columns. Each row-column entry consists of a single data item, and all data items in a given column are drawn from the same domain. Rows and columns can be viewed in any sequence. Each row contains a column or set of columns, called the primary key, that uniquely identifies the row. A foreign key is a column or set of columns that contains data item values drawn from the same domain as the column or columns that form the primary key of some other table. All relationships between tables are expressed by data stored in the tables. The relational model defines a number of relational operators that can be applied to tables. When a relational operator is applied to a table or group of tables, the result of the operation is always another table. The relational operators are union, intersection, difference, Cartesian product, select, project, inner join, outer join, and divide. The entity integrity rule states that no column that is part of a primary key can have a null value. The referential integrity rule states that a foreign key value must either match an existing primary key value or be wholly null.

Most database management systems provide for three levels of data definition: user views that are defined by the external schema, logical data models that are defined by the software schema, and physical data structures that are defined by the internal schema. In DB2, logical data models are defined in the form of tables. A user view is defined in the form of a DB2 view, which is a virtual table that is defined in terms of a relational operation that is performed on one or more base tables. DB2 physical data structures include indexes, table spaces, index spaces, databases, and storage groups. Indexes are used to define a table's primary key and can also be used to control the way a table is accessed. Tables are stored in table spaces, and indexes are stored in index spaces. A partitioned table space physically divides a table based on ranges of data item values. A DB2 database consists physically of a set of table spaces and their associated index spaces. A table space or index space can be associated with a particular group of DASD volumes, known as a storage group. The SQL language provides facilities for defining DB2 logical and physical storage structures, for retrieving and manipulating data, and for handling security, integrity, and recovery functions.

PART **II** **STRUCTURED QUERY LANGUAGE (SQL)**

As we learned in Part I, the main language of DB2 is *Structured Query Language* (SQL). Part II of this book examines the SQL language in detail and shows examples of its use. Chapter 4 shows how SQL can be used to formulate simple queries against DB2 tables. Chapter 5 presents examples of more complex queries. Chapter 6 examines the use of SQL for functions other than queries, including updating tables, creating and deleting tables and views, and granting authorization to perform operations on tables and views.

4 SIMPLE QUERIES

SQL is a powerful language that performs the functions of both a data definition language and a data manipulation language. SQL statements can be entered interactively at a terminal, executed as part of a stored procedure, or embedded in a program written in a host programming language. SQL provides a number of statements that are entered using an English-like syntax. As we will see in these chapters, SQL coding rules are simple and generally easy to remember. SQL is suitable for use by end users and also by trained information systems professionals.

EXECUTING SQL STATEMENTS A facility that is provided with the DB2 DBMS for executing SQL statements is a program called *DB2 Interactive* (DB2I). The main function of DB2I is to aid application developers in writing application programs that use embedded SQL statements to access DB2 tables. These facilities of DB2I are discussed in detail in Part IV of this book. DB2I also has a facility called *SQL Processor Using File Input* (SPUFI) that can be used to execute SQL statements interactively using a display terminal. Most installations that allow end users to execute SQL statements interactively, however, install the Query Management Facility (QMF). QMF is a separate program product that runs in conjunction with DB2 and provides more comprehensive support than SPUFI for interactive SQL users. For example, in addition to allowing SQL statements to be interactively executed, QMF also provides a comprehensive report formatter and allows end users to create graphics displays from the information stored in DB2 databases.

In this part of the book we examine SQL as a language, and these three chapters on SQL are independent of any particular implementation of the SQL language. We will show the results of SQL statements as if they had been entered using QMF; however, the examples all work using SPUFI as well. Most of the SQL statements shown here could also be executed by other products that support SQL. For example, the SQL examples in this book were initially developed on an IBM Personal Computer/AT using Oracle, a relational DBMS marketed by Oracle Corporation. The database management system that is part of the Extended Edition of IBM's OS/2 operating system for personal computers also supports SQL. Most products that implement SQL have introduced slight variations in the syntax, and many have added extensions to IBM's version of SQL. The SQL language has been accepted as an international standard, which has been published by the American National Standards Institute (ANSI). Again, the ANSI version of SQL is slightly different from IBM's. Unlike many languages, however, the various dialects of SQL are quite similar. A user who is familiar with IBM's version of SQL will find it easy to use another vendor's SQL product. It is safe to say that SQL will be implemented by great numbers of products in the coming years.

The SQL statements examined in this part of the book are those most commonly used for data retrieval and data manipulation and for logical data definition. Some statements used specifically in an application programming environment, such as those related to cursor processing, are introduced in Part IV. Statements associated with physical data definition and system administration functions are introduced in Part V.

THE SELECT STATEMENT

We will begin our investigation of SQL facilities by showing the results of simple examples of the SQL SELECT statement, which is used to retrieve data from DB2 tables. The SQL SELECT statement should not be confused with the *select* relational operator that we introduced in Chapter 2. The SELECT SQL statement can be used to perform all the various relational operations on tables and is not limited to the select relational operator. All SQL statements consist of a verb followed by one or more optional clauses. The basic form of the SELECT operation is as follows:

SELECT	some data (column names)
FROM	some place (a table name)
WHERE	conditions (comparisons on data item values)
ORDER BY	desired sequence (column names)

All SELECT statements must include a FROM clause, but the WHERE and ORDER BY clauses are optional. For the purposes of the SELECT statement examples in this chapter, we will assume that the tables shown in Fig. 4.1 have already been created and loaded and that they are available for our use.

INVENTORY

INVPART	PNAME	ONHAND
124	BOLT	900
125	BOLT	1000
105	GEAR	0
106	GEAR	700
171	GENERATOR	500
172	GENERATOR	400
134	NUT	900
135	NUT	1000
181	WHEEL	1000
205	BAND	450
206	MOTOR	225
221	AXLE	1500
222	AXLE	25
231	AXLE	75
232	AXLE	150
241	WHEEL	300

QUOTATIONS

QUOSUPP	QUOPART	PRICE	TIME	ONORD
51	124	1.25	5	400
51	125	0.55	5	0
51	134	0.40	5	500
51	135	0.39	5	1000
51	221	0.30	10	10000
51	231	0.10	10	5000
52	105	7.50	10	200
52	205	0.15	20	0
52	206	0.15	20	0
53	124	1.35	3	500
53	125	0.58	3	200
53	134	0.38	3	200
53	135	0.42	3	1000
53	222	0.25	15	10000
53	232	-	15	0
53	241	0.08	15	6000

SUPPLIERS

SUPSUPP	NAME	ADDRESS	CODE
51	DEFECTO PARTS	16 JUSTAMERE LANE, TACOMA WA	20
52	VESUVIUS INC.	512 ANCIENT BLVD., POMPEII NY	20
53	ATLANTIS CO.	8 OCEAN AVE., WASHINGTON DC	10
54	TITANIC PARTS	32 SINKING STREET, ATLANTIC CITY NJ	30
57	EAGLE HARDWARE	64 TRANQUILITY PLACE, APOLLO MN	30
61	SKYLAB PARTS	128 ORBIT BLVD., SYDNEY AUSTRALIA	10
64	KNIGHT LTD.	256 ARTHUR COURT, CAMELOT ENGLAND	20

Figure 4.1   Inventory, Quotations, and Suppliers tables.

SELECTING ALL COLUMNS, ALL ROWS

The simplest form of SQL query is to list all the data contained in a DB2 table. This can be done by using the * option of the SELECT statement. For example, the following SELECT statement displays all the rows from all the columns in the *Quotations* table:

```
SELECT      *
FROM        QUOTATIONS
```

Here are the results that would be displayed as a result of this query:

QUOSUPP	QUOPART	PRICE	TIME	ONORD
51	124	1.25	5	400
51	125	0.55	5	0
51	134	0.40	5	500
51	135	0.39	5	1000
51	221	0.30	10	10000
51	231	0.10	10	5000
52	105	7.50	10	200
52	205	0.15	20	0
52	206	0.15	20	0
53	124	1.35	3	500
53	125	0.58	3	200
53	134	0.38	3	200
53	135	0.42	3	1000
53	222	0.25	15	10000
53	232	-	15	0
53	241	0.08	15	6000

Keep in mind that the format of the resulting display may vary somewhat from the display shown here, depending on the particular SQL software that is being used. In the remaining SQL examples, we will follow each SQL statement by its result.

The asterisk following the keyword SELECT indicates that we would like all columns listed. The columns are displayed in the order in which they were defined when the table was created.

The SELECT statement can be used to generate a report that lists columns in a specified order, by listing the column names in the SELECT statement; SQL then displays the columns in the order in which we list them:

```
SELECT     QUOSUPP, QUOPART, TIME, ONORD, PRICE
FROM       QUOTATIONS
```

QUOSUPP	QUOPART	TIME	ONORD	PRICE
51	124	5	400	1.25
51	125	5	0	0.55
51	134	5	500	0.40
51	135	5	1000	0.39
51	221	10	10000	0.30
51	231	10	5000	0.10
52	105	10	200	7.50
52	205	20	0	0.15
52	206	20	0	0.15
53	124	3	500	1.35
53	125	3	200	0.58
53	134	3	200	0.38
53	135	3	1000	0.42
53	222	15	10000	0.25
53	232	15	0	–
53	241	15	6000	0.08

DISPLAYING SELECTED COLUMNS

We can use the SELECT statement to limit the number of columns that are displayed simply by omitting the names of the columns that we do not want displayed. Providing a list of only selected column names in a SELECT statement is equivalent to performing a *project* relational operation on the table. In the following example, we are displaying data from only three columns:

```
SELECT      QUOSUPP, QUOPART, PRICE
FROM        QUOTATIONS


QUOSUPP  QUOPART     PRICE
-------  -------    -------
     51      124       1.25
     51      125       0.55
     51      134       0.40
     51      135       0.39
     51      221       0.30
     51      231       0.10
     52      105       7.50
     52      205       0.15
     52      206       0.15
     53      124       1.35
     53      125       0.58
     53      134       0.38
     53      135       0.42
     53      222       0.25
     53      232         -
     53      241       0.08
```

DISPLAYING   We can include a WHERE clause in a SELECT state-
SELECTED ROWS   ment to cause SQL to display data from only selected
                             rows in the table. This use of a WHERE clause in a
SELECT statement is equivalent to performing a *select* relational operation on
the table. We use the WHERE clause to specify one or more conditions that
certain data item values in a row must meet in order for data from that row to
be displayed. For example, the following SELECT statement asks DB2 to display only the rows in the *Quotations* table for which the *Quopart* data item
value is 124:

```
SELECT      *
FROM        QUOTATIONS
WHERE       QUOPART = 124


QUOSUPP  QUOPART     PRICE      TIME     ONORD
-------  -------    -------   -------   -------
     51      124       1.25         5       400
     53      124       1.35         3       500
```

We used an equal comparison (QUOPART = 124) as the selection condition.
Other types of comparisons can also be used, including these:

>   greater than

>=   greater than or equal to

<   less than

<=   less than or equal to

¬ =   not equal to

¬ >   not greater than

¬ <   not less than

For example, the following statement asks for a list of all supplier, part, and price values for parts whose price is greater than $1.00:

```
SELECT    QUOSUPP, QUOPART, PRICE
FROM      QUOTATIONS
WHERE     PRICE > 1.00


QUOSUPP  QUOPART    PRICE
-------  -------  -------
     51      124     1.25
     52      105     7.50
     53      124     1.35
```

We can specify a WHERE condition that performs a comparison on data item values from a column that contains character data. To do this, we must enclose the comparison value in single quotation marks:

```
SELECT    *
FROM      INVENTORY
WHERE     PNAME = 'BOLT'


INVPART  PNAME            ONHAND
-------  ---------------  -------
    124  BOLT                 900
    125  BOLT                1000
```

SELECTION USING ARITHMETIC EXPRESSIONS

We can include arithmetic expressions in WHERE selection conditions. We can use these arithmetic operators in SELECT statements:

+   add

−   subtract

*   multiply

/   divide

The following SELECT statement will display all supplier and part values where the quotation amount *(Price × Onord)* is greater than $500.00:

```
SELECT      QUOSUPP, QUOPART
FROM        QUOTATIONS
WHERE       PRICE * ONORD > 500.00
```

```
QUOSUPP   QUOPART
-------   -------
     51       221
     52       105
     53       124
     53       222
```

SELECTION USING A LIST OR RANGE

We can use the IN and BETWEEN keywords to specify a list of values or a range of values in a WHERE condition. For example, we can specify a list of values in parentheses following the IN keyword. Whenever a row contains a data item value that matches one of the values in parentheses following the IN keyword, the row is selected. The following SELECT command displays supplier, part, and price values for part numbers *105, 135,* or *205:*

```
SELECT      QUOSUPP, QUOPART, PRICE
FROM        QUOTATIONS
WHERE       QUOPART IN (105, 135, 205)
```

```
QUOSUPP   QUOPART     PRICE
-------   -------   -------
     51       135      0.39
     52       105      7.50
     52       205      0.15
     53       135      0.42
```

We can use the BETWEEN keyword to specify a range of values. The following statement selects quotations for all parts in the range *105* through *135* (the range specified includes the values *105* and *135* as well as all values that fall between them):

```
SELECT      QUOSUPP, QUOPART, PRICE
FROM        QUOTATIONS
WHERE       QUOPART BETWEEN 105 AND 135
```

```
QUOSUPP   QUOPART     PRICE
-------   -------   -------
     51       124      1.25
     51       125      0.55
     51       134      0.40
     51       135      0.39
     52       105      7.50
     53       124      1.35
     53       125      0.58
     53       134      0.38
     53       135      0.42
```

The IN and BETWEEN keywords can also specify character values, in which case the values must be enclosed in single quotation marks.

PATTERN MATCHING

We can also base a selection on the occurrence of a particular pattern of characters in a data item. This is done by using the LIKE option. Selection using LIKE can only be done for columns that contain character or graphic data. We can specify that a variable number of characters may occur either before or after the desired value by using the percent sign (%). We might use the following SELECT statement to select suppliers located in the state of Minnesota:

```
SELECT     SUPSUPP, NAME, ADDRESS
FROM       SUPPLIERS
WHERE      ADDRESS LIKE '% MN%'
```

SUPSUPP	NAME	ADDRESS
57	EAGLE HARDWARE	64 Tranquility Place, Apollo, MN

The first % specifies that any number of other characters can precede '' MN'', and the second % character specifies that any number of characters can follow it. Of course, such queries must be carefully planned. All rows having the three-character string '' MN'' in the address column will be selected. We include a blank preceding the MN in the string to ensure that MN is preceded by at least one blank, thus ensuring that rows will not be selected that have the characters ''MN'' embedded in a street or city name.

We can also specify the number of characters that should precede or follow the desired value by using an underscore for each preceding or following character. The following SELECT statement could be used to display all parts for which the second character in the part name is ''O'':

```
SELECT     *
FROM       INVENTORY
WHERE      PNAME LIKE '_O%'
```

INVPART	PNAME	ONHAND
124	BOLT	900
125	BOLT	1000
206	MOTOR	225

This query could alternatively be performed using the SUBSTR function:

```
SELECT    *
FROM      INVENTORY
WHERE     SUBSTR (PNAME,2,1) = 'O'


INVPART  PNAME              ONHAND
-------  ----------------   -------
    124  BOLT                  900
    125  BOLT                 1000
    206  MOTOR                 225
```

The SUBSTR function is used to specify the starting position and length of a substring within a character or graphic data string. The substring can then be compared against the desired value.

ELIMINATING DUPLICATE ROWS   Depending on the selection criteria we specify and the columns that DB2 selects for display, it is possible for the result to contain duplicate rows. For example, the following SELECT displays suppliers that have quotations with an on-order quantity greater than *200:*

```
SELECT    QUOSUPP
FROM      QUOTATIONS
WHERE     ONORD > 200


QUOSUPP
-------
     51
     51
     51
     51
     51
     53
     53
     53
     53
```

In this example, suppliers *51* and *53* are each listed several times in the resulting display, since each has numerous parts for which on-order is greater than *200*. To produce a result that is equivalent to the result of a true select relational operation, we include the DISTINCT keyword before specifying column names. The DISTINCT keyword causes DB2 to eliminate duplicate rows from the result:

```
SELECT      DISTINCT QUOSUPP
FROM        QUOTATIONS
WHERE       ONORD > 200


QUOSUPP
-------
     51
     53
```

MULTIPLE CONDITIONS

Selection can be based on multiple conditions, by using the AND and OR boolean operators. The following statement selects quotations for part number *124* where the price is greater than *$1.30:*

```
SELECT      QUOSUPP, QUOPART, PRICE
FROM        QUOTATIONS
WHERE       QUOPART = 124 AND PRICE > 1.30


QUOSUPP   QUOPART    PRICE
-------   -------   -------
     53       124     1.35
```

Two conditions connected by AND select a row only if it satisfies both conditions. Two conditions connected by OR select a row if it meets either condition. We can specify any number of conditions using combinations of AND and OR, as in the following example:

```
SELECT      *
FROM        QUOTATIONS
WHERE       QUOPART < 200 AND (PRICE > 1.00 OR TIME < 10)


QUOSUPP  QUOPART    PRICE     TIME     ONORD
-------  -------   -------   -------   -------
     51      124     1.25         5       400
     51      125     0.55         5         0
     51      134     0.40         5       500
     51      135     0.39         5      1000
     52      105     7.50        10       200
     53      124     1.35         3       500
     53      125     0.58         3       200
     53      134     0.38         3       200
     53      135     0.42         3      1000
```

In a WHERE clause that uses ANDs and ORs, all the ANDs are evaluated first, followed by the ORs. We can use parentheses to control the order in which the conditions are to be evaluated, as in the previous example. Parentheses can also be used to add clarity:

```
SELECT      *
FROM        QUOTATIONS
WHERE       (QUOPART < 200 AND PRICE > 1.00) OR TIME < 10
```

QUOSUPP	QUOPART	PRICE	TIME	ONORD
51	124	1.25	5	400
51	125	0.55	5	0
51	134	0.40	5	500
51	135	0.39	5	1000
52	105	7.50	10	200
53	124	1.35	3	500
53	125	0.58	3	200
53	134	0.38	3	200
53	135	0.42	3	1000

Multiple levels of parentheses can be used if required.

NULL VALUES

Depending on how a table is defined, a column may be allowed to contain data items that have a null value. A null value means that no value has been entered for the data item in that row; it is not the same as a value of blanks or zero. When DB2 displays a null value, it typically displays it as a hyphen (-). The *Quotations* table shows an example of a null value. The entry for supplier *53* and part *232* has a null value for price. We can select specifically for null values by using the NULL keyword:

```
SELECT      *
FROM        QUOTATIONS
WHERE       PRICE IS NULL
```

QUOSUPP	QUOPART	PRICE	TIME	ONORD
53	232	-	15	0

Note that we used the keyword IS instead of the equal sign. The various comparison operators, $+$, $>$, $<$, etc., cannot be used to select a null value. Null is not considered greater than, less than, or equal to any value in evaluating conditional expressions. When any operation is performed using a null value, the result is null. So for the row shown, the arithmetic operation PRICE * ONORD results in a null value, not zero. NULL cannot be specified as one of the values in the list of values used with the IN keyword.

It is possible to specify that something other than the hyphen be displayed
for null values. This is done using the VALUE function:

```
SELECT      QUOSUPP, QUOPART, VALUE (PRICE, 0.00), TIME, ONORD
FROM        QUOTATIONS
WHERE       PRICE IS NULL
```

QUOSUPP	QUOPART	PRICE	TIME	ONORD
53	232	0.00	15	0

In this example, the value 0.00 is displayed for *Price* rather than the hyphen.
The value to be displayed must be consistent with the data type of the field in
question.

NEGATIVE CONDITIONS

We can specify the opposite of any condition by adding the keyword NOT to the beginning of the conditional expression. When NOT is used, rather than se-
lecting rows that meet the condition, DB2 selects rows that fail to meet the
condition. For example, NOT can be used with a comparison operator:

```
SELECT      *
FROM        QUOTATIONS
WHERE       NOT QUOPART = 124
```

QUOSUPP	QUOPART	PRICE	TIME	ONORD
51	125	0.55	5	0
51	134	0.40	5	500
51	135	0.39	5	1000
51	221	0.30	10	10000
51	231	0.10	10	5000
52	105	7.50	10	200
52	205	0.15	20	0
52	206	0.15	20	0
53	125	0.58	3	200
53	134	0.38	3	200
53	135	0.42	3	1000
53	222	0.25	15	10000
53	232	-	15	0
53	241	0.08	15	6000

This SELECT statement is equivalent to the following:

```
SELECT      *
FROM        QUOTATIONS
WHERE       QUOPART ¬= 124
```

QUOSUPP	QUOPART	PRICE	TIME	ONORD
51	125	0.55	5	0
51	134	0.40	5	500
51	135	0.39	5	1000
51	221	0.30	10	10000
51	231	0.10	10	5000
52	105	7.50	10	200
52	205	0.15	20	0
52	206	0.15	20	0
53	125	0.58	3	200
53	134	0.38	3	200
53	135	0.42	3	1000
53	222	0.25	15	10000
53	232	–	15	0
53	241	0.08	15	6000

Note that NOT precedes the entire condition. It would not be correct to code the following:

```
SELECT      *
FROM        QUOTATIONS
WHERE       QUOPART NOT = 124
```

USING THE NOT OPERATOR

The NOT Boolean operator can be used with multiple conditions that are connected by AND or OR. Again, it may be necessary to use parentheses to specify the part or parts of the conditions the NOT applies to. If parentheses are not used, the NOT applies only to the condition that immediately follows it. So

```
SELECT      *
FROM        QUOTATIONS
WHERE       NOT QUOPART < 200 AND (PRICE > 1.00 OR TIME < 10)
```

is equivalent to

```
SELECT      *
FROM        QUOTATIONS
WHERE       (NOT QUOPART < 200) AND (PRICE > 1.00 OR TIME < 10)
```

No rows would be selected by either of these SELECT statements.

To negate an entire expression, it is necessary to enclose the entire conditional expression in parentheses:

```
SELECT    *
FROM      QUOTATIONS
WHERE     NOT (QUOPART < 200 AND (PRICE > 1.00 OR TIME < 10))
```

QUOSUPP	QUOPART	PRICE	TIME	ONORD
51	221	0.30	10	10000
51	231	0.10	10	5000
52	205	0.15	20	0
52	206	0.15	20	0
53	222	0.25	15	10000
53	232	–	15	0
53	241	0.08	15	6000

This SELECT statement selects all rows where the part number is greater than or equal to *200* or the price is less than or equal to *1.00* and time is greater than or equal to *10*.

NOT can also be used with the IN, BETWEEN, and LIKE keywords. For example, the following SELECT statement lists rows with part numbers other than *105, 135,* or *205:*

```
SELECT    QUOSUPP, QUOPART, PRICE
FROM      QUOTATIONS
WHERE     QUOPART NOT IN (105, 135, 205)
```

QUOSUPP	QUOPART	PRICE
51	124	1.25
51	125	0.55
51	134	0.40
51	221	0.30
51	231	0.10
52	206	0.15
53	124	1.35
53	125	0.58
53	134	0.38
53	222	0.25
53	232	–
53	241	0.08

Similarly, this SELECT statement selects rows where the part number is less than *105* or greater than *135:*

```
SELECT      QUOSUPP, QUOPART, PRICE
FROM        QUOTATIONS
WHERE       QUOPART NOT BETWEEN 105 AND 135
```

QUOSUPP	QUOPART	PRICE
51	221	0.30
51	231	0.10
52	205	0.15
52	206	0.15
53	222	0.25
53	232	–
53	241	0.08

And this one selects suppliers whose address does not contain the value '' MN'':

```
SELECT      *
FROM        SUPPLIERS
WHERE       ADDRESS NOT LIKE '% MN%'
```

SUPSUPP	NAME	ADDRESS	CODE
51	DEFECTO PARTS	16 JUSTAMERE LANE, TACOMA WA	20
52	VESUVIUS INC.	512 ANCIENT BLVD., POMPEII NY	20
53	ATLANTIS CO.	8 OCEAN AVE., WASHINGTON DC	10
54	TITANIC PARTS	32 SINKING STREET, ATLANTIC CITY NJ	30
61	SKYLAB PARTS	128 ORBIT BLVD., SYDNEY AUSTRALIA	10
64	KNIGHT LTD.	256 ARTHUR COURT, CAMELOT ENGLAND	20

NOT can also be used with NULL, to select entries that do not have a null value. The following SELECT statement selects all rows in which the price is not a null value.

```
SELECT      *
FROM        QUOTATIONS
WHERE       PRICE IS NOT NULL
```

QUOSUPP	QUOPART	PRICE	TIME	ONORD
51	124	1.25	5	400
51	125	0.55	5	0
51	134	0.40	5	500
51	135	0.39	5	1000
51	221	0.30	10	10000
51	231	0.10	10	5000
52	105	7.50	10	200
52	205	0.15	20	0
52	206	0.15	20	0
53	124	1.35	3	500
53	125	0.58	3	200
53	134	0.38	3	200
53	135	0.42	3	1000
53	222	0.25	15	10000
53	241	0.08	15	6000

GENERATED COLUMNS

In addition to displaying columns selected from a table, it is possible to display values that are generated based on calculations performed on values from other columns. Earlier, we calculated the quotation amount by multiplying *Price* times *Onord* and used the result as part of a condition. We can also display the calculated amount as part of the resulting table:

```
SELECT      QUOSUPP, QUOPART, PRICE * ONORD
FROM        QUOTATIONS
WHERE       PRICE > 1.00


QUOSUPP    QUOPART   PRICE*ONORD
-------    -------   -----------
     51        124        500.00
     52        105       1500.00
     53        124        675.00
```

Different SQL implementations use various conventions for naming generated columns. For example, the SPUFI program that is part of DB2's DB2I facility leaves the names of generated columns blank. The version of SQL used with DB2 running under MVS assigns the name "COL1" to the first generated column, "COL2" to the second, and so on. The version of SQL that runs under the VM operating system names columns "EXPRESSION 1", "EXPRESSION 2", etc. Some SQL implementations use the expression itself as the column name, as in our example. We will adopt this convention in our examples to make the listings easier to read.

SEQUENCING THE ROWS

The rows that are displayed as the result of a query are displayed in the same sequence as they occur in the table from which they are selected. As we learned in Chapter 2, one of the characteristics of a DB2 table is that no sequence is associated with the rows of a table. If data is entered into a table in sequence, the table may appear to be sequenced when it is displayed, but this sequence may not be maintained.

When data is retrieved, we may want it displayed in a particular sequence. We can use the ORDER BY clause in the SELECT statement to sequence the rows in the displayed table. For example, the following SELECT statement lists the selected rows in ascending part number sequence and in descending price sequence for each part number:

```
SELECT    QUOPART, QUOSUPP, PRICE
FROM      QUOTATIONS
WHERE     QUOPART IN (124, 125, 134, 135)
ORDER BY  QUOPART, PRICE DESC
```

QUOPART	QUOSUPP	PRICE
124	53	1.35
124	51	1.25
125	53	0.58
125	51	0.55
134	51	0.40
134	53	0.38
135	53	0.42
135	51	0.39

The ORDER BY clause specifies the sequence used for the results. The first column name listed is the primary sequence. Additional column names, if used, specify minor sort sequences. So here the results are in sequence by part number, and by price within part number. The keyword DESC specifies descending sequence on the *Price* column. The default is ascending sequence, so part numbers are listed in ascending sequence. A column that we specify in an ORDER BY clause must be included in the list of columns specified in the SELECT statement (or by using the * option).

SORTING ON A GENERATED COLUMN

It is possible to use a generated column as one of the ORDER BY columns. However, since a calculated column does not have a name, we must refer to it by its column number. Here, since the generated column is the third one specified in the SELECT statement, we refer to it by the number *3* in the ORDER BY clause:

```
SELECT    QUOSUPP, QUOPART, PRICE * ONORD
FROM      QUOTATIONS
WHERE     PRICE > 1.00
ORDER BY  QUOPART, 3 DESC
```

QUOSUPP	QUOPART	PRICE*ONORD
52	105	1500
53	124	675
51	124	500

Column numbers can be used in place of column names for the other columns as well. The following SELECT statement is equivalent to the previous one:

```
SELECT     QUOSUPP, QUOPART, PRICE * ONORD
FROM       QUOTATIONS
WHERE      PRICE > 1.00
ORDER BY   2, 3 DESC
```

```
QUOSUPP   QUOPART   PRICE*ONORD
-------   -------   -----------
     52       105          1500
     53       124           675
     51       124           500
```

As the examples in this chapter show, the SQL SELECT statement has a great deal of power and versatility, even when used for relatively simple queries. Chapter 5 shows additional queries using the SQL SELECT statement that illustrate more complex relational operations.

5 COMPLEX QUERIES

In this chapter, we will look at examples of SQL SELECT statements that address some of the more complex types of queries that we can formulate using SQL. These examples will use the tables introduced in Chapter 4, repeated here in Fig. 5.1.

INVENTORY

INVPART	PNAME	ONHAND
124	BOLT	900
125	BOLT	1000
105	GEAR	0
106	GEAR	700
171	GENERATOR	500
172	GENERATOR	400
134	NUT	900
135	NUT	1000
181	WHEEL	1000
205	BAND	450
206	MOTOR	225
221	AXLE	1500
222	AXLE	25
231	AXLE	75
232	AXLE	150
241	WHEEL	300

QUOTATIONS

QUOSUPP	QUOPART	PRICE	TIME	ONORD
51	124	1.25	5	400
51	125	0.55	5	0
51	134	0.40	5	500
51	135	0.39	5	1000
51	221	0.30	10	10000
51	231	0.10	10	5000
52	105	7.50	10	200
52	205	0.15	20	0
52	206	0.15	20	0
53	124	1.35	3	500
53	125	0.58	3	200
53	134	0.38	3	200
53	135	0.42	3	1000
53	222	0.25	15	10000
53	232	–	15	0
53	241	0.08	15	6000

SUPPLIERS

SUPSUPP	NAME	ADDRESS	CODE
51	DEFECTO PARTS	16 JUSTAMERE LANE, TACOMA WA	20
52	VESUVIUS INC.	512 ANCIENT BLVD., POMPEII NY	20
53	ATLANTIS CO.	8 OCEAN AVE., WASHINGTON DC	10
54	TITANIC PARTS	32 SINKING STREET, ATLANTIC CITY NJ	30
57	EAGLE HARDWARE	64 TRANQUILITY PLACE, APOLLO MN	30
61	SKYLAB PARTS	128 ORBIT BLVD., SYDNEY AUSTRALIA	10
64	KNIGHT LTD.	256 ARTHUR COURT, CAMELOT ENGLAND	20

Figure 5.1 Inventory, Quotations, and Suppliers tables.

JOINING TABLES   The queries shown in Chapter 4 were all based on selecting data from a single table. SQL has the capability to allow data from multiple tables to be combined, in effect performing a *join* relational operation. As we discussed in Chapter 2, a join operation involves combining rows from one table with rows from another table, based on a comparison that is performed between the data item values in a column from the first table and the values from a column in the second table.

Suppose that we wished to list the part number, name, on-hand quantity, supplier, and on-order quantity for all parts for which there are quotations. To do this, we need to combine information from the *Inventory* and the *Quotations* tables. The following SELECT statement joins the two tables based on the *Invpart* column from the *Inventory* table and the *Quopart* column from the *Quotations* table:

```
SELECT     INVPART, PNAME, ONHAND, QUOSUPP, ONORD
FROM       INVENTORY, QUOTATIONS
WHERE      INVPART = QUOPART
ORDER BY   INVPART, QUOSUPP
```

INVPART	PNAME	ONHAND	QUOSUPP	ONORD
105	GEAR	0	52	200
124	BOLT	900	51	400
124	BOLT	900	53	500
125	BOLT	1000	51	0
125	BOLT	1000	53	200
134	NUT	900	51	500
134	NUT	900	53	200
135	NUT	1000	51	1000
135	NUT	1000	53	1000
205	BAND	450	52	0
206	MOTOR	225	52	0
221	AXLE	1500	51	10000
222	AXLE	25	53	10000
231	AXLE	75	51	5000
232	AXLE	150	53	0
241	WHEEL	300	53	6000

Notice in this SELECT statement that we listed column names from both tables and also identified both tables in the FROM clause. The WHERE clause specifies that we want an *equijoin* based on the *Invpart* and *Quopart* columns. For example, each row in the *Quotations* table that has a part number of *124* will be joined with the information for part *124* from the *Inventory* table. Only the rows for the part numbers that appear in both the *Quotations* and *Inventory* tables are included in the result.

The comparison used to join the tables does not have to be for equal values, although the equijoin is the most commonly used type of join in practice. It is also possible to join tables without specifying a condition. If we exclude the WHERE clause and name two tables, each row of the first table is joined with every row of the second table—in effect performing a *Cartesian product* relational operation. As we pointed out in Chapter 2, the result of a Cartesian product operation is a table that has a number of rows that is equal to the number of rows in the first table multiplied by the number of rows in the second table. A Cartesian product operation is allowed, but if the two tables are large, it could consume large amounts of computing resources.

In performing a join operation, we must take care in selecting the joining columns. In most cases, join operations are performed on columns that contain the same type of data, such as the part numbers in our most recent example. It is the user's responsibility to ensure that the values in the columns are drawn from the same domain and that it makes sense to compare them. For example, it would make no sense to perform a join based on the part number in the *Inventory* table and the on-order amount in the *Quotations* table, even though some of the values might possibly match. DB2 checks that the joining columns contain the appropriate type of data to be compared but performs no validation beyond this.

JOINING MORE THAN TWO TABLES

A join can involve more than two tables. Suppose that in our previous example we also wished to list the supplier name from the *Supplier* table. Here is a SELECT statement that will provide the required information:

```
SELECT      INVPART, PNAME, ONHAND, QUOSUPP, NAME, ONORD
FROM        INVENTORY, QUOTATIONS, SUPPLIERS
WHERE       INVPART = QUOPART
            AND QUOSUPP = SUPSUPP
ORDER BY    INVPART, QUOSUPP
```

INVPART	PNAME	ONHAND	QUOSUPP	NAME	ONORD
105	GEAR	0	52	VESUVIUS, INC.	200
124	BOLT	900	51	DEFECTO PARTS	400
124	BOLT	900	53	ATLANTIS CO.	500
125	BOLT	1000	51	DEFECTO PARTS	0
125	BOLT	1000	53	ATLANTIS CO.	200
134	NUT	900	51	DEFECTO PARTS	500
134	NUT	900	53	ATLANTIS CO.	200
135	NUT	1000	51	DEFECTOR PARTS	1000
135	NUT	1000	53	ATLANTIS CO.	1000
205	BAND	450	52	VESUVIUS, INC.	0
206	MOTOR	225	52	VESUVIUS, INC.	0
221	AXLE	1500	51	DEFECTO PARTS	10000
222	AXLE	25	53	ATLANTIS CO.	10000
231	AXLE	75	51	DEFECTO PARTS	5000
232	AXLE	150	53	ATLANTIS CO.	0
241	WHEEL	300	53	ATLANTIS CO.	6000

Notice that the comparisons we are asking DB2 to perform are reasonable. We are comparing part numbers in the *Inventory* and *Quotations* tables and supplier numbers in the *Quotations* and *Suppliers* tables.

DUPLICATE COLUMN NAMES

In the sample tables we have been using, all the column names are unique. However, this may not always be true. There may be occasions when columns in different tables have the same name. As shown in Chapter 2, this is often done to make clear the relationships that exist between tables. Suppose we named our columns as shown in Fig. 5.2. This naming scheme makes it clear

INVENTORY

PNUM	PNAME	ONHAND
124	BOLT	900
125	BOLT	1000
105	GEAR	0
106	GEAR	700
171	GENERATOR	500
172	GENERATOR	400
134	NUT	900
135	NUT	1000
181	WHEEL	1000
205	BAND	450
206	MOTOR	225
221	AXLE	1500
222	AXLE	25
231	AXLE	75
232	AXLE	150
241	WHEEL	300

QUOTATIONS

SNUM	PNUM	PRICE	TIME	ONORD
51	124	1.25	5	400
51	125	0.55	5	0
51	134	0.40	5	500
51	135	0.39	5	1000
51	221	0.30	10	10000
51	231	0.10	10	5000
52	105	7.50	10	200
52	205	0.15	20	0
52	206	0.15	20	0
53	124	1.35	3	500
53	125	0.58	3	200
53	134	0.38	3	200
53	135	0.42	3	1000
53	222	0.25	15	10000
53	232	–	15	0
53	241	0.08	15	6000

SUPPLIERS

SNUM	SNAME	SADDRESS	CODE
51	DEFECTO PARTS	16 JUSTAMERE LANE, TACOMA WA	20
52	VESUVIUS INC.	512 ANCIENT BLVD., POMPEII NY	20
53	ATLANTIS CO.	8 OCEAN AVE., WASHINGTON DC	10
54	TITANIC PARTS	32 SINKING STREET, ATLANTIC CITY NJ	30
57	EAGLE HARDWARE	64 TRANQUILITY PLACE, APOLLO MN	30
61	SKYLAB PARTS	128 ORBIT BLVD., SYDNEY AUSTRALIA	10
64	KNIGHT LTD.	256 ARTHUR COURT, CAMELOT ENGLAND	20

Figure 5.2   Column names need be unique only within the same table.

which columns contain part numbers *(pnum)* and which contain supplier numbers *(snum)*. Now when we join these tables, we need a way to indicate to which table a column belongs. One way to do this is to prefix the column name with the name of the appropriate table:

```
SELECT     QUOTATIONS.PNUM, PNAME, ONHAND, QUOTATIONS.SNUM, SNAME, ONORD
FROM       INVENTORY, QUOTATIONS, SUPPLIERS
WHERE      INVENTORY.PNUM = QUOTATIONS.PNUM
           AND QUOTATIONS.SNUM = SUPPLIERS.SNUM
ORDER BY   QUOTATIONS.PNUM, QUOTATIONS.SNUM
```

This can get cumbersome if table names are long. Another possibility is to assign a shorter name to each table, called a *join variable,* for the purpose of column identification. Join variables can be assigned in the FROM clause:

```
SELECT     Q.PNUM, PNAME, ONHAND, Q.SNUM, SNAME, ONORD
FROM       INVENTORY I, QUOTATIONS Q, SUPPLIERS S
WHERE      I.PNUM = Q.PNUM
           AND Q.SNUM = S.SNUM
ORDER BY   Q.PNUM, Q.SNUM
```

We are assigning the name *I* to the *Inventory* table, the name *Q* to the *Quotations* table and the name *S* to the *Suppliers* table. We are using these shorter names in place of the full table names to indicate the tables we are referencing.

BUILT-IN FUNCTIONS

SQL includes a set of built-in functions that can be used with the SELECT statement to perform operations on a table or on sets of rows from a table. The functions are as follows:

Function	Operation
SUM	Calculates a total
MIN	Calculates the minimum value
MAX	Calculates the maximum value
AVG	Calculates an average value
COUNT(*)	Counts the number of selected rows
COUNT (DISTINCT column name)	Counts unique values within a set of selected rows

Built-in functions can be applied to all the values in one or more columns in a table:

```
SELECT     SUM(ONORD), SUM(PRICE * ONORD), MAX(PRICE), AVG(PRICE)
FROM       QUOTATIONS
```

```
SUM(ONORD)   SUM(PRICE*ONORD)   MAX(PRICE)   AVG(PRICE)
----------   ----------------   ----------   ----------
     35000             10357         7.50   0.92333333
```

We can include the DISTINCT keyword with any of the functions in order to eliminate duplicate data values from the computation. For example, the following SELECT statement would calculate the average of all the unique price values in the *Price* column:

```
SELECT      AVG(DISTINCT PRICE)
FROM        QUOTATIONS


AVG(DISTINCTPRICE)
------------------
          0.978571
```

GROUPING ROWS

Built-in functions can also be applied to selected groups of rows in a table. To do this, we use the GROUP BY clause to indicate how rows should be grouped together. Generally, GROUP BY produces one row in the resulting table for each different value it finds in the column specified in the GROUP BY clause. The following SELECT uses a SUM function and a GROUP BY clause to produce a total of the *Onord* data item values for each different part number:

```
SELECT      QUOPART, SUM(ONORD)
FROM        QUOTATIONS
GROUP BY    QUOPART
ORDER BY    QUOPART


QUOPART   SUM(ONORD)
-------   ----------
    105          200
    124          900
    125          200
    134          700
    135         2000
    205            0
    206            0
    221        10000
    222        10000
    231         5000
    232            0
    241         6000
```

Here we group rows together on the basis of their part number values and apply the SUM function to the *Onord* values for each group of rows that have the same part number. Grouping rows does not guarantee that the results will be in sequence by the column specified. It is still necessary to include an ORDER BY clause, as shown, if the results are to be displayed in a particular sequence.

SUMMARY DATA IN CONDITIONS

Summary data calculated by grouping rows can be referenced in a conditional expression as well as displayed in a column. However, we use a HAVING clause instead of a WHERE clause to specify the conditional expression when the conditional expression references group data. For example, in this example, we use a conditional expression that references the results of a SUM function:

```
SELECT      QUOPART, SUM(ONORD)
FROM        QUOTATIONS
GROUP BY    QUOPART
HAVING      SUM(ONORD) > 0
ORDER BY    QUOPART
```

```
QUOPART   SUM(ONORD)
-------   ----------
    105          200
    124          900
    125          200
    134          700
    135         2000
    221        10000
    222        10000
    231         5000
    241         6000
```

The query results lists only parts that have a total on-order quantity that is greater than zero.

MULTIPLE COLUMNS IN A GROUP BY CLAUSE

If we specify more than one column name in the SELECT statement, other than those that specify built-in functions, we must list all of those columns in the associated GROUP BY clause. DB2 then generates a result row when the value changes in any of the specified columns. Suppose we have the table shown in Fig. 5.3. The following SELECT statement calculates the total invoice amount for each supplier/part pair:

```
SELECT      INVSUPP, INVPART, SUM(INVAMT)
FROM        INVOICES
GROUP BY    INVSUPP, INVPART
ORDER BY    INVSUPP, INVPART
```

```
INVSUPP   INVPART   SUM(INVAMT)
-------   -------   -----------
     51       124        500.00
     51       134        200.00
     51       135        390.00
     52       105       1500.00
     53       125        116.00
```

INVOICES

INVSUPP	INVPART	INVNUM	INVAMT
51	124	A103	200.00
51	124	A107	200.00
51	124	A111	100.00
51	134	A106	200.00
51	135	A120	200.00
51	135	A131	190.00
52	105	A115	1000.00
52	105	A127	500.00
53	125	A109	75.00
53	125	A122	25.00
53	125	A130	16.00

Figure 5.3   Invoices table.

NESTED QUERIES

One SELECT statement can be nested within an outer SELECT statement. The nested SELECT is known as a subselect or subquery. We can then reference the result of the subquery in the outer SELECT statement. Suppose we wished to list part numbers and prices for parts supplied by supplier *Vesuvius Inc*. To do this, we might use a subquery to determine the supplier number that corresponds to the name *Vesuvius Inc*. The following example shows how an outer SELECT statement references the result of the subquery:

```
SELECT     QUOPART, PRICE
FROM       QUOTATIONS
WHERE      QUOSUPP = (SELECT SUPSUPP
                      FROM SUPPLIERS
                      WHERE NAME = 'VESUVIUS INC.')


QUOPART    PRICE
-------    -------
    105     7.50
    205     0.15
    206     0.15
```

The inner SELECT is evaluated first and returns the value *52* for *Supsupp*. Based on this value, the outer SELECT is evaluated and returns the results shown. Note that the subquery must be entirely enclosed in parentheses. Generally, a subquery should be used when a value that is referenced in a WHERE or HAVING clause cannot be specified directly but must be determined on the basis of data retrieved from a table.

BUILT-IN FUNCTIONS IN SUBQUERIES

Built-in functions can be used in subqueries, as in the following example:

```
SELECT      QUOSUPP, QUOPART
FROM        QUOTATIONS
WHERE       PRICE > (SELECT AVG(PRICE)
                     FROM QUOTATIONS)


QUOSUPP   QUOPART
-------   -------
     51       124
     52       105
     53       124
```

Here the subquery determines the average price in the *Quotations* table (0.92), and then the main query selects supplier/part pairs that have a price higher than the average.

The following example shows a subquery used in a HAVING clause. Here we are selecting parts with a total on-order quantity greater than the average on-order quantity:

```
SELECT      QUOPART, SUM(ONORD)
FROM        QUOTATIONS
GROUP BY    QUOPART
HAVING      SUM(ONORD) > (SELECT AVG(ONORD)
                          FROM QUOTATIONS)


QUOPART   SUM(ONORD)
-------   ----------
    221        10000
    222        10000
    231         5000
    241         6000
```

SUBQUERIES THAT RETURN MULTIPLE VALUES

In the subquery examples used so far, the subquery immediately follows a comparison operator. For this to be valid, the subquery must return a single value, since we cannot perform a comparison operation on a set of values. We can, however, make use of subqueries that return multiple values by using the keywords IN, ANY, and ALL.

The following SELECT statement lists part numbers and prices for parts supplied by suppliers whose *Code* value is *20:*

```
SELECT       QUOPART, PRICE
FROM         QUOTATIONS
WHERE        QUOSUPP = ANY  (SELECT SUPSUPP
                             FROM SUPPLIERS
                             WHERE CODE = 20)



QUOPART     PRICE
-------     -------
    124      1.25
    125      0.55
    134      0.40
    135      0.39
    221      0.30
    231      0.10
    105      7.50
    205      0.15
    206      0.15
```

The subquery determines which suppliers have a code of *20* and returns a list of those supplier numbers. The main query then uses the ANY keyword to list part number and price for *every* row in *Quotations* that has a supplier number in the list returned by the subquery.

The keyword IN means the same thing as an equal comparison in combination with ANY. The following example lists all parts whose total on-order quantity is greater than 500:

```
SELECT       INVPART, PNAME, ONHAND
FROM         INVENTORY
WHERE        INVPART IN  (SELECT QUOPART
                          FROM QUOTATIONS
                          GROUP BY QUOPART
                          HAVING SUM(ONORD) > 500)



INVPART  PNAME              ONHAND
-------  ----------------   -------
    124  BOLT                  900
    134  NUT                   900
    135  NUT                  1000
    221  AXLE                 1500
    222  AXLE                   25
    231  AXLE                   75
    241  WHEEL                 300
```

If the comparison operation is other than an equal comparison, we must use ANY. In the following example, we are using it to find all distinct supplier/ part pairs with a price that is greater than any one of the prices for parts that have an on-order quantity of zero.

```
SELECT      DISTINCT QUOSUPP, QUOPART, PRICE
FROM        QUOTATIONS
WHERE       PRICE > ANY (SELECT PRICE
                         FROM QUOTATIONS
                         WHERE ONORD > 0)
```

QUOSUPP	QUOPART	PRICE
52	105	7.50
53	124	1.35
51	124	1.25
51	125	0.55
53	125	0.58
53	135	0.42
51	134	0.40
51	135	0.39
53	134	0.38
51	221	0.30
52	205	0.15
52	206	0.15
53	222	0.25
51	231	0.10

The ANY specifies that we arc selecting rows that have a price greater than the lowest price of any row that has an on-order quantity greater than zero. The lowest price value of these is *0.08* (null values are not included in the selection), so all rows except for the row with price *0.08* and the row with the null price value are included in the selection.

When we use ANY, the comparison must be true for only one of the values returned by the subquery in order for the row to be selected. If we specify the ALL keyword, the comparison must be true for all values returned by the subquery. Here we are using ALL to find the part or parts that have the highest average on-order quantity:

```
SELECT      QUOPART, AVG(ONORD)
FROM        QUOTATIONS
GROUP BY    QUOPART
HAVING      AVG(ONORD) >= ALL  (SELECT AVG(ONORD)
                                FROM QUOTATIONS
                                GROUP BY QUOPART)
```

QUOPART	AVG(ONORD)
221	10000
222	10000

USING NOT WITH ANY AND ALL

We must use care in testing for negative conditions involving ANY and ALL. Suppose we wished to list part number, name, and on-hand quantity for all parts that have a total on-order quantity of zero or are not included in the *Quotations* table. One way of doing this is by using a subquery to select part numbers with total on-order quantity greater than zero and then selecting part numbers that are not in this list:

```
SELECT      INVPART, PNAME, ONHAND
FROM        INVENTORY
WHERE       INVPART NOT IN (SELECT QUOPART
                            FROM QUOTATIONS
                            GROUP BY QUOPART
                            HAVING SUM(ONORD) > 0)
```

```
INVPART   PNAME              ONHAND
-------   ----------------   -------
    106   GEAR                  700
    171   GENERATOR             500
    172   GENERATOR             400
    181   WHEEL                1000
    205   BAND                  450
    206   MOTOR                 225
    232   AXLE                  150
```

Another way of performing the subquery is as follows:

```
WHERE       INVPART ¬= ALL (SELECT QUOPART
                            FROM QUOTATIONS
                            GROUP BY QUOPART
                            HAVING SUM(ONORD) > 0)
```

The WHERE clause, in effect, selects only rows whose part numbers are different from all the part numbers returned by the subquery. If we had inadvertently used ANY instead of ALL in this WHERE clause, it would select rows that have part numbers that are different from any one value in the list, thus selecting all the rows.

MULTIPLE LEVELS OF NESTING

If we like, we can perform subqueries within subqueries. Suppose we wish to select part information for parts supplied by suppliers whose *Code* value is *10*. We could do this with the following query:

```
SELECT      INVPART, PNAME, ONHAND
FROM        INVENTORY
WHERE       INVPART IN (SELECT QUOPART
                        FROM QUOTATIONS
                        WHERE QUOSUPP IN (SELECT SUPSUPP
                                          FROM SUPPLIERS
                                          WHERE CODE = 10))
```

```
INVPART   PNAME             ONHAND
-------   ---------------   -------
    124   BOLT                 900
    125   BOLT                1000
    134   NUT                  900
    135   NUT                 1000
    222   AXLE                  25
    232   AXLE                 150
    241   WHEEL                300
```

Nested queries are always evaluated from the innermost subquery outward. In the above example, the subquery at level 3 is evaluated first and returns a set of supplier numbers for suppliers that have a *Code* value of 10. The subquery at level 2 is then evaluated and selects part numbers for the parts supplied by those suppliers. The main query is then evaluated on the basis of the part numbers returned by the subquery at level 2.

DB2 does not limit the level of nesting that can be specified in a SELECT statement. However, performance considerations ordinarily make five levels a practical limit.

CORRELATED SUBQUERIES

In the subqueries we have examined so far, the subquery needed to be evaluated only once. In some cases, we need to use a subquery that is reevaluated for each row selected by the main query. This type of subquery is called a correlated subquery.

Suppose we wished to list the supplier number, part number, and price for the supplier that has the lowest price for each part. The following example shows how a correlated subquery can be used to produce the desired result:

```
SELECT     QUOSUPP, QUOPART, PRICE
FROM       QUOTATIONS ROWX
WHERE      PRICE = (SELECT MIN(PRICE)
                    FROM QUOTATIONS
                    WHERE QUOPART = ROWX.QUOPART
```

QUOSUPP	QUOPART	PRICE
51	124	1.25
51	125	0.55
51	135	0.39
51	221	0.30
51	231	0.10
52	105	7.50
52	205	0.15
52	206	0.15
53	134	0.38
53	222	0.25
53	241	0.08

The name ROWX following the table name in the FROM clause is known as a *correlation variable* or a *correlation name*. It serves to identify the current row that is being processed by the main query. Any name can be chosen. In the subquery, the correlation name is used as a prefix to identify the values that are to come from the row in the main query. In the example, the subquery is evaluated as each row from the *Quotations* table is processed. The subquery uses the part number from the current row to determine the minimum price offered for that part. If the price in the current row is equal to the minimum price, that row is selected. As each row is processed, the part number and the subquery result both change.

THE EXISTS KEYWORD

In addition to using a subquery to determine a value or set of values, a subquery can also be used to determine if a row exists that meets a specified condition. In its simple form, EXISTS can be used to perform the same type of processing as the IN keyword. In an earlier example, we used the following SELECT statement to list parts supplied by suppliers that have a *Code* value of *20:*

```
SELECT     QUOPART, PRICE
FROM       QUOTATIONS
WHERE      QUOSUPP IN (SELECT SUPSUPP
                       FROM SUPPLIERS
                       WHERE CODE = 20)
```

We could produce the identical results by using a correlated subquery in conjunction with the EXISTS keyword:

```
SELECT     QUOPART, PRICE
FROM       QUOTATIONS THISROW
WHERE      EXISTS (SELECT *
                   FROM SUPPLIERS
                   WHERE SUPSUPP = THISROW.QUOSUPP
                     AND CODE = 20)
```

QUOPART	PRICE
124	1.25
125	0.55
134	0.04
135	0.39
221	0.30
231	0.10
105	7.50
205	0.15
206	0.15

When we use EXISTS, the subquery does not return data item values. Instead, it returns an indication of whether or not any rows in the subquery meet the specified conditions. If one or more rows do meet the conditions, the EXISTS is considered to be true. Since no data is returned, it's not necessary to name specific columns in the SELECT clause of the subquery, and the form SELECT * is commonly used.

In the example just given, as each row in *Quotations* is processed by the main query, the subquery determines whether or not any rows exist in the *Suppliers* table with the current row's supplier number and a *Code* value of *20*. If such a row exists, the current row in the main query is selected.

USING NOT WITH EXISTS

We can also use the NOT keyword with EXISTS to select rows that do not meet specified conditions. For example, the following query lists all parts from the *Inventory* table that do not have entries in the *Quotations* table:

```
SELECT    INVPART, PNAME
FROM      INVENTORY ROWX
WHERE     NOT EXISTS (SELECT *
                      FROM QUOTATIONS
                      WHERE ROWX.INVPART = QUOPART)
```

```
INVPART  PNAME
-------  ----------------
    106  GEAR
    171  GENERATOR
    172  GENERATOR
    181  WHEEL
```

A row from the main query is selected only if no row exists in *Quotations* that has the same part number. Again, this query could be handled by using NOT IN instead of a correlated subquery.

USING EXISTS FOR ALL VALUES

The EXISTS keyword can be particularly useful in defining a conditional expression that must be met for all values in a particular column. For example, suppose we wish to list the parts that are supplied by all suppliers. This means that a part number is selected if, for every supplier number in *Suppliers,* there is a row in *Quotations* with that supplier and part number. We test for this type of condition in a negative manner. We select part numbers for which there *does not exist* a supplier number for which the corresponding supplier and part number pair *does not exist* in *Quotations*. Assuming the tables contain the values shown in Fig. 5.4, we could use the following query to obtain the desired results:

```
SELECT    QUOPART
FROM      QUOTATIONS ROWX
WHERE     NOT EXISTS (SELECT *
                      FROM SUPPLIERS ROWY
                      WHERE NOT EXISTS
                          (SELECT *
                           FROM QUOTATIONS
                           WHERE ROWY.SUPSUPP = QUOSUPP
                           AND ROWX.QUOPART = QUOPART))
```

```
QUOPART
-------
    124
    135
```

QUOTATIONS

QUOSUPP	QUOPART	PRICE	TIME	ONORD
51	124	1.25	5	400
51	125	0.55	5	0
51	134	0.40	5	500
51	135	0.39	5	1000
52	105	7.50	10	200
52	135	0.40	10	100
52	124	1.30	10	250
52	206	0.15	20	0
53	124	1.35	3	500
53	125	0.58	3	200
53	134	0.38	3	200
53	135	0.42	3	1000
53	222	0.25	15	10000

SUPPLIERS

SUPSUPP	NAME	ADDRESS	CODE
51	DEFECTO PARTS	16 JUSTAMERE LANE, TACOMA WA	20
52	VESUVIUS INC.	512 ANCIENT BLVD., POMPEII NY	20
53	ATLANTIS CO.	8 OCEAN AVE., WASHINGTON DC	10

Figure 5.4   Quotations and Suppliers tables.

For each of these part numbers, there is no supplier number in *Suppliers* for which there is not a corresponding supplier/part entry in *Quotations*. In other words, for all suppliers, there is a supplier/part entry in *Quotations*.

COMBINING SELECT STATEMENTS
We can use SELECT statements and the UNION keyword to perform a *union* relational operation on the results of two or more SELECT statements. With a UNION operation, the rows produced by each SELECT statement are interleaved and duplicate rows are eliminated. For a UNION operation to be valid, the results of each SELECT statement must be similar; they must have the same number of columns, and corresponding columns must be compatible data types. For example, corresponding columns must be either character or numeric data.

For example, suppose that we have three different *Quotations* tables: one for *A* parts, one for *B* parts, and one for *C* parts, as shown in Fig. 5.5. We wish to select all parts supplied by supplier *51*. We can perform this selection as follows:

```
SELECT      QUOPART, PRICE, 'A PART'
FROM        QUOTATIONS_A
WHERE       QUOSUPP = 51
   UNION
SELECT      QUOPART, PRICE, 'B PART'
FROM        QUOTATIONS_B
WHERE       QUOSUPP = 51
   UNION
SELECT      QUOPART, PRICE, 'C PART'
FROM        QUOTATIONS_C
WHERE       QUOSUPP = 51
ORDER BY    1


QUOPART     PRICE
-------    -------    ------
    124       1.25    C PART
    125       0.55    C PART
    134       0.40    C PART
    135       0.39    C PART
    171      21.00    A PART
    181      12.50    B PART
    221       0.30    C PART
    231       0.10    C PART
```

This example illustrates the use of a *descriptive column,* in which a constant value is assigned to that column for each row in the table. In this case, we are using the constant values to identify the table from which each result row came. A descriptive column can be used with any type of SELECT statement; however, it is most useful with a UNION operation, where the resulting column contains different data item values.

ORDER BY can be used to determine the sequence of the final merged results table. If used, the ORDER BY clause should follow the last SELECT statement. Also, column numbers rather than column names should be used in the ORDER BY clause, since the corresponding columns in the different SELECT statements may not always have the same names.

Duplicate rows in the final results table are automatically removed by the UNION operation; it is not necessary to specify DISTINCT to do this. The ALL keyword can be specified in conjunction with UNION to prevent duplicate rows from being eliminated. With UNION ALL, duplicate rows are left in the resulting table. Since eliminating duplicate rows usually causes DB2 to sort the results, UNION ALL can result in a more efficient query, even in cases where duplicate rows are not possible.

UNION cannot be used to connect subqueries. All the SELECT statements must be main (outermost) queries, although any of the SELECT statements could invoke subqueries if required. The results of SELECT statements that are joined by the UNION operator can be from different tables or from the same

QUOTATIONS_A

QUOSUPP	QUOPART	PRICE	TIME	ONORD
61	106	25.75	10	10
61	171	30.00	15	20
61	172	35.00	10	10
54	171	22.50	12	15
54	106	26.25	20	5
51	171	21.00	15	12

QUOTATIONS_B

QUOSUPP	QUOPART	PRICE	TIME	ONORD
51	181	12.50	10	25
57	181	13.00	7	30
57	206	15.75	15	50
64	181	12.75	10	15
64	206	16.00	15	75
61	206	15.50	20	10

QUOTATIONS_C

QUOSUPP	QUOPART	PRICE	TIME	ONORD
51	124	1.25	5	400
51	125	0.55	5	0
51	134	0.40	5	500
51	135	0.39	5	1000
51	221	0.30	10	10000
51	231	0.10	10	5000
52	105	7.50	10	200
52	205	0.15	20	0
52	206	0.15	20	0
53	124	1.35	3	500
53	125	0.58	3	200
53	134	0.38	3	200
53	135	0.42	3	1000
53	222	0.25	15	10000
53	232	–	15	0
53	241	0.08	15	6000

Figure 5.5   Multiple Quotations tables.

table. For example, the following two SELECT statements are joined by a UNION operator in order to flag preferred customers on the resulting display:

```
SELECT      SUPSUPP, NAME, 'PREFERRED'
FROM        SUPPLIERS
WHERE       CODE = 30
    UNION
SELECT      SUPSUPP, NAME,
FROM        SUPPLIERS
WHERE       CODE ¬= 30
ORDER BY    2
```

```
SUPSUPP    NAME
-------    ----------------    ---------
     53    ATLANTIC CO.
     51    DEFECTO PARTS
     57    EAGLE HARDWARE      PREFERRED
     64    KNIGHT LTD.
     61    SKYLAB PARTS
     54    TITANIC PARTS       PREFERRED
     52    VESUVIUS INC.
```

PERFORMING
AN OUTER JOIN

As we discussed in Chapter 2, the SQL language as implemented by DB2 is not capable of directly expressing *outer join* operations. It is possible to construct an *outer join* by combining SELECT statements with the UNION operator. Suppose we wish to list part numbers and the suppliers that supply them. If a part number has no supplier (i.e., has no entry in the *Quotations* table), it should be listed with blanks in the *Suppliers* column. This is an *outer join* of the *Inventory* and *Quotations* tables on part number values. This *outer join* operation can be performed with the following statements:

```
SELECT INVPART, QUOSUPP
FROM INVENTORY, QUOTATIONS
WHERE INVPART = QUOPART
        UNION
SELECT INVPART, '   '
FROM INVENTORY
WHERE INVPART NOT IN (SELECT QUOPART
                      FROM QUOTATIONS)
```

```
INVPART    QUOSUPP
-------    -------
    124         51
    125         51
    134         51
    135         51
    221         51
    231         51
    105         52
    205         52
    206         52
    124         53
    125         53
    134         53
    135         53
    222         53
    232         53
    241         53
    106
    171
    172
    181
```

In the above example, the first SELECT statement lists part numbers and suppliers for part numbers that appear in the *Quotations* table. The second SE-

LECT statement lists part numbers and blanks for all part numbers that do not appear in the *Quotations* table. If it were possible for a part number to appear in the *Quotations* table without also being in the *Inventory* table, we would have to use another UNION operator and a third SELECT statement to produce the *outer join:*

```
SELECT QUOPART, QUOSUPP
FROM QUOTATIONS
WHERE QUOPART NOT IN (SELECT INVPART
                      FROM INVENTORY)
```

The above third SELECT statement would list suppliers for part numbers that are in the *Quotations* table but not in the *Inventory* table.

6 ADVANCED FUNCTIONS

In this chapter, we examine additional SQL statements that can be used to perform functions other than queries. We see how to create tables, modify the information stored in tables, alter table definitions, delete entire tables, create and delete views, and work with authorizations.

CREATING TABLES   We create a new DB2 table by issuing a CREATE TABLE statement. Figure 6.1 shows the sample tables that we used in Chapters 4 and 5. We can create these tables using the following CREATE TABLE statements:

```
CREATE TABLE INVENTORY
        (INVPART        SMALLINT NOT NULL,
         PNAME          CHAR(10),
         ONHAND         INTEGER)
        IN DATABASE TABLE1D3

CREATE TABLE QUOTATIONS
        (QUOSUPP        SMALLINT NOT NULL,
         QUOPART        SMALLINT NOT NULL,
         PRICE          DECIMAL(5,2),
         TIME           SMALLINT,
         ONORD          INTEGER)
        IN DATABASE TABLE1D3

CREATE TABLE SUPPLIERS
        (SUPSUPP        SMALLINT NOT NULL,
         NAME           CHAR(15),
         ADDRESS        VARCHAR(35),
         CODE           SMALLINT)
        IN DATABASE TABLE1D3
```

INVENTORY

INVPART	PNAME	ONHAND
124	BOLT	900
125	BOLT	1000
105	GEAR	0
106	GEAR	700
171	GENERATOR	500
172	GENERATOR	400
134	NUT	900
135	NUT	1000
181	WHEEL	1000
205	BAND	450
206	MOTOR	225
221	AXLE	1500
222	AXLE	25
231	AXLE	75
232	AXLE	150
241	WHEEL	300

QUOTATIONS

QUOSUPP	QUOPART	PRICE	TIME	ONORD
51	124	1.25	5	400
51	125	0.55	5	0
51	134	0.40	5	500
51	135	0.39	5	1000
51	221	0.30	10	10000
51	231	0.10	10	5000
52	105	7.50	10	200
52	205	0.15	20	0
52	206	0.15	20	0
53	124	1.35	3	500
53	125	0.58	3	200
53	134	0.38	3	200
53	135	0.42	3	1000
53	222	0.25	15	10000
53	232	-	15	0
53	241	0.08	15	6000

SUPPLIERS

SUPSUPP	NAME	ADDRESS	CODE
51	DEFECTO PARTS	16 JUSTAMERE LANE, TACOMA WA	20
52	VESUVIUS INC.	512 ANCIENT BLVD., POMPEII NY	20
53	ATLANTIS CO.	8 OCEAN AVE., WASHINGTON DC	10
54	TITANIC PARTS	32 SINKING STREET, ATLANTIC CITY NJ	30
57	EAGLE HARDWARE	64 TRANQUILITY PLACE, APOLLO MN	30
61	SKYLAB PARTS	128 ORBIT BLVD., SYDNEY AUSTRALIA	10
64	KNIGHT LTD.	256 ARTHUR COURT, CAMELOT ENGLAND	20

Figure 6.1   Inventory, Quotations, and Suppliers tables.

TABLE NAMES

The table name must follow the keywords CREATE TABLE. It can be any length up to a maximum of 18 characters and must be made up of the following characters:

- Letters of the alphabet
- Digits
- The characters @, #, $, or __

Other special characters can also be used, but if they are, the name must be enclosed in single or double quotes when it is referenced in an SQL statement, including the CREATE TABLE statement that creates it.

The table name given in the CREATE statement can be qualified by adding the *authorization ID* of the person creating the table. Each user, or group of users, who accesses DB2 must have an authorization ID that identifies that user or group of users to DB2. The authorization ID of a user who accesses DB2 via TSO is generally the same as that user's TSO logon ID. So if the user issuing the CREATE statement has an authorization ID of KKC01, the full table name for the first table would be KKC01.INVENTORY. When you are using tables that you have created, it is not necessary to specify the authorization ID qualifier; DB2 uses the current authorization ID as the default qualifier. However, if you are accessing tables created by another user, you have to qualify the table name with the authorization ID of the person who created it in order to access the table.

COLUMN DEFINITIONS

Following the table name is a list of column definitions, separated with commas and enclosed in parentheses. Column names follow the same coding conventions as table names. The order in which the column names are listed determines the order in which data is stored in the table. A data type is specified for each column. Here are descriptions of the allowed data types:

- INTEGER: Used for integers in the range $\pm 2,147,483,647$.

- SMALLINT: Used for integers in the range $\pm 32,767$. Using SMALLINT rather than INTEGER, where possible, saves storage space.

- DECIMAL: Used for numbers with a fixed number of places after the decimal point. It is followed by two numbers in parentheses, where the first number indicates the number of digits in the number and the second the number of decimal positions.

- FLOAT: Used for floating-point numbers. The FLOAT keyword is followed by a number in parentheses that indicates the number of binary digits of precision that are to be used. This number can range from 0-54. A value less than 22 indicates single precision; a value of 22 or greater indicates double precision.

- CHAR: Used to define fixed-length character data. The length of the column is specified in parentheses following CHAR.

- VARCHAR: Used for variable-length character data with a length up to 254 characters. The maximum length for the column is specified in parentheses following VARCHAR.

- LONG VARCHAR: Used for variable-length character data up to 32,767 characters long. Columns defined with the LONG VARCHAR data type cannot be used in conditions, sorting, grouping, indexes, subqueries, COUNT, UNION, or inserting or updating queries.

- GRAPHIC, VARGRAPHIC, and LONG VARGRAPHIC: Used with double-byte character set (DBCS) data. DBCS data uses two bytes to represent each character to represent data in such languages as Japanese *kanji* and Arabic.

- DATE: Used for date values, which are stored in the format *yyyymmdd*. The value is stored as eight unsigned packed-decimal digits occupying four bytes.

- TIME: Used for time values, which are stored in the format *hhmmss*. A time value is stored as six unsigned packed-decimal digits occupying three bytes.

- TIMESTAMP: Used for values that combine a date value and a time value, where the time value includes microseconds. The format is *yyyymmddhhmmssnnnnnn*. Values are stored as 20 unsigned packed-decimal digits occupying ten bytes.

The above data types can be combined with various operators to form expressions that are used in clauses such as SELECT, WHERE, and HAVING. The different type of possible expressions are discussed in Appendix II.

NOT NULL SPECIFICATIONS

In addition to specifying the data type, a column specification can also specify the way in which null data values are to be handled in that column. If we specify NOT NULL for a column, null values will not be allowed in that column. Trying to enter a null value in that column will result in an error condition. If we specify NOT NULL WITH DEFAULT for a column, DB2 uses a default value for the data item value if no value is specified for the data item when a row is inserted or updated. The default value is based on data type, as follows:

Data Type	Default Value
Numeric data	0
Fixed-length character or graphic data	Blanks
Variable-length data	String of length 0
Date	Current date, as provided by the CURRENT DATE register
Time	Current time, as provided by the CURRENT TIME register
Timestamp	Current date and time, as provided by the CURRENT TIMESTAMP register

CURRENT DATE, CURRENT TIME, and CURRENT TIMESTAMP are the names of special registers that return current date and time values. These special registers are discussed further in Appendix II.

DATABASE NAME

Following the column definitions, the IN DATABASE clause specifies the name of the database in which the table should be built. The database to be used is normally assigned to a user by the part of the organization responsible for overall administration of DB2.

CREATING TABLES WITH REFERENTIAL CONSTRAINTS

When defining tables, we can define any referential constraints that exist between them. This is done by defining primary keys and foreign keys for the tables. When referential constraints are defined among a group of two or more tables, a table that contains a foreign key is called a *dependent table;* a table that contains a corresponding primary key is called a *parent table*.

Defining a Primary Key

The following example shows how we can define primary keys for the *Inventory* and *Suppliers* tables:

```
CREATE TABLE INVENTORY
        (INVPART        SMALLINT NOT NULL,
         PNAME          CHAR(10),
         ONHAND         INTEGER,
         PRIMARY KEY    (INVPART))
         IN DATABASE TABLE1D3

CREATE TABLE SUPPLIERS
        (SUPSUPP        SMALLINT NOT NULL,
         NAME           CHAR(15),
         ADDRESS        VARCHAR(35),
         CODE           SMALLINT,
         PRIMARY KEY    (SUPSUPP))
         IN DATABASE TABLE1D3
```

In these examples, each primary key consists of a single column. However, it is possible to define more than one column from a table as the primary key by listing all the column names in parentheses in the PRIMARY KEY clause. The column or columns that make up the primary key must have a unique value in each row and cannot be null. We cause DB2 to ensure this uniqueness by defining a unique index for the table, specifying the primary key as the index key. Index definition is discussed in Chapter 14.

Defining a Foreign Key

When defining a table with one or more foreign keys, each foreign key must exactly match its corresponding primary key in the parent table; it must consist of the same number of columns, and all the columns must be of the same data type and length as the columns that make up the primary key in the parent table. The following CREATE TABLE statement defines two foreign keys for the *Quotations* table, thus making it dependent on both the *Suppliers* and *Inventory* tables:

```
CREATE TABLE QUOTATIONS
       (QUOSUPP       SMALLINT NOT NULL,
        QUOPART       SMALLINT NOT NULL,
        PRICE         DECIMAL(5,2),
        TIME          SMALLINT,
        ONORD         INTEGER,
        FOREIGN KEY   (QUOSUPP) REFERENCES SUPPLIERS
        FOREIGN KEY   (QUOPART) REFERENCES INVENTORY)
       IN DATABASE TABLE1D3
```

As with a primary key definition, the FOREIGN KEY keywords are followed by the names of the columns that make up the foreign key. When a foreign key is defined, DB2 will ensure that each foreign key value exactly matches an existing primary key value in the corresponding parent table.

With the previous table definitions, DB2 will ensure that each supplier number value *(Quosupp)* in the *Quotations* table matches a corresponding supplier number value *(Supsupp)* in the *Suppliers* table and that each part number value *(Quopart)* in the *Quotations* table matches a part number value *(Invpart)* in the *Inventory* table. DB2 ensures this correspondence by enforcing constraints on inserting, updating, and deleting rows in the tables. We will discuss these constraints in the following sections in which we show how data manipulation functions are performed.

DATA MANIPULATION

Chapters 4 and 5 showed many examples of how data can be retrieved from tables. SQL statements are also available for adding, changing, and deleting data in tables. The statements for performing these functions are INSERT, UPDATE, and DELETE.

INSERTING DATA

We insert new rows into a table with the INSERT statement. The following INSERT statement could be used to add the first row to an empty *Inventory* table:

```
INSERT INTO INVENTORY
VALUES (126, 'BOLT', 0)
```

The VALUES clause is used to specify the data values to be inserted. The values must be listed in the same sequence in which the columns were defined in the CREATE TABLE statement. This sequence can be determined by issuing a SELECT * statement for the table. The data values must be consistent with the data types that were specified for the columns in the DEFINE TABLE statement; that is, they must be of the appropriate data types and lengths. If a column allows null values, the keyword NULL can be specified in place of a data value to insert a null value.

We could now issue a SELECT statement to see the results of the previous insertion:

```
SELECT * FROM INVENTORY


INVPART  PNAME              ONHAND
-------  ---------------    -------
    126  BOLT                     0
```

We can insert data into only selected columns by listing the column names in parentheses following the table name:

```
INSERT INTO INVENTORY (INVPART, PNAME)
VALUES (105, 'GEAR')
```

Null values or default values are inserted in any columns not included in the list of column names, depending on how each column was defined in the CREATE TABLE statement. So in this case, a null value will be entered for *Onhand:*

```
SELECT * FROM INVENTORY


INVPART  PNAME              ONHAND
-------  ---------------    -------
    126  BOLT                     0
    105  GEAR                     -
```

Data can also be copied from one table to another by coding a SELECT statement rather than a VALUES clause:

```
INSERT INTO INVENTORY (INVPART)
SELECT DISTINCT QUOPART
   FROM QUOTATIONS
   WHERE PRICE IS NOT NULL
```

The use of a SELECT statement rather than a VALUES clause allows us to add multiple rows to the table with a single INSERT statement. If we ran the IN-SERT statement in our example against an empty *Inventory* table, the result would be an *Inventory* table having only *Invpart* values in it:

```
SELECT * FROM INVENTORY


INVPART  PNAME              ONHAND
-------  ---------------    -------
    124  -                        -
    125  -                        -
    134  -                        -
    135  -                        -
    221  -                        -
    231  -                        -
    105  -                        -
    205  -                        -
    206  -                        -
    222  -                        -
    241  -                        -
```

If we are inserting rows into tables for which we have defined primary keys or foreign keys, DB2 places constraints on the values of the primary keys and foreign keys that we can supply in the rows being inserted.

If we are inserting a new row into a table for which we have defined a primary key, DB2 will reject the INSERT request if the row we are attempting to add has a primary key value that matches the key of a row already in the table. DB2 will also reject the INSERT request if we are attempting to add a row that has a null value in any of the columns that make up the key.

If we are inserting a new row into a table for which we have defined a foreign key, the foreign key value must be either wholly or partially null, or the foreign key value must match the primary key value of a row in the parent table. If the foreign key value is partially null, the entire key is considered null, and no part of the value is checked against primary key values in the parent table. DB2 rejects the INSERT request if the defined integrity constraints are not satisfied.

CHANGING DATA

We can modify the data stored in a table by using the UPDATE statement. We can make changes that apply to all rows or only to selected rows, and we can specify new values directly or specify calculations to be performed in processing the update. The following UPDATE statement modifies a single row in the *Quotations* table:

```
UPDATE QUOTATIONS
SET PRICE = 1.30, TIME = 10
WHERE QUOSUPP = 51 AND QUOPART = 124
```

To see the result of the update, we can use a SELECT statement:

```
SELECT * FROM QUOTATIONS
WHERE QUOSUPP = 51 AND QUOPART = 124
```

QUOSUPP	QUOPART	PRICE	TIME	ONORD
51	124	1.30	10	400

Only the columns specified in the SET clause are affected by the UPDATE statement. The WHERE clause specifies the row or rows to which the change applies. In the previous example, only one row was updated.

The following example increases by 10 percent the value of *Price* in all rows:

```
UPDATE QUOTATIONS
SET PRICE = PRICE * 1.10
```

Again, a SELECT statement shows the result of the update:

```
SELECT * FROM QUOTATIONS

QUOSUPP   QUOPART    PRICE      TIME     ONORD
-------   -------   -------   -------   -------
     51       124      1.43         5       400
     51       125      0.61         5         0
     51       134      0.44         5       500
     51       135      0.43         5      1000
     51       221      0.33        10     10000
     51       231      0.11        10      5000
     52       105      8.25        10       200
     52       205      0.17        20         0
     52       206      0.17        20         0
     53       124      1.49         3       500
     53       125      0.64         3       200
     53       134      0.42         3       200
     53       135      0.46         3      1000
     53       222      0.28        15     10000
     53       232         -        15         0
     53       241      0.09        15      6000
```

Notice that an arithmetic operation performed on a null value always results in a null value. The *Price* value for the next-to-last row still contains a null *Price* value after the update operation.

If we have defined a primary key for the table, DB2 enforces restrictions on the types of changes we can make to the values in columns that make up the primary key of the table. An UPDATE statement that changes any column in the primary key must update only one row. The uniqueness requirement of primary keys causes DB2 to reject an UPDATE request that gives a primary key column a null value or attempts to change a primary key value so that it matches the primary key of some other row.

Referential constraints that we have specified by defining foreign keys further restrict the changes that we can make to primary key values. DB2 will reject an UPDATE request that attempts to change a primary key value that has a matching foreign key value in a dependent table.

There are also restrictions to the types of changes that we can make to columns that make up a foreign key. If we attempt to change the value of a column that is part of a foreign key, the new foreign key value must be either wholly or partially null or it must match some other primary key value in the parent table.

DELETING DATA

We can delete rows from a table by issuing a DELETE statement. For example, the following example deletes all rows for supplier *53* from the *Quotations* table:

```
DELETE FROM QUOTATIONS
WHERE QUOSUPP = 53

SELECT * FROM QUOTATIONS

QUOSUPP   QUOPART     PRICE       TIME      ONORD
-------   -------     -------     -------   -------
     51       124        1.43           5         400
     51       125        0.61           5           0
     51       134        0.44           5         500
     51       135        0.43           5        1000
     51       221        0.33          10       10000
     51       231        0.11          10        5000
     52       105        8.25          10         200
     52       205        0.17          20           0
     52       206        0.17          20           0
```

If we delete all the rows from a table, the table still exists in an empty state. We can later insert new rows into an empty table without having to recreate it.

Referential constraints on a group of tables for which we have defined primary keys and foreign keys have an impact on DELETE operations. There are no restrictions on deleting rows in a dependent table, but referential constraints can affect DELETE requests for a parent table.

When we define a foreign key, we can include an ON DELETE clause in the FOREIGN KEY specification that defines a *delete rule* for the foreign key. The delete rule determines the way in which DB2 handles DELETE requests to ensure that referential constraints are enforced. The possible values for the ON clause are RESTRICT, CASCADE, and SET NULL. ON DELETE RESTRICT is the default value for the ON DELETE clause if we do not include an ON clause in the FOREIGN KEY specification.

With the DELETE RESTRICT rule in effect, we cannot delete a row in a parent table if there is a row in any dependent table that has a matching foreign key value. With the other two DELETE rules, we can delete rows in parent tables without restriction, but the DELETE request may affect the rows in dependent tables. With the DELETE CASCADE rule in effect, when we delete a row in a parent table, any rows in dependent tables that contain matching foreign key values are automatically deleted as well. With the DELETE SET NULL rule in effect, if we delete a row from a parent table, DB2 changes to null values all matching foreign key values in dependent tables.

The following example shows the use of the ON clause in a FOREIGN KEY specification:

```
CREATE TABLE QUOTATIONS
        (QUOSUPP       SMALLINT NOT NULL,
         QUOPART       SMALLINT NOT NULL,
         PRICE         DECIMAL(5,2),
         TIME          SMALLINT,
         ONORD         INTEGER,
         FOREIGN KEY   (QUOSUPP) REFERENCES SUPPLIERS
                       ON DELETE CASCADE
         FOREIGN KEY   (QUOPART) REFERENCES INVENTORY
                       ON DELETE SET NULL)
        IN DATABASE TABLE1D3
```

In some situations, complex referential constraints that involve multiple tables may restrict the choice of delete rules that are appropriate. These complex relationships are discussed in Appendix III.

ALTERING AND DROPPING TABLES

We can modify the characteristics of a table by using the ALTER TABLE statement. For example, the ALTER TABLE statement allows us to add a new column to a table:

```
ALTER TABLE INVENTORY
ADD BIN SMALLINT

SELECT * FROM INVENTORY
```

INVPART	PNAME	ONHAND	BIN
124	BOLT	900	-
125	BOLT	1000	-
105	GEAR	0	-
106	GEAR	700	-
171	GENERATOR	500	-
172	GENERATOR	400	-
134	NUT	900	-
135	NUT	1000	-
181	WHEEL	1000	-
205	BAND	450	-
206	MOTOR	225	-
221	AXLE	1500	-
222	AXLE	25	-
231	AXLE	75	-
232	AXLE	150	-
241	WHEEL	300	-

When we add a column to a table, we must specify a data type for it in the same manner as when defining a new table. When a new column is added to a table, DB2 inserts a null value for that column into each row in the table. Therefore, we cannot specify NOT NULL for a column that we are adding. After we have added a column, we can insert values into it by using INSERT statements.

We can also add referential constraints to tables by using ALTER to define a primary key or foreign key:

```
ALTER TABLE INVENTORY
      PRIMARY KEY (INVPART)

ALTER TABLE QUOTATIONS
      FOREIGN KEY PARTRC1 (QUOPART)
      REFERENCES INVENTORY
      ON DELETE SET NULL
```

Before a primary key can be defined with ALTER, a unique index must be created for the table to ensure that existing primary key values are valid.

When a foreign key is defined with ALTER, the table is marked as being in check pending status, and cannot be used until a utility is used to check the foreign key values to be sure they match primary keys. This is discussed further in Chapter 16. In the most recent example, we have explicitly assigned a name (PARTRC1) to this referential constraint. If we do not explicitly assign a name, as in the previous examples in this chapter, DB2 assigns the name of the first column that makes up the foreign key as the name of the referential constraint.

A referential constraint can be dropped by using an ALTER statement:

```
ALTER TABLE INVENTORY
      DROP PRIMARY KEY

ALTER TABLE QUOTATIONS
      DROP FOREIGN KEY PARTRC1
```

When a primary or foreign key is dropped with ALTER, the key columns and their data values are not dropped; only the relational constraint is removed. A relational constraint is also automatically dropped when either the parent or dependent table is dropped.

DELETING A TABLE

To delete an entire table, we must use a DROP statement rather than a DELETE statement:

```
DROP TABLE INVENTORY
```

A DROP TABLE statement removes both the data in the table and the table definition. The table must be re-created with a CREATE TABLE statement before it can be used again.

CREATING AND DROPPING SYNONYMS

We can use the CREATE SYNONYM statement to give an alternative name to a table. Use of the CREATE SYNONYM statement can make it easier to refer to a table. Suppose the *Inventory* table had been created by user KKC01MFG. Users other than KKC01MFG would have to refer to it using the table's full name: KKC01MFG.INVENTORY, which is rather cumbersome. We could use the following statement to assign a shorter name for it:

```
CREATE SYNONYM INV FOR KKC01MFG.INVENTORY
```

We can use the DROP statement to delete a synonym:

```
DROP SYNONYM INV
```

In addition to providing short names, synonyms can make it easier to deal with name changes. Suppose the *Inventory* table is deleted and re-created under authorization ID RGT03MFG. If stored queries use the synonym, the following statements will enable these queries to operate without change:

```
DROP SYNONYM INV
CREATE SYNONYM INV FOR RGT03MFG.INVENTORY
```

CREATING AND DROPPING VIEWS

We can use the CREATE VIEW statement to provide an alternative way of looking at data stored in tables. As we discussed in Part I, a view is a logical, or virtual, table that is derived from one or more base tables or other views. In general, views appear to the user as if they are real tables and can be operated on in the same manner as base tables. Views have several advantages:

- Views can reduce the perceived complexity of data by allowing simple versions of tables to be presented to users.

- Views can reduce the need for maintenance and can increase flexibility, eliminating much of the need for replication. Users can define views quickly with little or no increased overhead.

- Views can be individually protected, making it easy for authorized end users to make data available without compromising the security of sensitive data.

The following is an example of a single view, named *Mydata*, that incorporates data from all three of the sample tables:

```
CREATE VIEW MYDATA
        (SUPPNAME, D17PART, PARTNAME, LEADTIME,
        ONHAND, ONORDER, PRICE, TOTALPRICE)
    AS SELECT NAME, QUOPART, PNAME, TIME, ONHAND,
            ONORD, PRICE, PRICE * ONORD
        FROM INVENTORY, QUOTATIONS, SUPPLIERS
        WHERE INVPART = QUOPART
            AND SUPSUPP = QUOSUPP
            AND PNAME IN ('NUT', 'BOLT')
```

We could now list the content of the view as if it were a physical DB2 table, as follows:

```
:LECT * FROM MYDATA
```

PPNAME	D17PART	PARTNAME	LEADTIME	ONHAND	ONORDER	PRICE	TOTALPRICE
FECTO PARTS	124	BOLT	5	900	400	1.25	500
FECTO PARTS	125	BOLT	5	1000	0	0.55	0
FECTO PARTS	134	NUT	5	900	500	0.40	200
FECTO PARTS	135	NUT	5	1000	1000	0.39	390
LANTIS CO.	124	BOLT	3	900	500	1.35	675
LANTIS CO.	125	BOLT	3	1000	200	0.58	116
LANTIS CO.	134	NUT	3	900	200	0.38	76
LANTIS CO.	135	NUT	3	1000	1000	0.42	420

This display assumes the original content of the three tables, as shown in Fig. 6.1.

Any user who has the required authorization can now refer to *Mydata* in subsequent SQL statements as if it were an actual table structured as shown here. There are a few restrictions that apply to updating views:

- The INSERT, UPDATE, and DELETE statements cannot be used with a view if the view contains any of the following:
  Data from more than one table
  A column defined by a built-in function
  Data selected with DISTINCT or GROUP BY
  A subquery in the SELECT statement defining the view that references the same table as the outer SELECT statement.
- INSERT cannot be used if the view contains a column that is defined by an arithmetic expression, and UPDATE cannot be used for that column.
- INSERT cannot be used if there is a column in the underlying table that is not included in the view and the column does not have a default value specified.

Generally, a view can be referenced in a SELECT statement in the same manner as a base table is referenced. However, there are a few restrictions on using a column from a view if that column is *defined* by an expression or built-in function and the column is also *referenced* in an expression, built-in function, or GROUP BY clause. These restrictions are described in detail in the SQL reference manual.

In defining a view, we can use SELECT statements to select, rename, and rearrange columns. We can also use arithmetic expressions or built-in functions to create new columns. We can use any desired conditional expression in selecting rows that will appear in a view. We can use GROUP BY to provide summary data, and we can join tables in any desired manner. However, it is not valid to use ORDER BY or UNION in the SELECT statements that make up a view definition.

A view is dependent on the underlying table on which it is defined. When we insert, change, or delete data from a view, those changes are applied to the underlying base table. If we drop a base table, views based on that table are also dropped.

AUTHORIZATION   No query system would be complete without security provisions to prevent unauthorized access to data. GRANT and REVOKE are the two SQL statements that provide security facilities. We use the GRANT statement to give users authorization to perform certain operations on a table or view. We use the REVOKE statement to remove authorization previously granted.

Before we can create a table, we must have previously been granted the general authorization to create tables. If we are granted the authority to create a table, we are also automatically granted the authority to retrieve or modify data in the table, alter the table, and define and drop indexes and views based on the table. Other users will be allowed to access our tables only if they have specifically been granted the appropriate authorization. Authorization must also be granted to access a view created by another user. To create a view based on our tables, a user must have the authority to select data from the specific tables and views that are used in creating the view.

When using the GRANT statement in granting authorization, we specify the authority being granted in terms of the specific operations that specified users can perform:

```
GRANT SELECT ON SUPPLIERS
    TO KKC01, CLW01
```

This GRANT statement grants users KKC01 and CLW01 authorization to issue SELECT statements for the *Suppliers* table. Operations that can be specified in a GRANT statement for a table or view are ALTER, DELETE, INDEX, INSERT, SELECT, and UPDATE. We can also use the keyword ALL to indicate that authorization for all operations is granted. Also, when we grant UPDATE authorization, we can follow the UPDATE keyword with a list of column names in parentheses indicating the specific columns that are allowed to be changed:

```
GRANT SELECT, UPDATE (PNAME, ONHAND) ON INVENTORY
    TO DEL17PUR
```

We can add the clause WITH GRANT OPTION to a GRANT statement to give the specified users authorization to pass on their authorization to other users. With the following GRANT statement, we are allowing user DEL17PUR to grant other users authorization to select data from the INVENTORY table and to update its part name and on-hand values:

```
GRANT SELECT, UPDATE (PNAME, ONHAND) ON INVENTORY
    TO DEL17PUR
    WITH GRANT OPTION
```

We can use the TO PUBLIC clause to grant authorization to all users:

```
GRANT SELECT ON GENINFO
    TO PUBLIC
```

This statement allows all users to retrieve data from the *Geninfo* table.

We can revoke authorizations previously granted by issuing a REVOKE statement:

```
REVOKE SELECT ON SUPPLIERS
    FROM KKC01
```

It is not necessary to revoke all the operations that are granted, nor is it necessary to revoke authorizations from all the users to whom they were granted. The REVOKE statement specifies the operations and users to which the REVOKE applies.

REVOKE has similar options to GRANT. The following exceptions apply to REVOKE:

- In revoking authorization for UPDATE, columns cannot be listed. Revoking authorization for UPDATE always revokes authorization for updating all the columns for which it was granted.

- The WITH GRANT OPTION does not apply to REVOKE. If an authorization is revoked, it is revoked for the users listed and for any other users to whom they granted authorization.

When we drop a table, DB2 also drops any authorizations granted for that table or for views based on that table.

The DB2 authorization system and other security facilities are discussed in detail in Chapter 18.

SUMMARY OF PART II

The SQL SELECT statement is used to retrieve data from a table. A SELECT statement can specify that all columns and rows be retrieved, or it can specify that only selected columns and selected rows are to be displayed. Rows are selected by specifying, in a WHERE clause, selection conditions that are to be met. Selection conditions can include comparison operators, expressions, lists or ranges of values, or partial values. SELECT can also specify that duplicate rows are to be eliminated from the result. Multiple conditions can be connected with AND and OR operators. Selection conditions can specify null values. Negative conditions are also valid. An ORDER BY clause can be included to specify the sequence in which the results should be displayed. In addition to displaying values that are contained in table columns, calculated values can also be displayed.

The SQL SELECT statement can be used to perform *join* operations that combine data from multiple tables. Built-in functions, such as SUM and AVG, can be used to calculate values. These calculated values can be displayed, and they can also be included in selection conditions. Built-in functions can also be included in a GROUP BY clause. SELECT statements can be nested within other SELECT statements to create subqueries. A subquery is typically used to generate a value or set of values that is used as part of a selection condition. A correlated subquery is one that uses a value from the rows being processed by the main query. A correlated subquery is reevaluated for each row in the main query. In addition to returning values, a subquery can be used to determine whether or not a row exists that meets particular conditions. The UNION operator can be used to merge the results of two or more SELECT statements. The UNION operator can also be used to simulate the effect of an *outer join* relational operator.

SQL provides a CREATE statement for creating tables, views, and synonyms, an ALTER statement for adding columns to a table, and a DROP statement for deleting tables, views, and synonyms. Data modification statements are also provided, including an INSERT statement to add data, an UPDATE statement to change data, and a DELETE statement to delete data. The GRANT statement is used to allow users to perform specified operations on tables and views; authorization can be revoked using the REVOKE statement.

PART III QUERY MANAGEMENT
FACILITY (QMF)

In Part III of this book, we examine the Query Management Facility (QMF), a program product that is used in most DB2 installations to provide application developers and end users with interactive access to DB2 databases. QMF is an interactive query product that can be used to provide access to data stored in DB2 databases. It is a separate product from DB2, and there are versions of QMF that can be used in either the DB2 or SQL/DS environment. Most installations that use DB2 or SQL/DS also use QMF.

This chapter presents an overview of QMF facilities. Chapter 8 explores QMF report formatting capabilities and shows how to use QMF procedures to save and later execute queries. Chapter 9 introduces Query-by-Example (QBE), a second query language provided by QMF that can be used instead of or in conjunction with SQL.

7 THE QMF ENVIRONMENT

QUERY MANAGEMENT FACILITY QMF can be used by nontechnical end users or by data processing professionals to perform functions such as the following:

- Retrieve data from DB2 tables, browse through the data, and save the data for later use.
- Perform calculations on data retrieved from tables.
- Produce reports in various formats, either on the screen of a display terminal or in printed form. Formatting capabilities include the use of presentation graphics facilities.
- Add to, change, or delete table data.
- Create, modify, or delete tables, views, and synonyms.
- Save queries and other processes entered as part of a QMF session for use at a later time.

Nontechnical end users can easily use a display terminal to create a report, modify it interactively, and produce an enhanced version of it without assistance from data processing personnel. Data processing professionals can use QMF facilities to respond quickly to one-time requests or to develop procedures that end users can invoke as needed.

THE QMF INTERFACE After we log on to QMF, we interact with the software via a simple, end-user-oriented interface, which incorporates the following features:

- Commands to initiate query or reporting operations
- Program function (PF) keys that can be used instead of commands to initiate query or reporting operations
- Prompts designed to aid the user in entering correct data
- Helpful error messages
- Online HELP facilities

To access many functions, we simply press an appropriate PF key on the terminal. If information is missing or a query command is incomplete, QMF either prompts us for the missing information or displays an error message. HELP screens are always available to assist us.

CHOICE OF LANGUAGES

QMF provides a choice between two high-level languages to formulate queries: *Structured Query Language* (SQL) and *Query-by-Example* (QBE). The SQL language used within QMF is the same SQL language that is a part of DB2. All the SQL statements shown in Part II of this book can be entered interactively via QMF. QBE is based on graphic representation of data in tabular form. QMF allows us to formulate queries and perform other functions using either language.

QMF FUNCTIONS

To access data in a DB2 table using QMF, we formulate a query in either the SQL or QBE language. In response to our query, QMF displays a formatted report. We can then change the appearance of the report by calling up a screen panel that defines the report's format. By entering changes directly into the panel, we can change the format of the report to meet specific requirements.

The following are some typical functions that we might perform with QMF:

- Ad hoc query requests using SQL or QBE
- Report preparation
- Definition and execution of procedures containing predefined query or report requests
- Generation of graphic displays

QUERIES

We can employ either SQL or QBE to formulate retrieval requests using a terminal. The results of these queries are immediately displayed on the terminal screen. Scrolling commands can be used to browse through the data. We can then access the original query and modify it in order to obtain different results. We can save the data, print it, save the request that produced the data, or simply go on to another task.

REPORTS

Query results are normally displayed in the form of simple table such as the ones we looked at in the chapters in Part II. QMF automatically generates a screen panel that describes the default format it uses for the presentation of query results. Alternatively, we can identify a panel that we have created to override the QMF defaults. A user-defined panel is created by filling in and changing values in the QMF-generated panel.

QMF allows us to produce reports using a wide variety of formats. Once we are satisfied with the format of a report, we can request that selected data be redisplayed. QMF then reformats the report for us. Since preparing a report can often be an iterative process, QMF makes it easy to generate multiple versions of the same report, redisplaying the data until we are satisfied with its format.

PROCEDURES

For reports that will be requested periodically, we can create a procedure definition that stores the sequence of commands that must be issued to produce the report. We can then produce the report at any time by entering a single QMF command. A procedure can execute SQL statements, QBE queries, or both.

QMF makes it easy for us to create and alter queries and procedures. For example, we make corrections by simply typing over the incorrect information on the screen, we insert data by typing data into blank areas of the screen, and we delete data by blanking it out. QMF provides prompts and HELP panels to guide us in the performance of a task.

QMF SESSION

In order to begin interacting with QMF, we must first establish a QMF session. QMF interacts with us during a session by displaying a sequence of screen panels. We interact with QMF by issuing various QMF commands and by entering SQL statements or QBE queries. After we have logged on to QMF, QMF begins a session by displaying a QMF Home panel, shown in Fig. 7.1. QMF displays the Home panel at the beginning and at the end of each QMF session.

QMF COMMAND ENTRY

In conducting a session with QMF, we can specify functions to be performed either by pressing PF keys or by entering mnemonic commands. QMF always

```
QMF HOME PANEL                              Query
                                           Management
                                           Facility


_____

                                    ******    **    **      *********
                              **      **    ***   ***       **
                              **      **   ****  ****        *******
                              **          ** ** ** **      **     **
                              **    * **   **   ****    **  **
                              ******    **    **       ** **
                                          *

Type command on command line or use PF keys.  For help, press PF1 or type HELP.
_____


1=Help        2=List      3=Exit      4=          5=Chart      6=Query
7=Retrieve    8=          9=Form     10=Proc      11=Profile   12=Report
OK, you may enter a command
COMMAND ===>  _
```

Figure 7.1   QMF Home panel.

displays at the bottom of the screen the QMF PF-key functions that are available
while a particular QMF panel is displayed. Each SQL panel also has a command
line that we can use for entering mnemonic commands. QMF always displays
messages that it generates in response to commands (such as error messages)
between the PF-key line and the command line.

QMF ITEMS

The first thing that we normally do in a QMF session
is to specify the *QMF item* that we wish to access.
Box 7.1 lists the five types of items on which QMF can take action. The five
item types are listed in the PF-key line in the Home panel.

QMF COMMANDS

We can issue QMF commands to operate on any
QMF items. Some commonly used QMF commands
are listed in Box 7.2.

QMF QUERIES

In order to initiate a query function, we select the
query item type either by pressing PF6 or by entering
QUERY on the command line. In response to this, QMF displays a Query

BOX 7.1   QMF items

Query	A QMF *query* describes the data the user is interested in and the actions the user wants to perform on that data.
Form	A QMF *form* describes how formatted data should be formatted in a report.
Procedure	A QMF *procedure* is a named set of one or more QMF commands that are executed as a unit.
Profile	A QMF *profile* contains information unique to a particular QMF user. Each user has a user profile stored in the system that specifies language preference (SQL or QBE) and default values for report formats, such as report page length and width.
Report	A QMF *report* consists of the actual data that is retrieved and displayed as a result of a query request.

BOX 7.2   QMF commands

DISPLAY	Displays the contents of a QMF item
RUN	Executes a query or a procedure
PRINT	Prints the content of a QMF item or a DB2 table
SAVE	Saves a QMF item for future use
HELP	Obtains online assistance
ERASE	Deletes a QMF item or a DB2 table from the database
EXPORT	Transfers a QMF item from QMF to TSO or CMS
IMPORT	Transfers a QMF item from TSO or CMS to QMF
TSO	Allows a TSO command to be entered while in QMF
CMS	Allows a CMS command to be entered while in CMS

panel, as shown in Fig. 7.2.* If the current session has just begun, the Query panel will be empty, as it is in Fig. 7.2. In an ongoing session, the Query panel contains the query we last entered.

QMF displays either a SQL or QBE panel, depending on the choice indi-

*Actual screen formats may vary slightly from our examples, depending on whether you are using the MVS or VM version of QMF, and on the type of terminal and software release you are using.

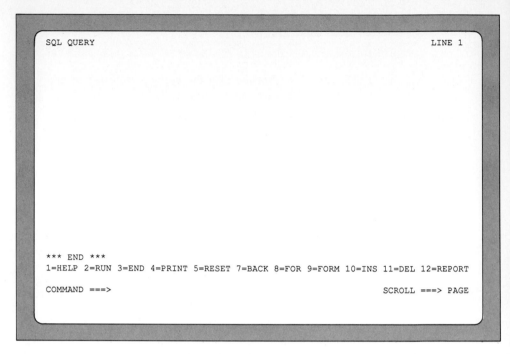

```
SQL QUERY                                                              LINE 1




















*** END ***
1=HELP 2=RUN 3=END 4=PRINT 5=RESET 7=BACK 8=FOR 9=FORM 10=INS 11=DEL 12=REPORT

COMMAND ===>                                                SCROLL ===> PAGE
```

Figure 7.2   SQL Query panel.

cated in our user profile. Figure 7.2 is an example of an SQL Query panel. We can display the current user profile by pressing PF11 while the Home panel is displayed. We can change the language choice at any time, simply by typing QBE or SQL over the current choice. An empty QBE or SQL panel can be obtained at any time during a session by issuing the RESET command.

SQL QUERIES

If the user profile indicates SQL, QMF automatically displays an SQL Query panel when we request the query function. The PF-key functions that are available while the Query panel is displayed are listed at the bottom of the screen. As with all QMF panels, a command line is also available for entering mnemonic commands.

Assume that we have available the tables that we used in Part II, which are repeated in Fig. 7.3, and that we want to display the supplier number, part number, price, and on-order quantity for all quotations that have an on-order quantity equal to *200*. We might use the following SQL query to obtain the required results:

```
SELECT     QUOSUPP, QUOPART, PRICE, ONORD
FROM       QUOTATIONS
WHERE      ONORD = 200
ORDER BY   PRICE
```

INVENTORY

INVPART	PNAME	ONHAND
124	BOLT	900
125	BOLT	1000
105	GEAR	0
106	GEAR	700
171	GENERATOR	500
172	GENERATOR	400
134	NUT	900
135	NUT	1000
181	WHEEL	1000
205	BAND	450
206	MOTOR	225
221	AXLE	1500
222	AXLE	25
231	AXLE	75
232	AXLE	150
241	WHEEL	300

QUOTATIONS

QUOSUPP	QUOPART	PRICE	TIME	ONORD
51	124	1.25	5	400
51	125	0.55	5	0
51	134	0.40	5	500
51	135	0.39	5	1000
51	221	0.30	10	10000
51	231	0.10	10	5000
52	105	7.50	10	200
52	205	0.15	20	0
52	206	0.15	20	0
53	124	1.35	3	500
53	125	0.58	3	200
53	134	0.38	3	200
53	135	0.42	3	1000
53	222	0.25	15	10000
53	232	-	15	0
53	241	0.08	15	6000

SUPPLIERS

SUPSUPP	NAME	ADDRESS	CODE
51	DEFECTO PARTS	16 JUSTAMERE LANE, TACOMA WA	20
52	VESUVIUS INC.	512 ANCIENT BLVD., POMPEII NY	20
53	ATLANTIS CO.	8 OCEAN AVE., WASHINGTON DC	10
54	TITANIC PARTS	32 SINKING STREET, ATLANTIC CITY NJ	30
57	EAGLE HARDWARE	64 TRANQUILITY PLACE, APOLLO MN	30
61	SKYLAB PARTS	128 ORBIT BLVD., SYDNEY AUSTRALIA	10
64	KNIGHT LTD.	256 ARTHUR COURT, CAMELOT ENGLAND	20

Figure 7.3 Inventory, Quotations, and Suppliers tables.

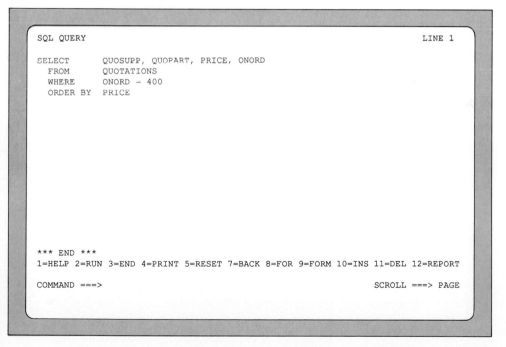

```
SQL QUERY                                                   LINE 1

SELECT      QUOSUPP, QUOPART, PRICE, ONORD
  FROM      QUOTATIONS
  WHERE     ONORD = 400
  ORDER BY  PRICE
```

```
*** END ***
1=HELP 2=RUN 3=END 4=PRINT 5=RESET 7=BACK 8=FOR 9=FORM 10=INS 11=DEL 12=REPORT

COMMAND ===>                                      SCROLL ===> PAGE
```

Figure 7.4 An SQL statement can be entered directly in the SQL Query panel.

We can enter this query directly into the SQL Query panel, as shown in Fig.
7.4.

QBE QUERIES

If we enter a QUERY command on the Home panel and our user profile indicates QBE, QMF displays a QBE Query panel instead of an SQL panel. To execute the same query as the previous SQL example, we begin by entering the name of the desired table, *Quotations,* on the command line and then press PF6 to select the DRAW function. Alternatively, we could enter DRAW QUOTATIONS on the command line.

In response to the request, QMF displays a skeleton of the *Quotations* table, as shown in Fig. 7.5. We now enter the query by entering information directly in the table, as shown in Fig. 7.6. We enter the "P." operator (for Print) under the columns that we want displayed. We then also enter *200* under the *Onord* column to indicate that we want only rows that contain *200* in the *Onord* column. We enter the operator "AO." under the *Price* column to indicate that we want rows displayed in ascending order by *Price* data item values. Chapter 9 describes the QBE language in detail.

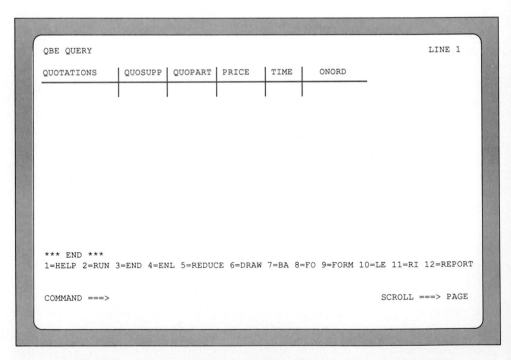

Figure 7.5   A skeleton diagram of the desired table is displayed in the QBE Query panel.

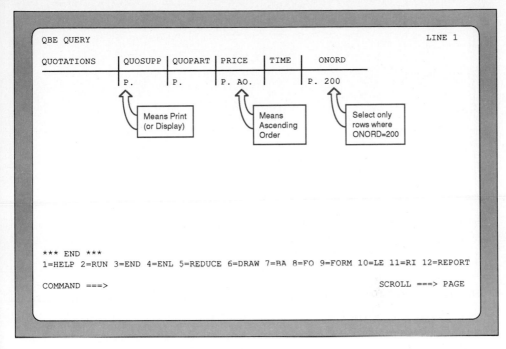

Figure 7.6 Operators and data values are entered in the table skeleton in formulating a QBE query.

GENERATING A REPORT

After we have entered our query using either the SQL or QBE language, we can obtain a response to the query in the form of a displayed report. To obtain the report, we either press PF2 or enter the RUN command. QMF interprets the query, retrieves the required information from the database, and displays the report on the terminal screen. The report corresponding to the SQL and QBE queries just described is shown in Fig. 7.7. The same report would be produced by either query.

PRINTING AND FORMATTING A REPORT

After QMF displays the report on our terminal screen, we can obtain a printed copy of the report either by pressing PF4 or by entering the PRINT RE-PORT command on the command line. We can change the report's format by using various QMF formatting facilities and then redisplay or print the new report. The format of a report is described on a Form panel that we can display either by pressing PF9 or by entering the FORM command on the command line. We then change the report's format by changing the information displayed on the Form panel.

```
REPORT                                                                  LINE 1

QUOSUPP   QUOPART    PRICE    ONORD
-------   -------   -------   -------
     53       134     0.38       200
     53       125     0.58       200
     52       105     7.50       200
*** END ***




















1=HELP  3=END  4=PRINT  6=QUERY  7=BACKWARD  8=FORWARD  9=FORM  10=LEFT  11=RIGHT


COMMAND ===>                                                SCROLL ===> PAGE
```

Figure 7.7 Query results are displayed in a Report panel for both SQL and QBE query results.

```
                              QMF HELP: FORM
FORMATTING NUMBERS

For character data (CHAR, VARCHAR, or LONG VARCHAR) use EDIT code C.
To show numbers in floating-point notation (for example, 1.23E-04), use E.

For numbers in other forms, you may put a number from 0 to 9 after the code
to tell how many decimal places to allow.  The examples below use 2 places.

To get this... use...   which allows for...

  -$12,345.67   D2      negative sign, dollar sign, punctuation
  -0012345.67   I2      negative sign, leading zeros, no punctuation
  00012345.67   J2      no negative sign, leading zeros, no punctuation
   -12,345.67   K2      negative sign, no leading zeros, punctuation
    -12345.67   L2      negative sign, no leading zeros, no punctuation

If you allow fewer decimal places than the data type of a DECIMAL number
allows, the number is rounded.  If you allow more, zeros are added.


PF keys: 3=END  7=UP  8=SKIP  10=BACK  11=NEXT

HELP SUBCOMMAND ===>  _
```

Figure 7.8 Sample QMF HELP screen.

HELP FACILITY

While working with any of the QMF panels, we can obtain assistance by pressing PF1 or by entering HELP on the command line. QMF then displays a HELP screen related to that panel. Figure 7.8 illustrates the HELP screen that would be displayed in conjunction with the Form panel.

DATA ENTRY AND UPDATE

We can use QMF to manipulate data in a variety of ways. As just shown in the SQL and QBE examples, we can execute queries and can format and print reports. In addition, we can use QMF to modify DB2 data. For example, we can perform functions such as the following:

- Update, insert, or delete information in tables.
- Add new tables to the database, change table definitions, or delete tables.
- Create or delete views.
- Grant or revoke authorization to other users to use tables and views.

8 REPORT FORMATTING AND QMF PROCEDURES

This chapter examines some QMF functions that can be performed using QMF commands and facilities rather than SQL or QBE statements. These features allow for the formatting of reports and for the saving and later execution of queries and QMF commands.

DISPLAYING OR PRINTING A REPORT After we enter a query using either the SQL or QBE language, we normally wish to see a response to the query. To obtain the response, we either press PF2 or enter the RUN command. QMF interprets the query, retrieves the requested information from the specified tables, and displays a formatted report on the terminal screen. Suppose we had the tables shown in Fig. 8.1 and we entered a query. For example, we might enter the following SQL query:

```
SELECT     QUOSUPP, QUOPART, PRICE, ONORD
FROM       QUOTATIONS
ORDER BY   QUOSUPP, QUOPART
```

Or we might enter the following QBE query, which is equivalent to the SQL query:

QUOSUPP	QUOPART	PRICE	TIME	ONORD
P. AO(1).	P. AO(2).	P.		P.

INVENTORY

INVPART	PNAME	ONHAND
124	BOLT	900
125	BOLT	1000
105	GEAR	0
106	GEAR	700
171	GENERATOR	500
172	GENERATOR	400
134	NUT	900
135	NUT	1000
181	WHEEL	1000
205	BAND	450
206	MOTOR	225
221	AXLE	1500
222	AXLE	25
231	AXLE	75
232	AXLE	150
241	WHEEL	300

QUOTATIONS

QUOSUPP	QUOPART	PRICE	TIME	ONORD
51	124	1.25	5	400
51	125	0.55	5	0
51	134	0.40	5	500
51	135	0.39	5	1000
51	221	0.30	10	10000
51	231	0.10	10	5000
52	105	7.50	10	200
52	205	0.15	20	0
52	206	0.15	20	0
53	124	1.35	3	500
53	125	0.58	3	200
53	134	0.38	3	200
53	135	0.42	3	1000
53	222	0.25	15	10000
53	232	–	15	0
53	241	0.08	15	6000

SUPPLIERS

SUPSUPP	NAME	ADDRESS	CODE
51	DEFECTO PARTS	16 JUSTAMERE LANE, TACOMA WA	20
52	VESUVIUS INC.	512 ANCIENT BLVD., POMPEII NY	20
53	ATLANTIS CO.	8 OCEAN AVE., WASHINGTON DC	10
54	TITANIC PARTS	32 SINKING STREET, ATLANTIC CITY NJ	30
57	EAGLE HARDWARE	64 TRANQUILITY PLACE, APOLLO MN	30
61	SKYLAB PARTS	128 ORBIT BLVD., SYDNEY AUSTRALIA	10
64	KNIGHT LTD.	256 ARTHUR COURT, CAMELOT ENGLAND	20

Figure 8.1   Inventory, Quotations, and Suppliers tables.

After we pressed PF2 or entered the RUN command, QMF would display the following report, whether we had entered the query using either SQL or QBE:

QUOSUPP	QUOPART	PRICE	ONORD
51	124	1.25	400
51	125	0.55	0
51	134	0.40	500
51	135	0.39	1000
51	221	0.30	10000
51	231	0.10	5000
52	105	7.50	200
52	205	0.15	0
52	206	0.15	0
53	124	1.35	500
53	125	0.58	200
53	134	0.38	200
53	135	0.42	1000
53	222	0.25	10000
53	232	–	0
53	241	0.08	6000

After QMF has displayed the report on the terminal screen, we can obtain a printed copy of it either by pressing PF4 or by entering the PRINT REPORT command on the command line.

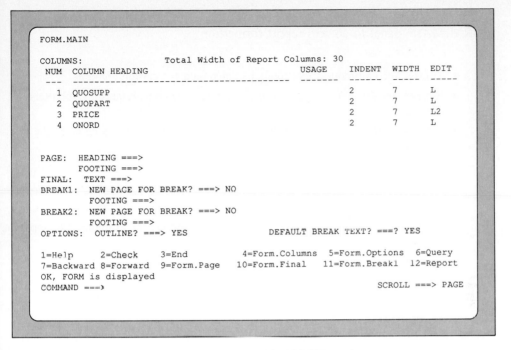

```
FORM.MAIN

COLUMNS:                    Total Width of Report Columns: 30
  NUM  COLUMN HEADING                          USAGE   INDENT  WIDTH  EDIT
  ---  ------------------------------------    -------  ------  -----  -----
    1  QUOSUPP                                               2      7  L
    2  QUOPART                                               2      7  L
    3  PRICE                                                 2      7  L2
    4  ONORD                                                 2      7  L


PAGE:   HEADING ===>
        FOOTING ===>
FINAL:  TEXT ===>
BREAK1:  NEW PAGE FOR BREAK? ===> NO
         FOOTING ===>
BREAK2:  NEW PAGE FOR BREAK? ===> NO
         FOOTING ===>
OPTIONS:  OUTLINE? ===> YES            DEFAULT BREAK TEXT? ===? YES

1=Help      2=Check     3=End        4=Form.Columns  5=Form.Options  6=Query
7=Backward 8=Forward  9=Form.Page  10=Form.Final   11=Form.Break1  12=Report
OK, FORM is displayed
COMMAND ===>                                     SCROLL ===> PAGE
```

Figure 8.2   Default FORM.MAIN panel.

CUSTOMIZING A REPORT

After seeing an initial version of the report that QMF displays, we might decide to alter the report's format. We can do this by calling up a set of FORM panels that describe the format of the report. We can do this by pressing PF9 or by entering the FORM command on the command line. QMF then displays the FORM.MAIN panel, as shown in Fig. 8.2.

The FORM panels created by QMF describe in detail the default report format, including the data to be displayed, the column headings, the number of blank spaces between columns, the width of each column, and the output format for each column of data. In addition to the FORM.MAIN panel, there are a number of additional FORM panels that can be used to modify the format of a report. We will look only at the FORM.MAIN panel in this book.

REPORT-CUSTOMIZING OPTIONS

We produce a customized report by making modifications to the FORM.MAIN panel and to any of the additional FORM panels that can be displayed. Here are some of the kinds of changes that we can make to the information in the FORM.MAIN panel to control report formatting:

- **Totals.** We can request that totals be calculated for certain columns.
- **Report Breaks.** We can request control breaks, such as requesting subtotals by supplier.
- **Output Edit.** We can add dollar signs and commas, for example, to the selected columns.
- **Text.** We can add explanatory text where required.
- **Page Heading.** We can print a heading at the top of each page.
- **Page Footing.** We can print a footing at the bottom of each page.
- **Grouping of Data.** We can group data in the report, for example, by supplier number.
- **Omissions.** We can omit specified columns of data from the report.

SAMPLE CUSTOMIZED REPORT

The modified FORM.MAIN panel illustrated in Fig. 8.3 shows how we can request changes to the format of our report. The changes that are specified in Fig. 8.3 are as follows:

- The SUPPLIER column heading causes QMF to display a more descriptive heading for the *Quosupp* column.
- BREAK1 under USAGE requests a break point in the report each time the value of *Quosupp* changes.
- The SUM keyword under USAGE causes QMF to display a subtotal of *Onord* values for each supplier and a total *Onord* value at the end of the report.
- The OMIT keyword under USAGE causes QMF to omit the *Price* column from the report.
- Changes under the WIDTH column cause QMF to widen the specified columns.
- The K entry under EDIT causes QMF to add commas to the *Onord* data.
- The entry after ''HEADING'' causes QMF to display a page heading at the top of each report page.

The following shows the format of the new report that QMF would produce using the enhancements described by the report form in Fig. 8.3.

```
                    QUOTATIONS REPORT


        SUPPLIER  QUOPART      ONORD
        --------  -------    ---------
            51      124          400
            51      125            0
            51      134          500
            51      135        1,000
            51      221       10,000
            51      231        5,000
                              ---------
                         *     16,900


            52      105          200
            52      205            0
            52      206            0
                              ---------
                         *        200


            53      124          500
            53      125          200
            53      134          200
            53      135        1,000
            53      222       10,000
            53      232            0
            53      241        6,000
                              ---------
                         *     17,900


                              =========
                                35,000
```

```
FORM.MAIN

COLUMNS:              Total Width of Report Columns: 30
  NUM  COLUMN HEADING                      USAGE    INDENT  WIDTH  EDIT
  ---  ----------------------------------  -------  ------  -----  ----
    1  SUPPLIER                            BREAK1      2       8    L
    2  QUOPART                                         2       7    L
    3  PRICE                               OMIT        2       7    L2
    4  ONORD                               SUM         2       9    K



PAGE:  HEADING ===> QUOTATIONS REPORT
       FOOTING ===>
FINAL: TEXT ===>
BREAK1:  NEW PAGE FOR BREAK? ===> NO
         FOOTING ===>
BREAK2:  NEW PAGE FOR BREAK? ===> NO
         FOOTING ===>
OPTIONS:  OUTLINE? ===> YES            DEFAULT BREAK TEXT? ===? YES


1=Help     2=Check    3=End      4=Form.Columns  5=Form.Options  6=Query
7=Backward 8=Forward  9=Form.Page  10=Form.Final   11=Form.Break1 12=Report
OK, FORM is displayed
COMMAND ===>                                      SCROLL ===> PAGE
```

Figure 8.3 Modified FORM.MAIN panel.

ADDITIONAL FORMATTING OPTIONS

QMF provides a number of additional processing options for formatting reports. For example, in addition to *summing* columns for control breaks, we can alternatively use any of the following functions:

AVERAGE	The average of the values in the column
COUNT	A count of the number of values in the column
FIRST	The first value in the column
LAST	The last value in the column
MAXIMUM	The maximum value in the column
MINIMUM	The minimum value in the column
STDEV	The standard deviation of the values in the column
CPCT	The cumulative percentage for each value in a column
CSUM	The cumulative sum for each value in a column
PCT	The percentage of the total that each value is
TCPCT	The total cumulative percentage for each value in a column
TPCT	The percentage of the column total that each value represents

We can also produce summary reports, where QMF displays a single line of summary data for each set of values in a column. We specify this by giving a usage of GROUP to the column. We can use the ACROSS option to produce a summary report with totals spread across a page rather than down it.

In addition to producing tabular reports, QMF can also generate output in the form of a chart by using various types of graphics. QMF provides support for various chart formats, including bar, pie, line, tower, polar, histogram, surface, and scatter charts.

SAVING A QUERY

One we have defined either an SQL or QBE query, we can give it a name and save it so we can execute again at a later time. This feature is useful for producing reports that need to be generated on a regular basis. We can also save a query's associated report form in order to produce a report having a customized format. Suppose we have formulated the following query:

```
SELECT    SUPSUPP, NAME, INVPART, PNAME, TIME, ONHAND, ONORD
FROM      SUPPLIERS, INVENTORY, QUOTATIONS
WHERE     INVPART = QUOPART
          AND SUPSUPP = QUOSUPP
          AND SUPSUPP = 53
```

Suppose also that we have customized the Form panels to produce this report:

```
SUPP   SUPPLIER          PART     PART           LEAD
NUMB   NAME              NUMBER   NAME           TIME   ON HAND   ON ORDER
----   ----------------  ------   ------------   ----   -------   --------
53     ATLANTIS CO.        124    BOLT             3       900        500
                           125    BOLT             3     1,000        200
                           134    NUT              3       900        200
                           135    NUT              3     1,000      1,000
                           222    AXLE            15        25     10,000
                           232    AXLE            15       150          0
                           241    WHEEL           15       300      6,000
                                                        -------   --------
TOTAL FOR SUPPLIER 53                                     4,275     17,900
```

We can save this query under the name SUPPQUERY by entering the following QMF command:

```
SAVE QUERY AS SUPPQUERY
```

We can save the information contained in the Form panels for the report under the name SUPPFORM by issuing this QMF command:

```
SAVE FORM AS SUPPFORM
```

Now, at any time, we can enter the following command to run the SUPPQUERY query and produce the report whose format is described by SUPPFORM:

```
RUN SUPPQUERY (FORM = SUPPFORM
```

Notice that it is not necessary to code a right parenthesis when parameters follow the name of the statement being run. A right parenthesis can be coded if desired, but the blank following SUPPFORM in the example is sufficient to terminate the command properly.

VARIABLES

The previous query was coded to display information only for supplier *53*. Suppose that we wished to be able to submit the query asking for information for any supplier. One way to do this is to display the query's code and change the supplier number in the WHERE clause before issuing the RUN command. However, an easier way is to specify the supplier number in the form of a variable. The variable then allows us to supply the supplier number at the time that we run the query without having to modify the code of the query. The following example shows how we can specify the supplier number in the form of a variable:

```
SELECT      SUPSUPP, NAME, INVPART, PNAME, PRICE, TIME, ONHAND, ONORD
FROM        SUPPLIERS, INVENTORY, QUOTATIONS
WHERE       INVPART = QUOPART
            AND SUPSUPP = QUOSUPP
            AND SUPSUPP = &SUPPLIER
```

An ampersand that precedes a name identifies the name as a variable. We supply a value for the variable at the time the query is run. We can issue a RUN command that does not supply a value for the variable, as in the following example:

```
RUN SUPPQUERY
```

QMF will then display a screen that asks us to enter a value for the &SUP-PLIER variable. After we enter the supplier number, QMF invokes the query and substitutes the supplier number that we enter for the &SUPPLIER variable.

Alternatively, we can supply a value for the variable in the RUN command, as in this example:

```
RUN SUPPQUERY (FORM = SUPPFORM &SUPPLIER = 52
```

QMF PROCEDURES

In the previous example, we gave a name to a single QMF query, saved it, and then ran it by supplying the query's name in a RUN statement. In a similar manner, we can save a *set* of commands in the form of a *procedure*. A QMF procedure can include any number of SQL or QBE queries and other QMF commands. We run the commands stored in a procedure by supplying its name in a RUN command. Suppose we wishcd to run the supplier query shown previously and produce a printed report of the results. To create a procedure to do this, we would first enter the command

```
RESET PROC
```

which causes QMF to display a blank procedure panel. We can then enter into the procedure panel the commands that make up the procedure:

```
RUN SUPPQUERY (FORM = SUPPFORM
PRINT REPORT
```

Again, the RUN statement could be terminated with a closing right parenthesis, but it is not necessary. We can then use the procedure panel to give the name PRINTSUPP to the procedure:

```
SAVE PROC AS PRINTSUPP
```

We would then issue the following command to run the PRINTSUPP procedure:

```
RUN PRINTSUPP
```

**PROCEDURE
VARIABLES**

We can also use variables within a procedure. We
could have created the previous procedure using the
following set of commands:

```
RUN SUPPQUERY (FORM = &FORMNAME
PRINT REPORT
```

Then when we execute the procedure, we can supply the form name in the RUN
command:

```
RUN PRINTSUPP (&FORMNAME = SUPPFORM2
```

It may also be necessary to supply values for variables that are used in the
queries that the procedure invokes. Suppose the SUPPQUERY query uses the
variable &SUPPLIER for supplier number, as shown earlier. When the procedure is executed, if no value has been specified for &SUPPLIER, QMF will
prompt us for a value. We can alternatively include the query variable value in
the RUN command:

```
RUN PRINTSUPP (&FORMNAME = SUPPFORM2 &&SUPPLIER = 51
```

Notice that we must use two ampersands in entering the variable that specifies the supplier number. This is because the variable is defined in a query that
the procedure invokes and is not defined in the procedure itself.

9 QUERY-BY-EXAMPLE (QBE)

In addition to supporting SQL, QMF supports a second language called *Query-by-Example* (QBE). This chapter shows how QBE can be used to perform many of the same functions that were shown in Part II using SQL. QBE uses a very different syntax from SQL. Rather than using English-like statements, QBE displays table structures on the terminal screen and allows the user to enter directly into the table the operators and data needed to define the operation to be performed. The user sees the tables on the screen, can fill them in, and can move command operators, such as PRINT, UPDATE, INSERT, and DELETE, to appropriate parts of the table. Users can have two or more tables on the screen at the same time and can link them. Using powerful operators, they can quickly formulate complex queries.

DISPLAYING TABLE STRUCTURES

We display a table structure by issuing the QMF DRAW command. We can do this by pressing the appropriate PF key or by entering the DRAW command on the command line. If we enter a DRAW command without specifying a table name, QBE prompts us for one. Alternatively, we can specify in the DRAW command the table we are interested in. QBE then responds by displaying an outline of the specified table. Figure 9.1 shows the tables we have been using. Based on these tables, QMF would display the following table structure if we entered DRAW QUOTATIONS on the command line:

QUOTATIONS	QUOSUPP	QUOPART	PRICE	TIME	ONORD

INVENTORY

INVPART	PNAME	ONHAND
124	BOLT	900
125	BOLT	1000
105	GEAR	0
106	GEAR	700
171	GENERATOR	500
172	GENERATOR	400
134	NUT	900
135	NUT	1000
181	WHEEL	1000
205	BAND	450
206	MOTOR	225
221	AXLE	1500
222	AXLE	25
231	AXLE	75
232	AXLE	150
241	WHEEL	300

QUOTATIONS

QUOSUPP	QUOPART	PRICE	TIME	ONORD
51	124	1.25	5	400
51	125	0.55	5	0
51	134	0.40	5	500
51	135	0.39	5	1000
51	221	0.30	10	10000
51	231	0.10	10	5000
52	105	7.50	10	200
52	205	0.15	20	0
52	206	0.15	20	0
53	124	1.35	3	500
53	125	0.58	3	200
53	134	0.38	3	200
53	135	0.42	3	1000
53	222	0.25	15	10000
53	232	–	15	0
53	241	0.08	15	6000

SUPPLIERS

SUPSUPP	NAME	ADDRESS	CODE
51	DEFECTO PARTS	16 JUSTAMERE LANE, TACOMA WA	20
52	VESUVIUS INC.	512 ANCIENT BLVD., POMPEII NY	20
53	ATLANTIS CO.	8 OCEAN AVE., WASHINGTON DC	10
54	TITANIC PARTS	32 SINKING STREET, ATLANTIC CITY NJ	30
57	EAGLE HARDWARE	64 TRANQUILITY PLACE, APOLLO MN	30
61	SKYLAB PARTS	128 ORBIT BLVD., SYDNEY AUSTRALIA	10
64	KNIGHT LTD.	256 ARTHUR COURT, CAMELOT ENGLAND	20

Figure 9.1   Inventory, Quotations, and Suppliers tables.

The table name appears on the left, followed by the table's column names, in the order in which the column names were defined when the table was created. Depending on the type of terminal that is used and the particular software version, QBE will display the outline of the table using various types of characters. In this book, we will show QBE column displays as in the previous example.

There may be times when not all the columns will fit on the screen. For large tables, PF keys can be used to scroll left and right through the table's columns. Once we have displayed a table's columns, we can tell QBE that we will not be working with certain columns. We place the cursor on a column we would like omitted from the display and press the appropriate PF key. QBE then eliminates that column from the display. This has no effect on the underlying table, just on the display.

ENTERING
A QBE QUERY

We define a query by entering operators and values in the table structure. For example, suppose we wanted to use QBE and the table structure shown previously to perform the following query, expressed in the form of an SQL SELECT statement:

```
SELECT      *
FROM        QUOTATIONS
WHERE       QUOPART = 124
```

We would enter the ''P.'' operator (meaning print) under the table name and the value ''124'' under the *Quopart* column:

QUOTATIONS	QUOSUPP	QUOPART	PRICE	TIME	ONORD
P.		124			

Entering a ''P.'' operator under a specific column indicates that we want values displayed for that column; entering the ''P.'' operator under the table name indicates that we want all columns displayed. Entering the value ''124'' in the *Quopart* column indicates that we want only rows that have a *Quopart* value of *124* displayed.

After we have entered our query, we press the PF key assigned to the RUN function or enter RUN QUERY on the command line and press ENTER. QMF then displays a screen that contains the identical results as if we had entered the equivalent SQL query:

```
QUOSUPP   QUOPART     PRICE      TIME     ONORD
-------   -------   -------   -------   -------
     51       124      1.25         5       400
     53       124      1.35         3       500
```

Here is another example:

SQL Query:

```
SELECT      INVPART, PNAME
FROM        INVENTORY
WHERE       PNAME = 'BOLT'
```

Equivalent QBE Query:

INVENTORY	INVPART	PNAME	ONHAND
	P.	P. BOLT	

Results:

```
INVPART   PNAME
-------   ----------------
    124   BOLT
    125   BOLT
```

Here we are specifying the ''P.'' operator only for selected columns. Note that QBE does not require that we use quotation marks with the value ''BOLT''.

Quotation marks are not necessary unless the value contains blanks, special characters other than #, $, or @, or DBCS characters.

If we specify no Boolean operator with the value, QBE assumes that we want an equal operator to be used in selecting the rows to display. We can explicitly supply the operator if we want some other type of comparison to be performed.

SQL Query:

```
SELECT      QUOSUPP, QUOPART, PRICE
FROM        QUOTATIONS
WHERE       PRICE > 1.00
```

Equivalent QBE Query:

QUOTATIONS	QUOSUPP	QUOPART	PRICE	TIME	ONORD
	P.	P.	P. >1.00		

Results:

```
QUOSUPP   QUOPART    PRICE
-------   -------    -------
     51       124       1.25
     52       105       7.50
     53       124       1.35
```

We can also use the NULL keyword to select only rows that contain null values:

SQL Query:

```
SELECT      *
FROM        QUOTATIONS
WHERE       PRICE IS NULL
```

Equivalent QBE Query:

QUOTATIONS	QUOSUPP	QUOPART	PRICE	TIME	ONORD
P.			NULL		

Results:

```
QUOSUPP   QUOPART    PRICE     TIME     ONORD
-------   -------    -------   -------   -------
     53       232         -        15         0
```

USE OF IN, BETWEEN, AND LIKE

QBE supports the use of IN and BETWEEN for multiple values in a condition and LIKE for partial values. (See Chapter 4 for a discussion of IN, BETWEEN, and LIKE operations.) Several SQL queries from Part II are repeated here, followed by their QBE equivalents:

SQL Query:

```
SELECT      QUOSUPP, QUOPART, PRICE
FROM        QUOTATIONS
WHERE       QUOPART IN (105, 135, 205)
```

Equivalent QBE Query:

QUOTATIONS	QUOSUPP	QUOPART	PRICE	TIME
	P.	P. IN (105, 135, 205)	P.	

Results:

QUOSUPP	QUOPART	PRICE
51	135	0.39
52	105	7.50
52	205	0.15
53	135	0.42

SQL Query:

```
SELECT      QUOSUPP, QUOPART, PRICE
FROM        QUOTATIONS
WHERE       QUOPART BETWEEN 105 AND 135
```

Equivalent QBE Query:

QUOTATIONS	QUOSUPP	QUOPART	PRICE	TIME
	P.	P. BT 105 AND 135	P.	

Results:

QUOSUPP	QUOPART	PRICE
51	124	1.25
51	125	0.55
51	134	0.40
51	135	0.39
52	105	7.50
53	124	1.35
53	125	0.58
53	134	0.38
53	135	0.42

SQL Query:

```
SELECT      SUPSUPP, NAME, ADDRESS
FROM        SUPPLIERS
WHERE       ADDRESS LIKE '% MN%'
```

Equivalent QBE Query:

SUPPLIERS	SUPSUPP	NAME	ADDRESS	CODE
	P.	P.	P. LIKE '% MN%'	

Results:

```
SUPSUPP  NAME              ADDRESS
-------  ---------------   -------------------------------------
    57   EAGLE HARDWARE    64 TRANQUILITY PLACE, APOLLO, MN
```

SQL Query:

```
SELECT      *
FROM        INVENTORY
WHERE       PNAME LIKE '_O%'
```

Equivalent QBE Query:

INVENTORY	INVPART	PNAME	ONHAND
P.		LIKE '_O%'	

Results:

```
INVPART  PNAME              ONHAND
-------  ---------------    -------
    124  BOLT                  900
    125  BOLT                 1000
    206  MOTOR                 225
```

UNIQUE ROWS

It is possible to eliminate duplicate rows from the displayed results. We specify this by including the ''UNQ.'' operator under the table name:

SQL Query:

```
SELECT      DISTINCT QUOSUPP
FROM        QUOTATIONS
WHERE       ONORD > 200
```

Equivalent QBE Query:

QUOTATIONS	QUOSUPP	QUOPART	PRICE	TIME	ONORD
UNQ.	P.				>200

Results:

```
          QUOSUPP
          -------
             51
             53
```

MULTIPLE CONDITIONS

We can specify multiple conditions by entering conditional expressions under more than one column. If we enter all the conditions on the same line, QBE assumes that we mean them to be connected by AND:

SQL Query:

```
SELECT      QUOSUPP, QUOPART, PRICE
FROM        QUOTATIONS
WHERE       QUOPART = 124 AND PRICE > 1.30
```

Equivalent QBE Query:

QUOTATIONS	QUOSUPP	QUOPART	PRICE	TIME	ONORD
	P.	P. 124	P. >1.30		

Results:

```
      QUOSUPP    QUOPART      PRICE
      -------    -------      -----
         53        124        1.35
```

If we want the conditions to be connected by OR, we must enter them on separate lines in the table structure. To expand the skeleton table to allow more than one line of input, we position the cursor in the table name column and press the PF key assigned to the ENLARGE function. This adds a line to the skeleton table. Here is an example of use of the OR operator:

SQL Query:

```
SELECT      QUOSUPP, QUOPART, PRICE, TIME
FROM        QUOTATIONS
WHERE       PRICE > 1.30 OR TIME > 10
```

Equivalent QBE Query:

QUOTATIONS	QUOSUPP	QUOPART	PRICE	TIME	ONORD
	P.	P.	P. >1.30	P.	
	P.	P.	P.	P. >10	

Results:

```
          QUOSUPP   QUOPART    PRICE     TIME
          -------   -------   -------   -------
               52       105      7.50        10
               52       205      0.15        20
               52       206      0.15        20
               53       124      1.35         3
               53       222      0.25        15
               53       232         -        15
               53       241      0.08        15
```

Here QBE selects a row if it meets the conditions specified in either line. We must include the ''P.'' operator in both lines, and we must include it in the same set of columns on both lines.

EXAMPLE ELEMENTS   In some cases, it is necessary to connect two or more tables that are displayed on the screen. To do this, we can enter *example elements* in the table structure. An example element is a name we assign to a column so that we can refer to that column elsewhere in the query. An example element name begins with an underscore (_) and consists of up to 18 alphabetic or numeric characters. One use for example elements is to specify selection conditions using a *condition box*.

CONDITION BOX   In some cases, it is easier to specify selection conditions by using SQL-style conditional expressions that explicitly state the AND and OR operators. To do this, we create a *condition box* by issuing the DRAW COND command. QBE then adds a special table structure to the screen in which we can enter selection conditions. We define a selection condition in the condition box and connect it to our table by using example elements, as in the following query:

SQL Query:

```
SELECT     *
FROM       QUOTATIONS
WHERE      QUOPART < 200 AND  (PRICE > 1.00 OR TIME < 10)
```

Equivalent QBE Query:

QUOTATIONS	QUOSUPP	QUOPART	PRICE	TIME	ONORD
P.		_QP	_PART	_TIME	

CONDITIONS
_QP < 200 AND (_PART > 1.00 OR _TIME < 10)

Results:

QUOSUPP	QUOPART	PRICE	TIME	ONORD
51	124	1.25	5	400
51	125	0.55	5	0
51	134	0.40	5	500
51	135	0.39	5	1000
52	105	7.50	10	200
53	124	1.35	3	500
53	125	0.58	3	200
53	134	0.38	3	200
53	135	0.42	3	1000

EXPRESSIONS IN CONDITIONS

We can use arithmetic expressions in defining selection conditions. If the arithmetic expression involves multiple columns, then we must use a condition box to specify the selection condition:

SQL Query:

```
SELECT    QUOSUPP, QUOPART
FROM      QUOTATIONS
WHERE     PRICE * ONORD > 500.00
```

Equivalent QBE Query:

QUOTATIONS	QUOSUPP	QUOPART	PRICE	TIME	ONORD
	P.	P.	_PRCE		_ORD

CONDITIONS
_PRCE * _ORD > 500.00

Results:

QUOSUPP	QUOPART
51	221
52	105
53	124
53	222

NEGATIVES

QBE allows us to use negative conditions in much the same way as SQL does. The NOT operator can be used in conjunction with NULL, IN, BETWEEN, and LIKE; it can also be used preceding any type of condition in a condition box. The comparison operator = can be preceded by NOT, or we can use ¬=. Operators involving >

or $<$ cannot be immediately preceded by either NOT or $\neg$; instead, the entire condition must be preceded by NOT:

QUOTATIONS	QUOSUPP	QUOPART	PRICE	TIME	ONORD
	P.	P.	_PRCE		_ORD

CONDITIONS
NOT _PRCE * _ORD > 500.00

COLUMNS OF CALCULATED VALUES

We can add columns to the table to display values that are calculated from other columns. In this example, we first delete the *Time* column by positioning the cursor in the *Time* column above the horizontal line and pressing the PF key assigned to the REDUCE function. (This is not required; we do this only to eliminate unnecessary information from the display.) We then position the cursor on the last column of the table *(Onord)*, above the horizontal line, and press the PF key assigned to the ENLARGE function. This adds an empty column to the table. We then enter the appropriate arithmetic expression into the new column:

SQL Query:

```
SELECT      QUOSUPP, QUOPART, PRICE * ONORD
FROM        QUOTATIONS
WHERE       PRICE > 1.00
```

Equivalent QBE Query:

QUOTATIONS	QUOSUPP	QUOPART	PRICE	ONORD	
	P.	P.	_PRCE	_ORD	P._PRCE * _ORD

CONDITIONS
_PRCE > 1.00

Results:

QUOSUPP	QUOPART	PRICE*ONORD
51	124	500.00
52	105	1500.00
53	124	675.00

Notice that we have used example elements in defining the column that contains the calculated values. We can use example elements anywhere that we need to refer to a column value.

SPECIFYING ROW SEQUENCE

We can use the "AO." and "DO." operators to specify columns used to sort the resulting display into a desired sequence. The "AO." operator indicates ascending sequence and "DO." descending sequence. If we specify multiple columns, we can include a number in parentheses following the operator to indicate which column is most significant, which is second, and so on.

SQL Query:

```
SELECT      QUOPART, QUOSUPP, PRICE
FROM        QUOTATIONS
ORDER BY    QUOPART, PRICE DESC
```

Equivalent QBE Query:

QUOTATIONS	QUOSUPP	QUOPART	PRICE	TIME	ONORD
	P.	P.AO(1).	P.DO(2).		

Results:

QUOSUPP	QUOPART	PRICE
52	105	7.50
53	124	1.35
51	124	1.25
53	125	0.58
51	125	0.55
51	134	0.40
53	134	0.38
53	135	0.42
51	135	0.39
52	205	0.15
52	206	0.15
51	221	0.30
53	222	0.25
51	231	0.10
53	232	-
53	241	0.08

We can also use a column of calculated values for sequencing the display by including the appropriate operator in the calculated column:

SQL Query:

```
SELECT      QUOSUPP, QUOPART, PRICE * ONORD
FROM        QUOTATIONS
WHERE       PRICE > 1.00
ORDER BY    QUOPART, 3 DESC
```

Equivalent QBE Query:

QUOTATIONS	QUOSUPP	QUOPART	PRICE	ONORD	
	P.	P. AO(1).	_PRCE	_ORD	P.DO(2)._PRCE * _ORD

CONDITIONS
_PRCE > 1.00

Results:

```
QUOSUPP   QUOPART   PRICE*ONORD
-------   -------   -----------
     52       105          1500
     53       124           675
     51       124           500
```

JOINING TABLES

We can define QBE queries that combine data from two or more tables. We begin by displaying all the tables that we are joining by issuing multiple DRAW commands, one for each table. We then specify the manner in which we want to join the tables by using example elements:

SQL Query:

```
SELECT    INVPART, PNAME, ONHAND, QUOSUPP, ONORD
FROM      INVENTORY, QUOTATIONS
WHERE     INVPART = QUOPART
```

Equivalent QBE Query:

INVENTORY	INVPART	PNAME	ONHAND		
P.	_PART			_SUPP	_OO

QUOTATIONS	QUOSUPP	QUOPART	PRICE	TIME	ONORD
	_SUPP	_PART			_OO

Results:

INVPART	PNAME	ONHAND	QUOSUPP	ONORD
105	GEAR	0	52	200
124	BOLT	900	51	400
124	BOLT	900	53	500
125	BOLT	1000	51	0
125	BOLT	1000	53	200
134	NUT	900	51	500
134	NUT	900	53	200
135	NUT	1000	51	1000
135	NUT	1000	53	1000
205	BAND	450	52	0
206	MOTOR	225	52	0
221	AXLE	1500	51	10000
222	AXLE	25	53	10000
231	AXLE	75	51	5000
232	AXLE	150	53	0
241	WHEEL	300	53	6000

Here we are using the example element ''_PART'' to join the two tables together based on part number values. QBE selects data only where a row in *Inventory* and a row in *Quotations* have the same value for part number. In QBE, the comparison used for joining is assumed to be an equal comparison (equijoin) between any columns in which we have entered the same example element name.

The results of a QBE query always take the form of a single table. Therefore, we can specify ''P.'' operators in only one of the tables displayed on the screen. In this example, we are using the *Inventory* table to specify the columns that we want displayed. Since we want data displayed from both the *Inventory* and the *Quotations* tables, we have added two empty columns in the *Inventory* table and have used example elements (''_SUPP'' and ''_OO'') to identify the columns from the *Quotations* table that we want displayed in addition to columns that come directly from the *Inventory* table.

BUILT-IN FUNCTIONS AND GROUP BY

QBE supports the use of the same built-in functions as SQL, both for the entire table and for subsets of rows based on grouping by a specified column or columns. The following example shows how we can use built-in functions for an entire table. Notice that we show the table in two parts, but on the terminal the entire table is displayed horizontally. We use the horizontal scroll functions to display a portion of the table if it is too wide to fit on the screen.

SQL Query:

```
SELECT    SUM(ONORD), SUM(PRICE * ONORD), MAX(PRICE), AVG(PRICE)
FROM      QUOTATIONS
```

Equivalent QBE Query:

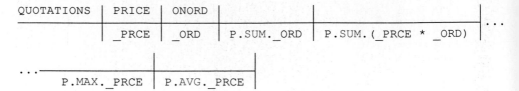

```
QUOTATIONS | PRICE | ONORD |                   |                        |
           | _PRCE | _ORD  | P.SUM._ORD | P.SUM.(_PRCE * _ORD) |  ...

    ...
        | P.MAX._PRCE | P.AVG._PRCE |
```

Results:

SUM(ONORD)	SUM(PRICE*ONORD)	MAX(PRICE)	AVG(PRICE)
35000	10357.00	7.50	0.92333333

In this example, we are using the example elements "_PRCE" and "_ORD" to specify the columns that will be used with the built-in functions. The built-in functions are then specified in unnamed columns. The first unnamed column, for example, uses the SUM built-in function to total on-order quantities.

We use the "G." operator to specify grouping, as in the following example:

SQL Query:

```
SELECT     PNAME, SUM(ONHAND)
FROM       INVENTORY
GROUP BY   PNAME
```

Equivalent QBE Query:

```
INVENTORY | INVPART | PNAME | ONHAND |              |
          |         | G.P.  | _OH    | P.SUM.(_OH)  |
```

Results:

PNAME	SUM(ONHAND)
AXLE	1750
BAND	450
BOLT	1900
GEAR	700
GENERATOR	900
MOTOR	225
NUT	1900
WHEEL	1300

In this example, we are grouping on the content of the PNAME column and thus are calculating total *Onhand* amounts for groups of parts having the same name. When we use "G.", we must not specify "P." for a column unless it has a single value for the group of rows we are specifying. For example, specifying "P." for the *Invpart* column would be invalid, since there can be multiple values of part number for each part name value.

LINKED QUERIES   QBE does not support subqueries in the same manner as SQL; however, by linking tables with example elements, it is possible to perform some of the types of queries that can be requested using SQL subqueries. Generally, the linking is done to determine a condition value.

CONDITION VALUE   The condition value may be in a different table than
IN A DIFFERENT   that being used to display data:
TABLE

SQL Query:

```
SELECT      QUOPART, PRICE
FROM        QUOTATIONS
WHERE       QUOSUPP IN (SELECT SUPSUPP
                        FROM SUPPLIERS
                        WHERE CODE = 20)
```

Equivalent QBE Query:

QUOTATIONS	QUOSUPP	QUOPART	PRICE	TIME	ONORD
	_SUPP	P.	P.		

SUPPLIERS	SUPSUPP	NAME	ADDRESS	CODE
	_SUPP			20

Results:

QUOPART	PRICE
124	1.25
125	0.55
134	0.40
135	0.39
221	0.30
231	0.10
105	7.50
205	0.15
206	0.15

Here the query in the *Suppliers* table finds all the supplier numbers for which CODE is 20. We are then using these supplier numbers to select rows from the *Quotations* table.

We can use built-in functions and grouping when linking tables:

SQL Query:

```
SELECT      INVPART, PNAME, ONHAND
FROM        INVENTORY
WHERE       INVPART IN (SELECT QUOPART
                        FROM QUOTATIONS
                        GROUP BY QUOPART
                        HAVING SUM(ONORD) > 500)
```

Equivalent QBE Query:

INVENTORY	INVPART	PNAME	ONHAND
P.	_PART		

QUOTATIONS	QUOSUPP	QUOPART	PRICE	TIME	ONORD
		G._PART			_ORD

CONDITIONS
SUM._ORD > 500

Results:

```
INVPART  PNAME              ONHAND
-------  ---------------    -------
    124  BOLT                   900
    134  NUT                    900
    135  NUT                   1000
    221  AXLE                  1500
    222  AXLE                    25
    231  AXLE                    75
    241  WHEEL                  300
```

In this example, we are summarizing on-order quantity by part number. We are selecting part numbers where the on-order sum is greater than 500. We are then displaying information from the *Inventory* table for the selected part numbers.

CONDITION VALUE IN THE SAME TABLE

It is also possible to link a table to itself. We can do this by using two copies of the same table structure, or we can enter two queries in the same table structure. Here is an example using two separate table structures:

SQL Query:

```
SELECT      DISTINCT QUOSUPP, QUOPART, PRICE
FROM        QUOTATIONS
WHERE       PRICE > ANY  (SELECT PRICE
                          FROM QUOTATIONS
                          WHERE ONORD > 0)
```

Equivalent QBE Query:

QUOTATIONS	QUOSUPP	QUOPART	PRICE	TIME	ONORD
			_PRCE		>0

QUOTATIONS	QUOSUPP	QUOPART	PRICE	TIME	ONORD
UNQ.	P.	P.	P. >MIN._PRCE		

Results:

QUOSUPP	QUOPART	PRICE
51	124	1.25
51	125	0.55
51	134	0.40
51	135	0.39
51	221	0.30
51	231	0.10
52	105	7.50
52	205	0.15
52	206	0.15
53	124	1.35
53	125	0.58
53	134	0.38
53	135	0.42
53	222	0.25

The first query selects all values for price where the on-order quantity is greater than *0*. The second query determines the minimum value selected by the first query and selects distinct rows with a price greater than the minimum.

The following example shows how we can use grouped data by linking a table to itself:

SQL Query:

```
SELECT      QUOSUPP, QUOPART, PRICE
FROM        QUOTATIONS ROWQ
WHERE       PRICE = (SELECT MIN(PRICE)
                     FROM QUOTATIONS
                     WHERE QUOPART = ROWQ.QUOPART)
```

Equivalent QBE Query:

QUOTATIONS	QUOSUPP	QUOPART	PRICE	TIME	ONORD
	P.	G._QP P._QP	_PRCE P̄.MIN._PRCE		

Results:

```
QUOSUPP   QUOPART    PRICE
-------   -------   -------
     51       124      1.25
     51       125      0.55
     51       135      0.39
     51       221      0.30
     51       231      0.10
     52       105      7.50
     52       205      0.15
     52       206      0.15
     53       134      0.38
     53       222      0.25
     53       241      0.08
```

Here the first query groups prices by part number. The second query then determines the minimum price for each part number and selects the row or rows for that part number with a price equal to the minimum price.

COMBINING QUERY RESULTS

We can perform a *union* relational operation to combine the results from two or more queries. We do this by specifying multiple query lines, where each line contains a "P." operator. The following is an example of a *union* operation:

SQL Query:

```
SELECT     SUPSUPP, NAME, 'PREFERRED'
FROM       SUPPLIERS
WHERE      CODE = 30
    UNION
SELECT     SUPSUPP, NAME,
FROM       SUPPLIERS
WHERE      CODE ¬= 30
```

Equivalent QBE Query:

SUPPLIERS	SUPSUPP	NAME	CODE	
	P.	P.	30	P. 'PREFERRED'
	P.	P.	¬= 30	P. ' '

```
SUPSUPP    NAME
-------    ----------------    ---------
     51    DEFECTO PARTS
     52    VESUVIUS INC.
     53    ATLANTIS CO.
     54    TITANIC PARTS       PREFERRED
     57    EAGLE HARDWARE      PREFERRED
     61    SKYLAB PARTS
     64    KNIGHT LTD.
```

To combine queries in this manner, the two queries must select the same number of columns and the columns must be of the same data type. The columns selected can be from different tables as long as they meet the number and type restrictions.

UPDATING TABLES   In addition to retrieving data from tables, QBE allows us to add, change, or delete data from tables, using the "I.", "U.", and "D." operators. We can insert data directly by entering it in the table structure, or we can copy data from another table. When we insert data directly, we can enter more than one row on the screen if we like:

INVENTORY	INVPART	PNAME	ONHAND
I.	126	BOLT	0
I.	107	GEAR	25

We can also update data values by using the "U." operator:

SQL Query:

```
UPDATE QUOTATIONS
SET PRICE = 1.30, TIME = 10
WHERE QUOSUPP = 51 AND QUOPART = 124
```

Equivalent QBE Query:

QUOTATIONS	QUOSUPP	QUOPART	PRICE	TIME	ONORD
	51	124	U. 1.30	U. 10	

In this example, the values we have entered for supplier and part identify the row to be updated. The values for price and time, which we have preceded with a "U." operator, represent the new values for the row.

We can delete rows from a table by using the "D." operator:

QUOTATIONS	QUOSUPP	QUOPART	PRICE	TIME	ONORD
D.	52				

This deletes all rows for supplier 52.

Keep in mind that if the tables we are accessing have referential constraints defined for them through the use of primary keys and foreign keys, the same inserting, updating, and deleting restrictions apply as for the SQL updating that we discussed in Chapter 6.

OPERATIONS NOT SUPPORTED

QBE does not support the following operations:

- Creating, altering, or dropping a table
- Creating or dropping a synonym
- Creating or dropping a view
- Granting or revoking authorizations

SQL statements must be used to perform these functions.

SUMMARY OF PART III

QMF allows DB2 data to be accessed interactively using either SQL or QBE. Using QMF, queries can be formulated and run, the results of a query displayed at the terminal or printed, query results formatted in various ways including graphic presentation, and QMF queries and commands stored and executed as procedures. QMF can also be used to update, insert, and delete data; to create, alter, and drop tables; to create and drop views; and to grant and revoke authorizations.

QMF automatically formats data retrieved as the result of a query for display at a terminal or for printing. A user can modify the QMF formatting to produce customized reports. Report-formatting capabilities include control breaks, totals, editing, headings and footings, functions, summarization, and graphical presentation. Queries, report forms, and sets of QMF commands, called procedures, can be saved and executed at a later time. QMF queries and procedures can include variables whose values are specified at the time the query or procedure is run.

QBE uses a graphical approach to query formulation. A table structure is displayed and the query formed by entering operators and data into the skeleton structure. The "P." operator indicates columns to be displayed. Comparison operators, expressions, lists and ranges of values, and partial values can be used in conditions. Multiple conditions can be specified. Columns can be added to the table to display values calculated from other columns. A sequence can be specified for displaying the results. Two or more tables can be joined by specifying example elements. Built-in functions can be specified for an entire table or for groups of rows. Multiple queries can be linked using example elements to determine a value or set of values to be used as part of a condition. The linked queries can be for different tables or the same table. The results of two or more queries can be merged. QBE can also be used to insert, update, and delete data. DB2's implementation of QBE does not support creating or dropping tables, views or synonyms, altering a table, or granting or revoking authorizations.

PART **IV** APPLICATION PROGRAMMING

In the chapters of Parts II and III, we looked at examples of SQL statements that we invoked interactively using a facility such as SPUFI or QMF. We can also include SQL statements in application program, thus allowing us to access DB2 data in an application system. In this part of the book, we will examine the use of SQL in application programs and discuss the steps involved in the DB2 application development process.

In this chapter, we examine the syntax of embedded SQL statements, discuss the general processing requirements associated with the use of DB2 data in an application program, and walk through a sample program that illustrates how we can retrieve data from DB2 tables by issuing SELECT in an application program. In Chapter 11, we present the steps involved in the program development process, including precompilation, compilation, link editing, binding, and execution. In Chapter 12, we show additional coding examples that illustrate how we can load data into a table and modify the data in tables. Chapter 13 discusses the use of dynamic SQL statements that are generated at execution time rather than being compiled into the source code.

10 EMBEDDED SQL STATEMENTS

DB2 PROGRAMMING ENVIRONMENT DB2 supports interfaces for application programs that are written in a number of fourth-generation languages (4GLs) and conventional programming languages, including COBOL, PL/I, C, FORTRAN, APL, C, and Assembler, that run in the following subsystem environments:

- **TSO.** A program running under TSO can run either in foreground or in background under the control of the Terminal Monitor Program.
- **CICS.** A CICS program uses the CICS Attachment Facility to access DB2.
- **IMS.** An IMS program using IMD/DC runs as a message processing program (MPP), a batch message processing program (BMP), or a Fast Path program. IMS batch programs can also access DB2 tables.

Not all languages are supported in all environments. Consult your IBM documentation for an up-to-date description of the languages that are supported in your particular subsystem environment.

Figure 10.1 illustrates the software environments that support DB2 applications. As shown in the diagram, an application that runs under CICS or IMS can access IMS databases as well as DB2 databases. However, the application does not access IMS databases via DB2 facilities by issuing SELECT statements. Instead, the normal CICS and IMS CALL interfaces to IMS databases are used.

SYNTAX FOR EMBEDDED SQL STATEMENTS SQL statements that are embedded in an application program follow the same general syntax rules as those that we saw in Part II. In COBOL, PL/I, C, FORTRAN, and Assembler programs, an SQL state-

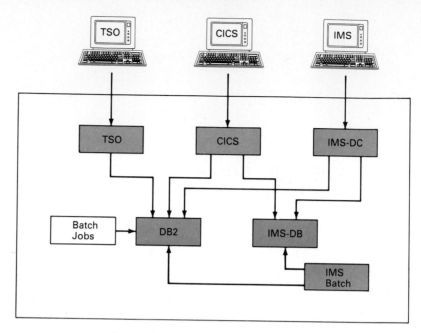

Figure 10.1   DB2 subsystem environment.

ment begins with the keywords "EXEC SQL". Each language requires that SQL statements be terminated in a particular way:

Language	Terminator
COBOL	"END-EXEC."
PL/I	";"
C	";"
FORTRAN	No continuation character in column 6 of the next line
Assembler	No continuation character in column 72

Figure 10.2 shows examples of SELECT statements coded in COBOL, PL/I, C, FORTRAN, and Assembler. Other languages may require that SQL statements be delimited in other ways. Consult the documentation for your particular language before attempting to compile a DB2 program.

HOST VARIABLES

The names to which SQL statements refer can either be names known to DB2, such as the names of DB2 table columns, or names known to the application program, such as the names of data items defined by the application program. Names known to DB2 are coded in the normal manner, such as the table column names *Supsupp* and *Code*

COBOL

```
EXEC SQL SELECT SUPSUPP, CODE
        INTO :SUPPNO, :SUPPCODE
        FROM SUPPLIERS
        WHERE NAME = :SUPPNAME
    END-EXEC.
```

PL/I

```
EXEC SQL SELECT SUPSUPP, CODE
        INTO :SUPPNO, :SUPPCODE
        FROM SUPPLIERS
        WHERE NAME = :SUPPNAME;
```

C

```
EXEC SQL SELECT SUPSUPP, CODE
        INTO :SUPPNO, :SUPPCODE
        FROM SUPPLIERS
        WHERE NAME = :SUPPNAME;
```

FORTRAN

```
 EXEC SQL SELECT SUPSUPP, CODE
C        INTO :SUPPNO, :SUPPCODE
C        FROM SUPPLIERS
C        WHERE NAME = :SUPPNAME
```

Assembler

```
EXEC SQL SELECT SUPSUPP, CODE                                    *
        INTO :SUPPNO, :SUPPCODE                                  *
        FROM SUPPLIERS                                           *
        WHERE NAME = :SUPPNAME
```

Figure 10.2   Embedded SQL statements.

and the table name *Suppliers* in the following COBOL SQL statement repeated from Fig. 10.2:

```
EXEC SQL SELECT SUPSUPP, CODE
        INTO :SUPPNO, :SUPPCODE
        FROM SUPPLIERS
        WHERE NAME = :SUPPNAME
    END-EXEC.
```

Names that are known to the application program and not to DB2 are called *host variables*. A host variable is generally a data item that is defined in the normal way in the application program. A host variable name is distinguished from a DB2 name in an embedded SQL statement by preceding the host variable's name with a colon (:).

Host variables can be used to provide input to the SQL statement. For example, the :SUPPNAME host variable in the previous example supplies the value for the *Name* column of the *Suppliers* table to be used in evaluating the WHERE clause conditional expression. A host variable can also be used to receive the results of an SQL statement's processing, such as the :SUPPNO and :SUPPCODE host variables in the previous example. In an application program that issues the query, the program must store an appropriate value in the :SUPPNAME host variable before executing the query. When the SQL statement is executed, DB2 performs the processing specified by the SQL statement and places the results of the query into the :SUPPNO and :SUPPCODE host variables. The program can then use the results of the query for any desired processing.

PROCESSING QUERY RESULTS

When we execute an SQL query interactively, the results of the query are normally displayed on the terminal screen. When a query is embedded in an application program, the query results are normally passed to the program for processing. For example, when an SQL SELECT statement returns a single value for each specified column, the values can be placed directly into host variables using an INTO clause, as shown in the examples in Fig. 10.2. The SELECT statement returns a single supplier number value and a single code value, so the INTO clause causes the returned values to be stored directly into the :SUPPNO and :SUPPCODE host variables. Application programs often issue SQL queries that return multiple rows. The sample retrieval program that we will look at in this chapter is an example of such a program.

DB2 RETRIEVAL PROGRAM

Figure 10.3 contains the partial coding for a COBOL program that issues embedded SQL statements. We have included only the coding that is specifically related to DB2. This program, though simple, demonstrates the basic coding requirements for an application program that accesses DB2 data. We will next discuss this sample program, one piece at a time.

The program shown in Fig. 10.3 uses the following SQL query to produce a report about part information stored in the *Inventory* and *Quotations* tables:

```
SELECT INVPART, PNAME, QUOSUPP, PRICE, ONHAND, ONORD
    FROM INVENTORY, QUOTATIONS
    WHERE INVPART = QUOPART AND PRICE > :MINPRICE
    ORDER BY INVPART, QUOSUPP
```

```
DATA DIVISION.

WORKING-STORAGE SECTION.

    EXEC SQL DECLARE PARTROW CURSOR FOR
        SELECT INVPART, PNAME, QUOSUPP, PRICE, ONHAND, ONORD
            FROM INVENTORY, QUOTATIONS
            WHERE INVPART = QUOPART AND PRICE > :MINPRICE
            ORDER BY INVPART, QUOSUPP
        END-EXEC.

    EXEC SQL INCLUDE SQLCA END-EXEC.

77  NO-DATA         PIC S9(9)   COMP   VALUE +100.
77  MINPRICE        PIC S999V99 COMP-3.

01  PARTINFO.
    05  PARTNO      PIC S9(4)   COMP.
    05  PARTNAME    PIC X(15).
    05  SUPPNO      PIC S9(4)   COMP.
    05  PRICE       PIC S999V99 COMP-3.
    05  ONHAND      PIC S9(5)   COMP.
    05  ONORD       PIC S9(5)   COMP.

PROCEDURE DIVISION.

    [Initialize processing and store
     minimum price in MINPRICE.]

PROCESS-PART.
    EXEC SQL OPEN PARTROW END-EXEC.
    EXEC SQL FETCH PARTROW INTO :PARTINFO END-EXEC.
    IF SQLCODE = NO-DATA
        PERFORM NOINFO-MSG
    ELSE
        PERFORM PROCESS-PARTLINE UNTIL
            SQLCODE = NO-DATA.

    EXEC SQL CLOSE PARTROW END-EXEC.

    STOP RUN.

PROCESS-PARTLINE.
    PERFORM PRINT-PARTLINE.
    EXEC SQL FETCH PARTROW INTO :PARTINFO END-EXEC.

PRINT-PARTLINE.
    [Print Part Report.]

NOINFO-MSG.
    [Print no-data-found message.]
```

This statement declares a cursor and its associated SQL statement.

This statement prepares the cursor for processing.

This statement fetches the first row of the query results.

This statement closes the cursor.

This statement fetches subsequent rows of the query results.

Figure 10.3 Sample COBOL DB2 program.

INVENTORY

INVPART	PNAME	ONHAND
124	BOLT	900
125	BOLT	1000
105	GEAR	0
106	GEAR	700
171	GENERATOR	500
172	GENERATOR	400
134	NUT	900
135	NUT	1000
181	WHEEL	1000
205	BAND	450
206	MOTOR	225
221	AXLE	1500
222	AXLE	25
231	AXLE	75
232	AXLE	150
241	WHEEL	300

QUOTATIONS

QUOSUPP	QUOPART	PRICE	TIME	ONORD
51	124	1.25	5	400
51	125	0.55	5	0
51	134	0.40	5	500
51	135	0.39	5	1000
51	221	0.30	10	10000
51	231	0.10	10	5000
52	105	7.50	10	200
52	205	0.15	20	0
52	206	0.15	20	0
53	124	1.35	3	500
53	125	0.58	3	200
53	134	0.38	3	200
53	135	0.42	3	1000
53	222	0.25	15	10000
53	232	-	15	0
53	241	0.08	15	6000

Figure 10.4   Inventory and Quotations tables.

If we processed a similar query using an interactive facility against the table content shown in Fig. 10.4 and a value of 0.50 substituted for :MINPRICE, we would receive the following results:

INVPART	PNAME	QUOSUPP	PRICE	ONHAND	ONORD
105	GEAR	52	7.50	0	200
124	BOLT	51	1.25	900	400
124	BOLT	53	1.35	900	500
125	BOLT	51	0.55	1000	0
125	BOLT	53	0.58	1000	200

USING A CURSOR   When an SQL query is expected to return multiple rows, we cannot simply assign the values it returns to host variables as in the embedded SELECT statement example we examined previously. Instead, we must declare a *cursor* with an associated SQL query. We then use the cursor to access successively the individual rows that the query returns. The following code, taken from the WORKING-STORAGE SECTION of our sample program, declares a cursor and its associated query:

```
EXEC SQL DECLARE PARTROW CURSOR FOR
    SELECT INVPART, PNAME, QUOSUPP, PRICE, ONHAND, ONORD
        FROM INVENTORY, QUOTATIONS
        WHERE INVPART = QUOPART AND PRICE > :MINPRICE
        ORDER BY INVPART, QUOSUPP
    END-EXEC.
```

This coding associates a cursor named PARTROW with the results that will be returned by the SELECT statement included in the cursor declaration.

Because the cursor and query declaration is included in the WORKING-STORAGE SECTION, program coding in the PROCEDURE DIVISION must reference this declaration in order to process the query. To process the query initially and to prepare the cursor for processing, we issue an OPEN statement:

```
EXEC SQL OPEN PARTROW END-EXEC.
```

After the OPEN has been executed, we process the first row of the results, by issuing a FETCH statement:

```
EXEC SQL FETCH PARTROW
         INTO :PARTINFO
      END-EXEC.
```

The FETCH statement causes a single row from the query results to be placed into the specified data area. In this case, the specified data area is a structure whose data item types and lengths match the six data items that are returned by the SELECT statement:

```
01   PARTINFO.
     05   PARTNO      PIC S9(4)    COMP.
     05   PARTNAME    PIC X(15).
     05   SUPPNO      PIC S9(4)    COMP.
     05   PRICE       PIC S999V99 COMP-3.
     05   ONHAND      PIC S9(5)    COMP.
     05   ONORD       PIC S9(5)    COMP.
```

After accessing the first row, the program tests a field in the *SQL Communications Area* (SQLCA). The SQLCA contains fields that describe the results of an embedded SQL statement's execution. DB2 provides a description of the SQLCA that can be brought into a DB2 program through the use of an INCLUDE statement:

```
EXEC SQL INCLUDE SQLCA END-EXEC.
```

This INCLUDE statement allows the program to refer by name to the various fields in the SQLCA. Later in this chapter, we will discuss the SQLCA in detail. For now, we are interested only in an SQLCA field named SQLCODE. It contains a return code that describes the results of an SQL statement's execution. DB2 places a return code value of $+100$ in SQLCODE after a FETCH when there is no data available to satisfy the FETCH request. The following IF statement follows the initial FETCH:

```
IF SQLCODE = NO-DATA
      PERFORM NOINFO-MSG
   ELSE
      PERFORM PROCESS-PARTLINE UNTIL
         SQLCODE = NO-DATA.
```

If there is no data available after the first FETCH, the program assumes that there is no data in the table that satisfies the condition of the SELECT statement, issues a message, and then terminates the program's execution. If the first FETCH does return a row, the program prints the values returned for the first row and then attempts to fetch and print the next row of the results:

```
PROCESS-PARTLINE.
    PERFORM PRINT-PARTLINE.
    EXEC SQL FETCH PARTROW INTO :PARTINFO END-EXEC.

PRINT-PARTLINE.
    [Print Part Report.]
```

The UNTIL clause in the PERFORM statement that executes PROCESS-PARTLINE causes the program to execute PROCESS-PARTLINE repeatedly, examining SQLCODE after each execution of the FETCH statement. After the program has processed the last row of the results, DB2 returns a value of $+100$ in SQLCODE. This causes the program to execute a CLOSE statement for the cursor:

```
EXEC SQL CLOSE PARTROW END-EXEC.
```

By closing the cursor, the program can later open the cursor again, if desired, to use the SQL query to produce a new set of results.

THE SQL COMMUNICATION AREA (SQLCA)
As we discussed, our sample program uses a field in the SQL Communication Area (SQLCA) to determine the results of SQL statement processing. The SQLCA must be described by every program that interfaces with DB2, usually by using the INCLUDE statement we saw in the sample program:

```
EXEC SQL INCLUDE SQLCA END-EXEC.
```

The fields that are contained in the SQLCA are described in Box 10.1.

As we saw in the sample program, an important field in the SQLCA is the SQLCODE field. It contains a value that describes the results of an SQL statement's execution. A value of zero in SQLCODE indicates that execution was successful. A negative value in SQLCODE indicates an error condition. A positive value in SQLCODE indicates that the statement executed successfully but that an exception condition occurred. For example, the SQLCODE value of $+100$ that we tested for in the sample program indicates that there is no more data to process.

A DB2 program references the six SQLERRD fields in the SQLCA using an index. Generally, only SQLERRD(3) is of interest to an application program. An update program normally examines the value in the SQLERRD(3) field following an SQL INSERT, UPDATE, or DELETE statement. The value contained in SQLERRD(3) specifies the number of rows in the table that were affected by the statement.

BOX 10.1 SQLCA contents

Field	Type	Contents
SQLCAID	CHAR(8)	An 8-byte field that contains the character string "SQLCA"
SQLCABC	INTEGER	A fullword field that specifies the length of the SQLCA and always contains the value 136
SQLCODE	INTEGER	A fullword field that contains a return code that describes the results of the processing of the most recently executed SQL statement
SQLERRM	VARCHAR(70)	A variable-length field that contains a character string that provides a description of an error condition
SQLERRD(1) through SQLERRD(6)	INTEGER	A set of six fullword fields that contain values related to the SQL statement most recently executed
SQLWARN0 through SQLWARN7	CHAR(1)	A set of eight 1-byte fields, of which only six are currently used, that provide warnings when certain conditions occur. An SQLWARN field contains either a blank or a "W"

BOX 10.2 SQLWARN fields

SQLWARN0	Contains "W" if one or more of the other SQLWARN fields contains a "W". When SQLWARN0 contains a blank, all other SQLWARN fields also contain blanks.
SQLWARN1	Contains "W" if a column's value was truncated when it was stored in a host variable.
SQLWARN2	Contains "W" if a null value was eliminated from the argument set of a function.
SQLWARN3	Contains "W" if the number of host variables specified is unequal to the number of columns in the table or view being accessed.
SQLWARN4	Contains "W" if a dynamic UPDATE or DELETE statement does not include a WHERE clause.
SQLWARN5	Contains "W" if a program tries to execute a statement that applies only to SQL/DS.

A program can refer to the eight SQLWARN fields using the individual data item names SQLWARN0 through SQLWARN7. The values that DB2 stores in the eight SQLWARN fields are useful in a number of situations. Box 10.2 lists the different conditions that are indicated by various values that DB2 stores in the SQLWARN fields.

PROCESSING SQL RETURN CODES

As an alternative to explicit testing of fields in the SQL communication area, an application program can use a WHENEVER statement for processing SQL return codes. A WHENEVER statement is different in scope from an IF statement. An IF statement test is applied only when the IF statement is executed; a WHENEVER statement specifies processing that is to be performed whenever a particular type of condition occurs and applies to *all* SQL statements that follow it in the source listing. There are three conditions that can be specified in a WHENEVER statement:

- **WHENEVER SQLERROR** . . . SQLERROR causes DB2 to test for any negative return code value.
- **WHENEVER NOT FOUND** . . . NOT FOUND causes DB2 to test for a return code of +100 and indicates that no row was found that satisfied the specified conditions.
- **WHENEVER SQLWARNING** . . . SQLWARNING causes DB2 to test for a positive return code value of other than +100 or a value of ''W'' in one or more of the SQLWARN fields.

A WHENEVER statement can specify one of two actions:

```
WHENEVER condition CONTINUE.
```

or

```
WHENEVER condition GO TO label.
```

CONTINUE causes the program to continue execution with the next program statement when the condition occurs. GO TO passes control to the statement having the specified label.

The processing specified in a WHENEVER statement applies to all SQL statements that follow it *in the source listing*, not in the execution path. If we include a single WHENEVER statement at the beginning of the PROCEDURE DIVISION, it applies to all the other SQL statements that are executed by the program. If we include a second WHENEVER statement later in the program, the first WHENEVER statement would apply to all SQL statements between the first WHENEVER statement and the second WHENEVER statement; the second

WHENEVER statement would apply to all the SQL statements that follow it in the source listing.

   Figure 10.5 shows a version of the sample program from Fig. 10.3, in which we are using a WHENEVER statement to handle the SQLCODE value of +100 that indicates the end of data. In this version of the program, we do

```
DATA DIVISION.

WORKING-STORAGE SECTION.

    EXEC SQL DECLARE PARTROW CURSOR FOR
        SELECT INVPART, PNAME, QUOSUPP, PRICE, ONHAND, ONORD
            FROM INVENTORY, QUOTATIONS
            WHERE INVPART = QUOPART AND PRICE > :MINPRICE
            ORDER BY INVPART, QUOSUPP
        END-EXEC.

    EXEC SQL INCLUDE SQLCA END-EXEC.

77  NO-DATA         PIC S9(9)   COMP   VALUE +100.
77  MINPRICE        PIC S999V99 COMP-3.

01  PARTINFO.
    05  PARTNO      PIC S9(4)   COMP.
    05  PARTNAME    PIC X(15).
    05  SUPPNO      PIC S9(4)   COMP.
    05  PRICE       PIC S999V99 COMP-3.
    05  ONHAND      PIC S9(5)   COMP.
    05  ONORD       PIC S9(5)   COMP.

PROCEDURE DIVISION.

    [Initialize processing and store minimum price in MINPRICE.]

PROCESS-PART.

    EXEC SQL WHENEVER NOT FOUND
        GO TO END-JOB
        END-EXEC.
    EXEC SQL OPEN PARTROW END-EXEC.

GET-ROW.

    EXEC SQL FETCH PARTROW INTO :PARTINFO END-EXEC.
    PERFORM PRINT-PARTLINE.
    GO TO GET-ROW.

END-JOB.

    EXEC SQL CLOSE PARTROW END-EXEC.

    STOP RUN.

PRINT-PARTLINE.
    [Print Part Report.]
```

A WHENEVER statement applies to all SQL statements that follow it in the source listing.

Figure 10.5   Using the WHENEVER statement.

```
DATA DIVISION.

WORKING-STORAGE SECTION.

     EXEC SQL DECLARE PARTROW CURSOR FOR
          SELECT INVPART, PNAME, QUOSUPP, PRICE, ONHAND, ONORD
              FROM INVENTORY, QUOTATIONS
              WHERE INVPART = QUOPART AND PRICE > :MINPRICE
              ORDER BY INVPART, QUOSUPP
          END-EXEC.

     EXEC SQL INCLUDE SQLCA END-EXEC.

     EXEC SQL DECLARE INVENTORY TABLE
              (INVPART SMALLINT NOT NULL,
               PNAME    CHAR (15),
               ONHAND   INTEGER)
          END-EXEC.

     EXEC SQL DECLARE QUOTATIONS TABLE
              (QUOSUPP SMALLINT NOT NULL,
               QUOPART SMALLINT NOT NULL,
               PRICE   DECIMAL (5,2),
               TIME    SMALLINT,
               ONORD   INTEGER)
          END-EXEC.

77  NO-DATA          PIC S9(9)   COMP   VALUE +100.
77  MINPRICE         PIC S999V99 COMP-3.

01  PARTINFO.
    05  PARTNO       PIC S9(4)   COMP.
    05  PARTNAME     PIC X(15).
    05  SUPPNO       PIC S9(4)   COMP.
    05  PRICE        PIC S999V99 COMP-3.
    05  ONHAND       PIC S9(5)   COMP.
    05  ONORD        PIC S9(5)   COMP.

PROCEDURE DIVISION.

     [Initialize processing and store minimum price in MINPRICE.]

PROCESS-PART.
     EXEC SQL OPEN PARTROW END-EXEC.
     EXEC SQL FETCH PARTROW INTO :PARTINFO END-EXEC.
     IF SQLCODE = NO-DATA
         PERFORM NOINFO-MSG
     ELSE
         PERFORM PROCESS-PARTLINE UNTIL
             SQLCODE = NO-DATA.

     EXEC SQL CLOSE PARTROW END-EXEC.

     STOP RUN.

PROCESS-PARTLINE.
     PERFORM PRINT-PARTLINE.
     EXEC SQL FETCH PARTROW INTO :PARTINFO END-EXEC.

PRINT-PARTLINE.
     [Print Part Report.]

NOINFO-MSG.
     [Print no-data-found message.]
```

> Optional table declarations look similar to the statements used to define the tables.

Figure 10.6   Declaring tables.

not print a message when the initial FETCH returns no values. We simply terminate the program when the end of data is reached.

DECLARING TABLES AND VIEWS

As shown in our sample program, it is not necessary to describe explicitly the formats of the tables and views that a DB2 program accesses; this information is available to DB2 through other sources. However, it is sometimes advantageous to include explicit descriptions of table columns. Declarations included in the program serve as valuable documentation, providing the names and data types of the table columns the program accesses. If a program includes table or view declarations, DB2 checks these and validates the column names and data types that are referenced by SQL statements that the program issues.

A table or view can be explicitly described by issuing a DECLARE statement that has a format similar to the DEFINE command:

```
EXEC SQL DECLARE INVENTORY TABLE
         (INVPART    SMALLINT NOT NULL,
          PNAME      CHAR(10),
          ONHAND     INTEGER)
     END-EXEC.
```

Figure 10.6 shows a version of our sample retrieval program in which we have included explicit declarations of the *Inventory* and *Quotations* table formats.

THE DCLGEN FACILITY

DB2 includes a facility that automatically generates DECLARE statements based on information about tables and views that it extracts from the DB2 catalog. This facility, called DCLGEN, automatically generates both an SQL DECLARE statement and a corresponding record description in the appropriate language. We will describe the DCLGEN facility in Chapter 11, as part of the overall program development process.

11 DB2 PROGRAM DEVELOPMENT

A program with embedded SQL statements requires some special processing to prepare it for execution. In this chapter, we will look at the program development process that is employed in developing DB2 applications. This process includes the steps of precompilation, compilation or assembly, link editing, binding, and execution. The DB2 program preparation process is illustrated in Fig. 11.1. This chapter discusses each of the steps shown in the figure. We also introduce some of the aids provided by DB2 to help in the program development process.

PRECOMPILATION

Before a program can be compiled or assembled, it must be processed by the DB2 precompiler. As part of precompilation, the embedded SQL statements are converted into host-language statements that can be processed by the host-language compiler or assembler. In addition to replacing SQL statements with host-language statements, the DB2 precompiler performs the following functions:

- **Validate SQL statements.** The variable names used in SQL statements and their definitions are checked to be sure they are valid. If there are any problems, they are flagged in the precompiler output.

- **Detect SQL statement syntax errors.** The SQL statements are also checked for syntax errors. If any are detected, they are described in the precompiler output listing.

- **Produce a database request module.** A module known as a *database request module* (DBRM) is produced containing information about the SQL statements contained in the application program. This module is used as part of the bind processing.

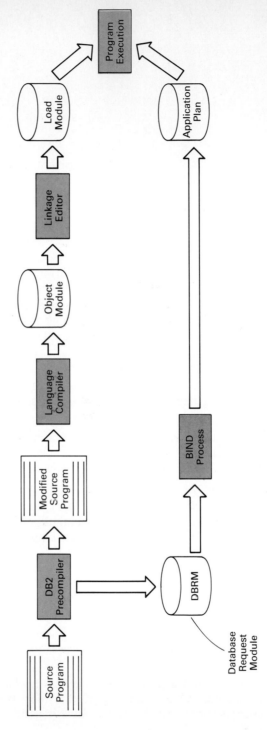

Figure 11.1 DB2 program preparation.

The primary input to the precompiler consists of the source statements that make up the application program. In addition, input can also come from a specified library by using an SQL INCLUDE statement in the program. The output of the precompiler consists of a modified source program in which the SQL statements have been replaced with host-language statements, the DBRM, and several output listings. The output includes a listing of source statements, a listing of diagnostic messages, and a cross-reference listing. The cross-reference listing shows the line numbers of SQL statements that reference each host variable or column name.

The DB2 precompiler does not access DB2 catalog information during its processing; therefore, DB2 does not have to be active at the time that the precompilation is run. If the application program contains CICS commands, it needs to be processed by the CICS command language translator before being compiled or assembled. The command language translation step can be done either before or after the DB2 precompilation step; however, IBM recommends that the DB2 precompilation step be performed first.

COMPILATION AND LINK EDITING

After the DB2 precompilation has been performed, the source program is ready to be compiled or assembled, using the appropriate host-language compiler or assembler to produce an object module. Once the program has been compiled or assembled without error, the object module can be link-edited in the normal manner to produce a load module. DB2 requires no special processing for these steps. As with other programs, a DB2 program can consist of multiple source modules that are each compiled or assembled separately. The individual object modules can then be combined in a single link-edit step. Individual DB2 program modules communicate with one another using conventional linkage techniques.

BINDING

Before a DB2 application program can be executed, a process called *binding* must be performed. Binding establishes a linkage between the application program and the DB2 data it accesses. The bind process does not involve the application program itself; instead, the input to the bind process consists only of the database request module (DBRM) that was produced by the DB2 precompiler. The DBRM contains descriptions of all the SQL statements in the application program, along with information about host variables that they reference. The bind process uses information from the DBRM along with information from the DB2 catalog to perform DB2-related activities that prepare the application program for execution. The activities performed as part of binding include these:

- **Validate SQL statements.** DB2 checks the table, view, and column names used in SQL statements against the DB2 catalog to ensure that the names and definitions are valid.

- **Verify authority.** DB2 checks to make sure that the user performing the bind process has the authority to perform the data access and manipulation operations that are specified in the program. It is possible, however, to request that this check be deferred until the program is executed.

- **Select access paths.** DB2 determines the indexes and other methods that will be used to access the data that is processed by this program.

- **Prepare an application plan.** DB2 produces an application plan, which is a control structure that describes the actions that need to be taken in order to execute each SQL statement. The application plan produced during the bind step is used by DB2 when the application program is executed.

Since the bind process does not involve the application program itself, but only its DBRM, the bind step can be run immediately after the precompilation step if desired. Also, if a DB2 application consists of multiple source modules, the DBRMs from all the source modules must be combined in a single bind step to produce an overall application plan. The compilation or assembly and the link-edit steps can be performed either before or after the bind step.

PROGRAM EXECUTION

Once the bind process has been successfully completed for a program, the program is ready to execute. The program can be executed any number of times without repeating any of the steps we have just described using the application plan produced by the bind step.

When a program is executed, DB2 checks the information in the application plan to be sure it is still consistent with the corresponding information in the DB2 catalog. If any changes have been made, either to the data structures or indexes used by the program or to the user's authorization to access these structures, DB2 will automatically rebind the application. The user can also explicitly request a rebind at any time to take advantage of new database structures, for example, a new index that the program may be able to take advantage of.

AUTHORIZATION

No special authorizations are required to code, precompile, compile, or link-edit a DB2 application program. However, the user who binds or executes programs must have been granted appropriate authorizations to perform those functions. The user must have appropriate table privileges, based on the types of operations performed by the program. These can include authorization to select data, to insert, update, or delete data, or to create new tables.

A user performing a bind must have specific authorization to perform a bind for that program. If authority is verified at the time of the bind, the user must also have been granted the appropriate table privileges.

A user executing the program must have specific authorization to perform the execution. If authority was verified at the time of the bind, the user executing the program does not also need table privileges. If authority verification was deferred until execution time, then the user must have been granted appropriate table privileges in order to execute the program. The process of granting authorizations is discussed in Chapter 18.

USING DB2I

There are several ways in which the program preparation steps can be run. They can be invoked directly, in batch mode, by preparing the appropriate JCL. They can be invoked at a TSO terminal using a CLIST called DSNH. Or they can be executed using a special DB2 facility called *DB2 Interactive* (DB2I). DB2I is an interactive

```
                        DB2I PRIMARY OPTION MENU
===> 3_

Select one of the following DB2 functions and press ENTER.

   1   SPUFI                (Process SQL statements)
   2   DCLGEN               (Generate SQL and source language declarations)
   3   PROGRAM PREPARATION  (Prepare a DB2 application program to run)
   4   PRECOMPILE           (Invoke DB2 precompiler)
   5   BIND/REBIND/FREE     (BIND, REBIND, or FREE application plans)
   6   RUN                  (RUN an SQL program)
   7   DB2 COMMANDS         (Issue DB2 commands)
   8   UTILITIES            (Invoke DB2 utilities)
   D   DB2I DEFAULTS        (Set global parameters)
   X   EXIT                 (Leave DB2I)




PRESS:  END to exit       HELP for more information
```

Figure 11.2   DB2I Primary Option Menu panel.

facility that runs in the TSO environment. It provides a number of screen panels that can be used to precompile, compile, link, bind, and run a DB2 application program. DB2I also provides panels that give access to tools that can be helpful in the application programming process, including these:

- **DCLGEN.** DCLGEN is a declaration generator that can be used to generate DECLARE statements and record descriptions to be included in an application program.
- **SPUFI.** SPUFI is a facility that can be used to execute SQL statements interactively. SPUFI can be useful for the initial testing of SQL statements that will later be embedded in an application program. However, most DB2 installations use QMF for interactive access to DB2 databases.
- **HELP.** HELP panels are available that provide tutorial information about DB2I functions.

DB2I is accessed via ISPF as one of the options on the ISPF main menu. DB2I then has a primary option menu that lists the facilities it offers. The DB2I Primary Option Menu panel is shown in Fig. 11.2. We will examine here only the options associated with application programming and the program preparation process.

DB2I PROGRAM PREPARATION

The DB2I Program Preparation panel, shown in Fig. 11.3, can be used to take an application program through all of the steps of precompilation, compilation or assembly, link editing, and binding. In using this panel, we specify the name of the program and provide other information about its environment. We then specify the program preparation steps that we wish to execute at this time. We can also specify if we want to see the DB2I panel for each step or if each step should be executed directly.

DB2I Precompile

Figure 11.4 shows the DB2I Precompile panel. We can invoke this panel either directly from the primary option menu or through the program preparation panel. This panel specifies the program name and the name of any libraries that contain members to be included in the program. Various precompile processing options can also be specified.

DB2I Bind

We can reach the DB2I Bind panel, shown in Fig. 11.5, either directly from the primary options menu or from the program preparation panel. We specify in this panel the name or names of the DBRMs to be processed by the bind. Various bind options can also be specified.

```
                  DB2 PROGRAM PREPARATION
===>

Enter the following:
 1  INPUT DATA SET NAME .... ===> SAMPLEPG.COBOL
 2  DATA SET NAME QUALIFIER  ===> TEMP      (for building data set names)
 3  PREPARATION ENVIRONMENT  ===> FOREGROUND (FOREGROUND, BACKGROUND, EDITJCL)
 4  RUN TIME ENVIRONMENT ... ===> TSO       (TSO, CICS, IMS)
 5  STOP IF RETURN CODE >=   ===> 8         (Lowest terminating return code)
 6  OTHER OPTIONS ===>

Select functions           Display panel?        Perform function?
 7  CHANGE DEFAULTS ........ ===> Y  (Y/N)       ............
 8  PL/I MACRO PHASE ....... ===> N  (Y/N)       ===> N  (Y/N
 9  PRECOMPILE ............. ===> Y  (Y/N)       ===> Y  (Y/N
10  CICS COMMAND TRANSLATION ............         ===> N  (Y/N
11  BIND ................... ===> Y  (Y/N)       ===> Y  (Y/N
12  COMPILE OR ASSEMBLE .... ===> Y  (Y/N)       ===> Y  (Y/N
13  LINK ................... ===> N  (Y/N)       ===> Y  (Y/N
14  RUN .................... ===> N  (Y/N)       ===> Y  (Y/N


PRESS:   ENTER to process      END to exit      HELP for more information
```

Figure 11.3   DB2 Program Preparation panel.

```
                        PRECOMPILE
===>

Enter precompiler data sets:
 1  INPUT DATA SET .... ===> SAMPLEPG.COBOL
 2  INCLUDE LIBRARY ... ===> SRCLIB.DATA

 3  DSNAME QUALIFIER .. ===> TEMP        (For building data set names)
 4  DBRM DATA SET ..... ===>

Enter processing options as desired:
 5  WHERE TO PRECOMPILE ===> FOREGROUND  (FOREGROUND, BACKGROUND, or EDITJCL)
 6  OTHER OPTIONS ..... ===>








PRESS:   ENTER to process    END to exit    HELP for more information
```

Figure 11.4   DB2 Precompiler panel.

```
                            BIND
===>

Enter DBRM data set name(s):
 1  LIBRARY(s)    ===> TEMP.DBRM
 2  MEMBER(s)     ===> SAMPLEPG
 3  PASSWORD(s) ===>

 4  MORE DBRMS? ===> NO

Enter options as desired:
 5  PLAN NAME ............... ===> SAMPLEPG    (Required to create a plan)
 6  ACTION ON PLAN .......... ===> REPLACE     (REPLACE or ADD)
 7  RETAIN EXECUTION AUTHORITY ===> YES        (YES to retain user list)
 8  ISOLATION LEVEL ......... ===> RR          (RR or CS)
 9  PLAN VALIDATION TIME ..... ===> BIND       (RUN or BIND)
10  RESOURCE ACQUISITION TIME  ===> USE        (USE OR ALLOCATE)
11  RESOURCE RELEASE TIME .... ===> COMMIT     (COMMIT OR DEALLOCATE)
12  EXPLAIN PATH SELECTION ... ===> NO         (NO or YES)




PRESS:   ENTER to process      END to exit    HELP for more information
```

Figure 11.5   DB2 Bind panel.

```
                PROGRAM PREPARATION: COMPILE, LINK, AND RUN
===>

 Enter compiler or assembler options:
  1  INCLUDE LIBRARY ===> SRCLIB.DATA
  2  INCLUDE LIBRARY ===>
  3  OPTIONS ....... ===> NUM, OPTIMIZE, ADV

 Enter linkage editor options:
  4  INCLUDE LIBRARY ===> SAMPLIB.COBOL
  5  INCLUDE LIBRARY ===>
  6  INCLUDE LIBRARY ===>
  7  LOAD LIBRARY .. ===> RUNLIB.LOAD
  8  OPTIONS ....... ===>

 Enter run options:
  9  PARAMETERS .... ===> D01, D02, D03/
 10  SYSIN DATA SET  ===> TERM
 11  SYSPRINT DS ... ===> TERM




PRESS: ENTER to proceed     END to exit    HELP for more information
```

Figure 11.6   DB2 Compile, Link, and Run panel.

DB2I Compile, Link, and Run

A single panel is provided for the steps of compiling or assembling, link-editing, and executing a DB2 program. Figure 11.6 illustrates this panel. The panel includes separate sections for each of the steps, in which we can specify library names and processing options.

DCLGEN

In addition to assisting with program development, we can use DB2I to generate DECLARE statements for the tables and views used in an application program. The DCLGEN panel, shown in Fig. 11.7, is provided for this purpose. We specify in the DCLGEN panel the name of the table or view for which the DECLARE is to be generated and a data set name. The DECLARE statement is stored in the specified data set, which can then later be included in the source program, using an EXEC SQL INCLUDE statement. Processing options can also be specified using the DCLGEN panel.

When DB2 generates a DECLARE for a COBOL program, it also generates a record description corresponding to the table or view. For PL/I, DB2 produces a structure declaration. Using DCLGEN to generate declarations saves

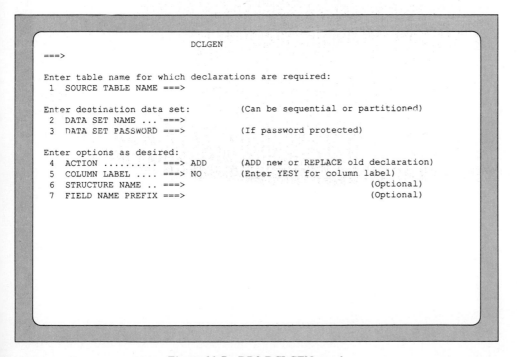

Figure 11.7   DB2 DCLGEN panel.

programming coding time and eliminates an important source of errors. Using DCLGEN also makes it easier to update application programs when table structures are changed.

SPUFI

As we mentioned in Chapter 1, DB2I provides a tool that allows SQL statements to be tested interactively. This tool is called *SQL Processor Using File Input* (SPUFI). SPUFI allows SQL statements to be entered and executed in an interactive fashion. By using SPUFI, we can request that the results of an SQL statement be either displayed on the terminal screen or stored in a data set. SPUFI provides many of the same facilities as QMF but lacks the sophisticated report-formatting features of QMF.

The SPUFI main panel is shown in Fig. 11.8. Using this panel, we specify the input data set that contains the SQL statements to be executed, the output data set into which results are to be placed, and the desired processing options.

```
                           SPUFI
        ===>

    Enter the input data set name:         (Can be sequential or partitioned)
    1   DATA SET NAME ... ===>
    2   VOLUME SERIAL ... ===>             (Enter if not cataloged)
    3   DATA SET PASSWORD ===>             (Enter if password protected)

    Enter the output data set name:        (Must be a sequential data set)
    4   DATA SET NAME ... ===>

    Specify processing options:
    5   CHANGE DEFAULTS   ===> YES         (Y/N - Display SPUFI defauults panel?)
    6   EDIT INPUT ...... ===> YES         (Y/N - Enter SQL statements?)
    7   EXECUTE ......... ===> YES         (Y/N - Execute SQL statements?)
    8   AUTOCOMMIT ...... ==-> YES         (Y/N - Commit after successful run?)
    9   BROWSE OUTPUT ... ===> YES         (Y/N - Browse output data set?)




    PRESS: ENTER to process    END to exit    HELP for more information
```

Figure 11.8   DB2 SPUFI panel.

SPUFI INPUT

SPUFI requires that SQL statements to be executed be stored in a data set. One way to use SPUFI is to create the data set prior to executing SPUFI. We can then make any desired changes to the data set using editing facilities provided by SPUFI before executing the statements stored in it. Alternatively, we can begin a SPUFI session and use the editing facilities of SPUFI to create a data set into which we can place our SQL statements.

The format used for SQL statements in SPUFI is generally similar to that used in QMF. The statements must not be preceded by EXEC SQL, and they cannot reference host variables. We must replace host variables with literals in order to test them using SPUFI. Unlike QMF, SPUFI requires that each SQL statement be terminated with a semicolon. SQL statements whose functions are specifically related to use within an application program, such as OPEN, CLOSE, FETCH, DECLARE, and INCLUDE, are not supported by SPUFI.

SPUFI OUTPUT

As SQL statements are processed by SPUFI, the results they generate are stored in a data set. The stored data includes a copy of each SQL statement followed by its results. For a SELECT statement, the results include both the data retrieved and the value of SQLCODE that is returned.

By invoking the browse option, we can cause the output data set to be displayed on the terminal. We can use the ISPF browse facilities to move around within the displayed data. SPUFI also provides limited formatting options that we can use to specify how the data in the output data set is displayed or printed. These formatting options can be set using the SPUFI defaults panel.

Application programming in the DB2 environment is sometimes complex. However, DB2I facilities like DCLGEN, SPUFI, and the program preparation process help make the application development process manageable.

12 LOADING AND UPDATING TABLES

So far we have examined application programs that retrieve data from tables. In this chapter, we examine programs that update tables. We will begin by examining SQL statements that can be used to load data into new tables. We then look at examples of application programs that insert, delete, and update rows in existing tables. Finally, we examine the DB2 change commitment process and its role in preserving data integrity during update processing.

LOADING DATA INTO TABLES

A number of facilities are available as part of the DB2 family of products to aid in initially loading data into tables. The method that we discuss in this chapter concerns writing specialized application programs that insert data into tables by using the SQL INSERT statement. An INSERT statement can be used to insert rows one at a time or to copy data from one table to another, processing multiple rows with a single statement.

As an alternative to specialized load programs, DB2 provides a LOAD utility (discussed in Chapter 16) that can be used to load data into DB2 tables from input data sets. The LOAD utility is often used in conjunction with a separate program product called *Data Extract* (DXT) (discussed in Chapter 17) that can be used to extract data from various sources and to reformat it for loading into DB2 tables. Tables can also be loaded manually by issuing INSERT statements via an interactive facility, such as SPUFI or QMF. QBE can also be used to load data into a table.

The various methods available for loading DB2 databases are summarized in Fig. 12.1. We will begin our investigation of DB2 table loading by discussing the various loading methods that can be implemented using the SQL INSERT statement.

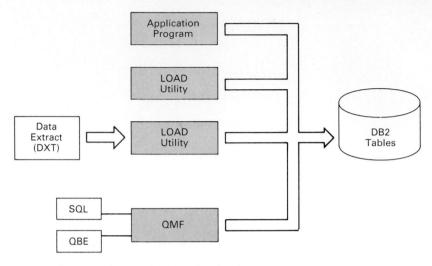

Figure 12.1 DB2 tables can be loaded using a variety of methods.

LOADING TABLES WITH INSERT

When we load data into a DB2 table using INSERT statements embedded in an application program, we can insert data into the table one row at a time, as in the following COBOL example:

```
EXEC SQL INSERT INTO INVENTORY
           VALUES (:TRPART, :TRNAME, :TRONHAND)
        END-EXEC.
```

This statement inserts one row of data at a time into the *Inventory* table, using host variables to specify data item values for the three table columns.

We can also insert data into selected columns by naming the columns:

```
EXEC SQL INSERT INTO INVENTORY (INVPART, PNAME)
           VALUES (:TRPART, :TRNAME)
        END-EXEC.
```

Null values are inserted in any columns not included in the list of column names; in this example, a null value is entered for the *Onhand* column.

Using an application program with embedded INSERT statements is useful when the input data does not yet exist in the required form but must be edited or reformatted before it can be loaded into the table.

INSERTING MULTIPLE ROWS

We can also issue INSERT statements that copy data from one table to another by including a SELECT statement rather than a VALUES clause in the INSERT statement:

```
        EXEC SQL INSERT INTO INVENTORY (INVPART)
                 SELECT DISTINCT QUOPART
                 FROM QUOTATIONS
                 WHERE PRICE IS NOT NULL
            END-EXEC.
```

With this type of INSERT statement, data is inserted into multiple rows with a single execution of the INSERT statement. Copying from one table to another is often done to create test tables that contain data that is extracted from a production database.

Certain conditions apply when a SELECT statement is embedded in an INSERT:

- The UNION and ORDER BY options of the SELECT statement cannot be used.

- The INSERT and SELECT statements must both reference the same number of columns, and the data type of each column referenced in the INSERT statement must be compatible with its corresponding column in the SELECT statement.

- An insertion sequence must not be specified for the rows being inserted.

If the rows are inserted successfully, the SQLERRD(3) field of SQLCA will contain a value that indicates the number of rows that were inserted. If the SELECT statement returns no rows, SQLCODE will be set to +100. If an error occurs during the execution of the INSERT statement, SQLCODE will be set to a negative value, and no rows will be inserted into the table.

MODIFYING DATA

DB2 application programs can include SQL statements that perform all the traditional update operations of row insertion, row modification, and row deletion. Figure 12.2 contains the partial coding for a program that updates the *Quotations* table. The first routine in the program, ADD-QUOT, adds a new row to the table with an INSERT statement. The data item values for the row being added are supplied using host variables. Following the INSERT statement, the program tests the SQLCODE field for a value of *−803*. This return code value indicates that an attempt was made to add a row with a duplicate key value to a table that has been defined as having a unique key. When this happens, DB2 does not insert the row and instead returns the negative return code.

The second routine, CHANGE-QUOT, uses an UPDATE statement to modify the data in an existing row. Again, the values used for the update are supplied using host variables. Following the UPDATE statement, the program tests for a return code of +100. This value indicates that no row was found with the values indicated in the WHERE clause.

The third routine, DELETE-QUOT, issues a DELETE statement to delete a row. Host variables are used to identify the row to be deleted. As with the UPDATE statement, the program tests SQLCODE for a value of $+100$, which indicates that the specified row was not found.

MODIFYING MULTIPLE ROWS

The program in Fig. 12.2 uses INSERT, UPDATE, and DELETE statements that affect one row of the table at a time. However, just as with interactive SQL, a program can issue SQL statements that update multiple rows. For example, the following statement could be used to update all the rows for a given supplier:

```
EXEC SQL UPDATE QUOTATIONS
            SET PRICE = PRICE * 1.10
            WHERE QUOSUPP = :QUOSUPP-TRANS
      END-EXEC.
```

Similarly, we could issue a single statement that deletes multiple rows:

```
EXEC SQL DELETE FROM QUOTATIONS
            WHERE QUOSUPP = :QUOSUPP-TRANS
      END-EXEC.
```

And we can add multiple rows to a table, in the same way that we load data into a new table, by selecting data from some other table:

```
EXEC SQL INSERT INTO QUOTATIONS
            (QUOSUPP, QUOPART, PRICE)
            SELECT SUPPNO, PARTNO, QUOTPRICE
            FROM NEWSUPP
      END-EXEC.
```

In this example, we are assuming that there is a table named *Newsupp* that contains the supplier number, part numbers, and prices for a new supplier that we are adding to the *Quotations* table.

As we mentioned in Chapter 10, the SQLCA contains a field that is often useful when issuing SQL statements that affect multiple rows. The third of the six SQLERRD fields, referred to as SQLERRD(3), indicates the number of rows that were affected by the previous SQL statement. After issuing an INSERT, SQLERRD(3) contains the number of rows that were added to the table; after an UPDATE, it contains the number of rows that were changed; and after a DELETE, it contains the number of rows that were deleted.

UPDATING USING A CURSOR

As an alternative to the types of statements just discussed, a program can use a cursor to handle multiple updates one row at a time. The partial program in Fig. 12.3 shows an example of updating using a cursor. In this program, we are

```
DATA DIVISION.

WORKING-STORAGE SECTION.

    EXEC SQL DECLARE QUOTATIONS TABLE
             (QUOSUPP  SMALLINT NOT NULL,
              QUOPART  SMALLINT NOT NULL,
              PRICE    DECIMAL(5,2),
              TIME     SMALLINT,
              ONORD    INTEGER)
        END-EXEC.

01  QUOT-TRANS.
    02  QUOSUPP-TRANS     PIC S9(4)    COMP.
    02  QUOPART-TRANS     PIC S9(4)    COMP.
    02  PRICE-TRANS       PIC S999V99  COMP.
    02  TIME-TRANS        PIC S9(4)    COMP.
    02  ONORD-TRANS       PIC S9(5)    COMP.
    02  TYPE-TRANS        PIC X.
    .
    .
    .

PROCEDURE DIVISION.

    [Initialize processing, get transaction, edit, determine type,
     and perform appropriate processing routine.]

ADD-QUOT.
    EXEC SQL INSERT INTO QUOTATIONS
             (QUOSUPP, QUOPART, PRICE, TIME, ONORD)
             VALUES
             (:QUOSUPP-TRANS, :QUOPART-TRANS, :PRICE-TRANS,
              :TIME-TRANS, :ONORD-TRANS)
        END-EXEC.
    IF SQLCODE = -803
        PERFORM DUPLICATE-ADD.

CHANGE-QUOT.
    EXEC SQL UPDATE QUOTATIONS
             SET PRICE = :PRICE-TRANS,
                 TIME  = :TIME-TRANS
                 ONORD = :ONORD-TRANS
             WHERE QUOSUPP = :QUOSUPP-TRANS
               AND QUOPART = :QUOPART-TRANS
        END-EXEC.
    IF SQL-CODE = +100
        PERFORM TRANS-NOT-FOUND.

DELETE-QUOT.
    EXEC SQL DELETE FROM QUOTATIONS
             WHERE QUOSUPP = :QUOSUPP-TRANS
               AND QUOPART = :QUOPART-TRANS
        END-EXEC.
    IF SQLCODE = +100
        PERFORM TRANS-NOT-FOUND.
```

← Routine to add a row to the QUOTATIONS table.

← Routine to update a row in the QUOTATIONS table.

← Routine to delete a row from the QUOTATIONS table.

Figure 12.2   Modifying DB2 table data.

```
DATA DIVISION.

WORKING-STORAGE SECTION.

    EXEC SQL DECLARE QUOT-CURSOR CURSOR FOR
             SELECT * FROM QUOTATIONS
                  WHERE QUOSUPP = :SUPPNO-IN
                  FOR UPDATE OF PRICE
         END-EXEC.

77  NO-DATA         PIC S9(9)     COMP VALUE +100.
77  SUPPNO-IN       PIC 999.
77  CALC-PRICE      PIC S999V99  COMP-3.

01  QUOT-INFO.
    02  SUPPNO      PIC S9(4)     COMP.
    02  PARTNO      PIC S9(4)     COMP.
    02  PRICE       PIC S999V99  COMP-3.
    02  TIME        PIC S9(4)     COMP.
    02  ONORD       PIC S9(5)     COMP.

PROCEDURE DIVISION.

    [Initialize processing]

    EXEC SQL WHENEVER SQLERROR
           GO TO SQL-PROBLEM
         END-EXEC.

    [Get supplier number.]

    PERFORM CHANGE-SUPP.
      .
      .
CHANGE-SUPP.
    EXEC SQL OPEN QUOT-CURSOR
         END-EXEC.
    EXEC SQL FETCH QUOT-CURSOR INTO :QUOT-INFO
         END-EXEC.
    IF SQLCODE = NO-DATA
       PERFORM SUPP-NOT-FOUND
    ELSE
       PERFORM PROCESS-SUPP UNTIL SQLCODE = NO-DATA.
    EXEC SQL CLOSE QUOT-CURSOR
         END-EXEC.

PROCESS-SUPP.
    PERFORM CHECK-PRICE-CHANGE.
    IF CHANGE-OK
       EXEC SQL UPDATE QUOTATIONS
                  SET PRICE = :CALC-PRICE
                  WHERE CURRENT OF QUOT-CURSOR
            END-EXEC.
    EXEC SQL FETCH QUOT-CURSOR INTO :QUOT-INFO
         END-EXEC.

SQL-PROBLEM.

    [Print message with SQLCODE and SQLERRM values.]

    STOP RUN.
```

> This statement updates the row to which the cursor currently refers.

Figure 12.3   Using a cursor for updating.

using a cursor and its associated SELECT statement to process all the rows from the *Quotations* table for a particular supplier number. We retrieve each row using a FETCH statement and perform the CHECK-PRICE-CHANGE routine to determine if the price should be increased. If so, we issue an UPDATE statement, referencing the row currently pointed to by the cursor, to change the *Price* value in that row. The UPDATE statement clause that refers to the row currently referenced by the cursor is

```
WHERE CURRENT OF QUOT-CURSOR
```

In order to update a column using a WHERE CURRENT OF cursor clause, the DECLARE statement for the cursor must specify that the column is eligible for updating. The pertinent clause in the DECLARE statement for QUOT-CURSOR is

```
FOR UPDATE OF PRICE
```

Our example specifies that a single column is eligible for updating; however, multiple columns can be specified in the FOR UPDATE clause if desired. They can then be included in the SET clause of the UPDATE statement.

There is one restriction concerning updating table columns with a cursor. A column that is part of a primary key cannot be updated using a cursor.

DELETING DATA USING A CURSOR

Rows can also be deleted a row at a time when results are being processed using a cursor. The following is an example of a DELETE statement that could be used to delete the row currently referenced by the cursor:

```
EXEC SQL DELETE FROM QUOTATIONS
            WHERE CURRENT OF QUOT-CURSOR
      END-EXEC.
```

It is not necessary to specify column names in a FOR UPDATE clause in the DECLARE CURSOR statement in order to delete rows.

CHANGE COMMITMENT AND CONCURRENCY

When data is updated in an environment that allows concurrent access to data, precautions must be taken to ensure that data integrity problems do not occur. For example, if two programs were permitted to change the same row of a table at the same time, these changes might be recorded incorrectly. DB2 uses a system of resource locks to prevent problems associated with concurrent access. Before a program is allowed to make a change to data in a table, DB2 places locks on any resources needed to make the change and then releases the locks when the change processing is completed.

No other user can access the resources until the locks are released. Chapter 19 discusses DB2 locking facilities in detail.

DB2 handles the placing and releasing of locks automatically. However, an application program can affect how long locks are held through a process known as *change commitment*. An application program is able to specify during its execution either that changes made up to that point are to be considered committed, or permanent, or that the changes should be rolled back, or undone. The point in a program where changes are committed or rolled back is known as a *commit point*. When a commit point is reached, any locks being held on resources are released.

SPECIFYING COMMIT POINTS

The termination of a program's execution is always considered to be a commit point. If the program terminates normally, all changes made to that point are committed; if the program terminates abnormally, changes are rolled back.

For application programs that run under TSO, either in foreground or in batch mode, the SQL statements COMMIT and ROLLBACK can be used to define additional commit points. Figure 12.4 shows a portion of a program that

```
      .
      .
CHANGE-QUOT.
    EXEC SQL WHENEVER SQLERROR
             GO TO UNDO
         END-EXEC.
    EXEC SQL UPDATE QUOTATIONS
             SET PRICE = :PRICE-TRANS,
                 TIME  = :TIME-TRANS,
                 ONORD = :ONORD-TRANS
             WHERE QUOSUPP = :QUOSUPP-TRANS
               AND QUOPART = :QUOPART-TRANS
         END-EXEC.
    IF SQL-CODE = NO-DATA
        PERFORM TRANS-NOT-FOUND
    ELSE
        EXEC SQL COMMIT END-EXEC.

CHANGE-QUOT-EXIT.
    EXIT.

UNDO.
    EXEC SQL ROLLBACK END-EXEC.
    EXIT.

TRANS-NOT-FOUND.
    EXEC SQL ROLLBACK END-EXEC.
      .
      .
```

The COMMIT statement commits all changes that have been made since the previous commit point.

The ROLLBACK statements cause DB2 to undo any changes that were made since the previous commit point.

Figure 12.4 Commit points

issues these statements. In this program example, we are updating the *Quotations* table. If the update is successful, the change is committed. If it is not successful and the SQL return code is negative, the WHENEVER statement causes the ROLLBACK statement to be executed, causing DB2 to undo any changes the program made to the database up to that point.

For application programs that run under CICS or IMS, similar facilities are available, but the program does not issue the SQL COMMIT or ROLLBACK statements. In the CICS environment, the CICS SYNCPOINT command and its ROLLBACK option can be used to define a commit point. DB2 and CICS coordinate their processing so that changes to both DB2 and non-DB2 data are committed or rolled back appropriately and that all data is kept in a consistent state of updating. In an IMS environment, CHKP, SYNC, ROLL, and ROLLB DL/I calls can be used to define commit points. DB2 works cooperatively with IMS to process commit points and to keep DB2 and non-DB2 data consistent.

UNIT OF RECOVERY

The period of time from one commit point to the next is called a *unit of recovery*. A unit of recovery always begins at the start of a program's execution and ends when a commit point is reached. The program can explicitly define a commit point by executing a statement such as COMMIT or ROLLBACK, or it can implicitly define a commit point by terminating normally or abnormally. When a unit of recovery ends, all changes are either committed or rolled back. If a system failure occurs during a unit of recovery, all changes made during that unit are rolled back so that data is restored to the condition that existed at the beginning of the unit of recovery.

When a program does not explicitly define commit points, the unit of recovery encompasses the entire execution of the program. This is illustrated in Fig. 12.5, where the program starts, defines no explicit commit points, and then terminates. This type of processing might be appropriate for a program that executes quickly, possibly processing a single transaction each time it executes. Program termination automatically generates the necessary commit point.

If a program executes for a longer period of time, perhaps processing a series of transactions where each transaction is independent of the others, it is often better to define a separate commit point after processing each transaction. With this approach, the program creates a separate unit of recovery for each

```
                                    ⎧ Program Start.
                                    ⎪      .
                                    ⎪      .
                      Unit of       ⎨    [Program processing code.]
                      recovery      ⎪      .
                                    ⎪      .
   Figure 12.5  Single unit of recovery.   ⎩ Program End.
```

```
                    Program Start.
Unit of          ⎧        .
recovery 1       ⎨        .
                 ⎩   [Commit/rollback for transaction 1.]

Unit of          ⎧        .
recovery 2       ⎨        .
                 ⎩   [Commit/rollback for transaction 2.]

                          .
                          .

Unit of          ⎧        .
recovery n       ⎨        .
                 ⎩   [Commit/rollback for transaction n.]

Unit of          ⎧        .
recovery n+1     ⎨        .

                    Program End.
```

Figure 12.6 Multiple units of recovery.

QUOTATIONS

QUOSUPP	QUOPART	PRICE	TIME	ONORD
51	124	1.25	5	400
51	125	0.55	5	0
51	134	0.40	5	500
51	135	0.39	5	1000
51	221	0.30	10	10000
51	231	0.10	10	5000
52	105	7.50	10	200
52	205	0.15	20	0
52	206	0.15	20	0
53	124	1.35	3	500
53	125	0.58	3	200
53	134	0.38	3	200
53	135	0.42	3	1000
53	222	0.25	15	10000
53	232	–	15	0
53	241	0.08	15	6000

SUPPLIERS

SUPSUPP	NAME	ADDRESS	CODE
51	DEFECTO PARTS	16 JUSTAMERE LANE, TACOMA WA	20
52	VESUVIUS INC.	512 ANCIENT BLVD., POMPEII NY	20
53	ATLANTIS CO.	8 OCEAN AVE., WASHINGTON DC	10
54	TITANIC PARTS	32 SINKING STREET, ATLANTIC CITY NJ	30
57	EAGLE HARDWARE	64 TRANQUILITY PLACE, APOLLO MN	30
61	SKYLAB PARTS	128 ORBIT BLVD., SYDNEY AUSTRALIA	10
64	KNIGHT LTD.	256 ARTHUR COURT, CAMELOT ENGLAND	20

Figure 12.7 Quotations and Suppliers tables.

transaction, as illustrated in Fig. 12.6. If a long-running program does not explicitly define commit points during its execution, it may interfere with other programs that may require concurrent access to the same databases. The DB2 locking facilities that handle concurrent access by multiple programs to the same databases are discussed in Chapter 19.

PROCESSING RELATED TRANSACTIONS   It is not always appropriate to create a separate unit of recovery for each transaction that is processed. For example, suppose we were processing the *Suppliers* and *Quotations* tables, shown in Fig. 12.7, and we wanted to change a supplier number value in both tables. We would probably not want to commit the changes until we know that both tables have been suc-

```
         .
         .
CHANGE-SUPPNO.
    EXEC SQL WHENEVER SQLERROR GO TO UNDO
         END-EXEC.
    EXEC SQL UPDATE SUPPLIERS
         SET SUPPNO = :NEW-SUPP
         WHERE SUPPNO - :CURR-SUPP
         END-EXEC.
    IF SQLCODE = NO-DATA
         PERFORM SUPP-NOT-FOUND
    ELSE
         PERFORM CHANGE-QUOT.
CHANGE-SUPPNO-EXIT.
    EXIT.

UNDO.
    EXEC SQL ROLLBACK END-EXEC.
    GO TO CHANGE-SUPPNO-EXIT
```
This statement rolls back all changes if an error occurs during the execution of any SQL statement.
```
CHANGE-QUOT.
    EXEC SQL OPEN QUOT-CURSOR END-EXEC.
    EXEC SQL FETCH QUOT-CURSOR INTO :QUOT-INFO
         END-EXEC.
    PERFORM PROC-QUOT UNTIL SQLCODE = NO-DATA.
    EXEC SQL COMMIT END-EXEC.
    EXEC SQL CLOSE QUOT-CURSOR END-EXEC.
```
This statement commits changes after all updates have been successfully completed.
```
PROC-QUOT.
    EXEC SQL UPDATE QUOTATIONS
         SET QUOSUPP = :NEW-SUPP
         WHERE CURRENT OF QUOT-CURSOR
         END-EXEC.
    EXEC SQL FETCH QUOT-CURSOR INTO :QUOT-INFO
         END-EXEC.
         .
         .
```

Figure 12.8   A single unit of recovery can be used to process a group of related transactions.

cessfully changed; otherwise, it might be possible for the following sequence of events to occur:

1. Update the *Suppliers* table.
2. Commit the change to the *Suppliers* table.
3. Update the *Inventory* table.
4. An error occurs.
5. The change to the *Inventory* table is backed out.

At this point, we have a situation in which the *Suppliers* table has been updated but the *Inventory* table has not.

The approach of processing multiple transactions in a single unit of recovery is illustrated in Fig. 12.8. If an error occurs during processing of either table, the WHENEVER statement will cause the ROLLBACK to be executed, and any changes made to that point will be rolled back. If both tables are updated successfully, the COMMIT statement causes all changes to be committed.

13 DYNAMIC SQL

DB2 supports a facility known as *dynamic SQL*. With dynamic SQL, an application program can construct SQL statements as it executes rather than compiling the SQL statements directly into the source code. In this chapter, we examine the processing required to construct and execute SQL statements dynamically. All the examples of SQL statements in application programs we have looked at so far are examples of *static SQL statements;* we knew the statement type and general structure of each statement ahead of time, and we coded the SQL statements directly into the program. The SQL statements were then processed by the DB2 precompiler before program execution. In static SQL statements, we generally use host variables to change the way a statement executes, as shown in the following SQL statement example:

```
EXEC SQL UPDATE QUOTATIONS
        SET PRICE = :PRICE-TRANS,
            TIME  = :TIME-TRANS,
            ONORD = :ONORD-TRANS
        WHERE QUOSUPP = :QUOSUPP-TRANS
          AND QUOPART = :QUOPART-TRANS
    END-EXEC.
```

With dynamic SQL, the application program can construct an SQL statement at run time, based on inputs available to the program, and then execute the generated statement. SPUFI is an example of a program that executes dynamic SQL. It takes character strings from an input data set, builds SQL statements from those strings, and then executes the resulting SQL statements dynamically. Not all SQL statements can be constructed and executed dynamically. Box 13.1 lists the statements that cannot execute dynamically. Also, the process used for preparing and executing a dynamic SQL statement varies with the type of statement.

BOX 13.1   SQL statements that cannot be executed dynamically

CLOSE

DECLARE

DESCRIBE

EXECUTE

EXECUTE IMMEDIATE

FETCH

INCLUDE

OPEN

PREPARE

WHENEVER

NON-SELECT STATEMENTS

The process used for dynamically executing an SQL statement is simplest if we know that the generated statement will not be a SELECT statement. For this type of dynamic SQL statement, the following steps are involved:

1. Construct an image of the SQL statement in a data area and verify that it is of an appropriate type to execute dynamically.
2. Execute the statement by issuing an EXECUTE IMMEDIATE statement that refers to the data area containing the image of the SQL statement to be executed.
3. Handle any error conditions that may occur.

The EXECUTE IMMEDIATE statement performs the same functions that are performed when an application program is precompiled and bound and then executes the dynamic SQL statement.

FIXED-LIST SELECT STATEMENTS

A dynamic SELECT statement that always returns the same number and type of data items is known as a *fixed-list SELECT statement*. Since the number and types of the data items to be returned are known ahead of time, appropriate host variables can be defined in the application program's source code. The program executes a dynamic SELECT statement of the fixed-list variety in the following manner:

1. Construct an image of the SELECT statement in a data area.

2. Issue a PREPARE statement that refers to the data area containing the SELECT statement image. The PREPARE statement translates the image of the SELECT statement into executable form.

3. Declare a cursor that references the name of the data area that contains the SELECT statement image.

4. Use the cursor to process the SELECT statement by opening the cursor, fetching rows, and closing the cursor.

5. Handle any error conditions that may occur.

Although the number, type, and size of the data items returned by a fixed-list dynamic SELECT statement cannot be changed at execution time, a fixed-list SELECT statement is often useful when the SELECT statement must be able to refer to different tables of the same type or when the program wishes to vary the selection conditions that are specified in the SELECT statement's WHERE clause.

VARYING-LIST SELECT STATEMENTS

If the definition of the variables to be returned by a SELECT statement is to be modified dynamically, the process of executing a dynamic SELECT statement becomes more complex. Since the number and types of the data items to be returned are not known in advance and cannot be compiled into the source code, appropriate host variables cannot be defined. This means that storage for the data items returned must be allocated dynamically by the application program and that address pointers to the values returned must be established at execution time. The process used for executing a varying-list SELECT statement is as follows:

1. Construct an image of the SELECT statement in a data area.

2. Declare a cursor for the SELECT statement naming the data area that contains the image of the SELECT statement.

3. Issue a PREPARE statement to translate the SELECT statement into executable form.

4. Issue a DESCRIBE statement, which returns information about the type and size of each of the data items that will be returned.

5. Determine the amount of storage that will be required for a row of retrieved data, based on the information returned by the DESCRIBE statement, and allocate the storage required.

6. Determine an address for each item of retrieved data that will be returned by the SELECT statement and insert these addresses in the appropriate place in the SQL descriptor area (SQLDA). This tells DB2 where to store each retrieved item.

7. Open the cursor, fetch rows, and close the cursor.

8. Free the storage allocated for the retrieved data items.

9. Handle any error conditions that may occur.

Generally, dynamic SQL applications can be coded using any of the conventional programming languages that DB2 supports. However, the addressing and storage allocation requirements associated with varying-list SELECT statements generally limit their use to applications coded in languages like PL/I, Assembler, and C that permit easy access to operating system facilities. For example, it is difficult in a COBOL or FORTRAN program to handle storage allocation and the storing of the data item addresses in the SQLDA without resorting to Assembler subroutines.

DESIGNING DYNAMIC SQL APPLICATIONS

Dynamic SQL is a very powerful feature but also a very complex one. It is generally employed by system programmers who are implementing special-purpose applications and is not often used in conventional application programs. IBM supplies examples of programs that use dynamic SQL in the manual *IBM DATABASE 2 Sample Application Guide*. Be warned that the program listings in that publication are long and complex and require detailed study.

SUMMARY OF PART IV

DB2 application programs can be written in a variety of 4GLs and in conventional programming languages. Programs can be run in conjunction with TSO, CICS, or IMS. SQL statements embedded in an application program begin with the keywords "EXEC SQL" and end in a manner specific to the particular language employed. Host variables defined in the program can be used in an SQL statement to provide or receive values. A host-variable name is preceded by a colon when used in an SQL statement. When a SELECT statement may return multiple rows, a cursor is used to allow the program to process the rows individually. The cursor is defined for a particular SELECT statement and is processed using OPEN, FETCH, and CLOSE statements. The SQL communication area (SQLCA) provides information about the execution of SQL statements, including a return code and error indicators. A WHENEVER statement can be used to specify general processing for different conditions, including a negative return code, no row found, or an SQL warning code. The SQL DECLARE statement can be used to describe tables and views in the program. It is not always necessary to describe DB2 data using DECLARE, but it is often helpful to do so.

The program development process includes precompilation, compilation or assembly, link editing, binding, and execution. Precompilation checks SQL statements for validity and syntax errors, translates them into host-language source statements, and produces a database request module (DBRM). The DBRM contains information about the SQL statements in the program. Compilation and link editing are performed in the normal manner. Binding establishes a linkage between an application program and the data it will use. The bind process further validates the SQL statements, checks that the user has the proper authorizations to perform the requested operations, selects access paths to be used, and prepares an application plan. An application plan is a control structure that describes the actions to be taken in executing each SQL statement. The application plan is used when the program is executed. In order to execute an application program, the user invoking the program must be authorized to perform the DB2 operations specified in the program and must also be authorized to execute the application plan. DB2 Interactive (DB2I) is an interactive facility that provides support for all the steps in the program preparation process. It also provides a declaration generator (DCLGEN) and a facility for executing SQL statements interactively (SPUFI).

An application program can insert, modify, and delete data in DB2 tables. When a cursor is used to process multiple rows, individual rows can be modified or deleted using a WHERE CURRENT OF clause. Changes made by an application program can be either committed (made permanent) or rolled back (undone). A program that runs under TSO uses the SQL COMMIT and ROLLBACK statements to specify commit points. Programs that run under CICS or IMS use the appropriate CICS or IMS facilities to define commit points.

Dynamic SQL allows an application program to construct and execute SQL statements during program execution. The process used depends on the type of dynamic SQL statement being constructed.

PART V DB2 SYSTEM ADMINISTRATION

The previous parts of this book examined the DB2 facilities most often used by end users and by application programmers who need access to DB2 data. DB2 also includes facilities designed to assist with overall administration of the DB2 system. Part V of this book explores these system administration facilities.

We begin Part V with an examination of the various DB2 objects, including tables, views, indexes, table spaces, databases, and storage groups, and the DB2 facilities used to define them. Chapter 15 introduces the DB2 utilities that are available to assist in DB2 system administration. Chapter 16 discusses the DB2 LOAD utility in detail and shows how it can be used to load data into tables. Chapter 17 presents the functions of Data Extract (DXT), a separate program product that is often used in conjunction with the LOAD utility for loading tables. Chapter 18 presents the facilities that can be used with DB2 to provide for data security, concentrating on the authorization system that allows privileges to be granted and revoked. Chapter 19 ends this book by examining the locking mechanism that DB2 uses in providing multiple users concurrent access to the same DB2 objects.

14 DB2 STORAGE STRUCTURES

DB2 OBJECTS   A key element in DB2 system administration is the management of the various DB2 objects that are created by the DB2 software. We introduced the various DB2 objects in Chapter 3. These objects include the tables and views that are used by application programmers and end users as part of application processing. DB2 objects also include objects not usually visible at the application level, such as table spaces, indexes, databases, and storage groups. In this chapter, we will see how each type of DB2 object is defined and managed.

DB2 Databases

A DB2 database consists of a set of tables and their associated indexes. By defining the tables and indexes that make up a particular database, we can give them a name, and we can then start and stop them in a single operation. Also, we can grant authorization for access to all the objects in the database as a single unit.

Table Spaces

A *table space* is an area of storage that contains one or more DB2 tables. Physically, a table space consists of from 1 to 64 VSAM entry-sequenced data sets (ESDS) and may contain up to 64 gigabytes of data. A table space is divided into *pages,* each of which can be read from or written to a direct-access storage device (DASD) in a single operation.

Table spaces can be either *simple, partitioned,* or *segmented.* A simple table space contains one or more complete tables. A partitioned table space is divided into units called *partitions,* each of which can contain part of a table. The division of the table into partitions is based on the definition of a clustering index for the table. Only one table can be stored in a partitioned table space. A segmented table space is divided into equal-size segments. A given segment contains rows from only one table. A segmented table space offers improved performance over a simple table space for storing multiple tables, since only the segments belonging to a given table need to be processed when that table is scanned or locked.

A table space represents DB2's basic unit of database recovery. If a table space contains multiple tables, all will be recovered as a unit. However, with a partitioned table space, each partition can be recovered separately. An entire database can also be recovered as a unit if desired, by specifying the name of the database rather than the name of the table space during recovery processing.

Indexes

An *index* consists of a set of pointers to the rows in a table. An index that is defined for a table can be used for a variety of purposes. For example, an index can be used to provide more efficient access to data by allowing individual or multiple rows to be accessed directly rather than by scanning through all the rows in the table.

A *unique index* is a particular type of index that can be used to ensure that no two rows in a table have the same key values. A *cluster index* is another type of index that can be used to control the order in which table rows are stored. A cluster index can also determine how rows are divided between partitions in a partitioned table space.

Each index is stored in an area of storage called an *index space*. An index space, like a table space, consists of from 1 to 64 VSAM ESDSs. Once an index is defined, DB2 automatically creates and maintains it. DB2 also decides, as part of selecting the access path specified in the application plan, whether or not to use an index in processing a particular SQL statement. Application programs and interactive users do not explicitly request the use of an index and, except possibly for noticing differences in performance, are generally not aware of when DB2 uses an index.

Storage Groups

DB2 uses storage groups to control the way in which DB2 data is physically stored on DASD volumes. A storage group consists of a set of DASD volumes, all of which must reside on the same type of device. Each storage group has a name, and a storage group name is used to assign a table space to a particular storage group.

A simple table space must be stored in a single storage group. With a partitioned table space, different partitions can be stored in different storage groups. An index space is also assigned to a storage group, and an index space may or may not be assigned to the same storage group as its associated table.

The relationships of table spaces, index spaces, and storage groups are illustrated in Fig. 14.1. We will see next how each type of DB2 object is defined.

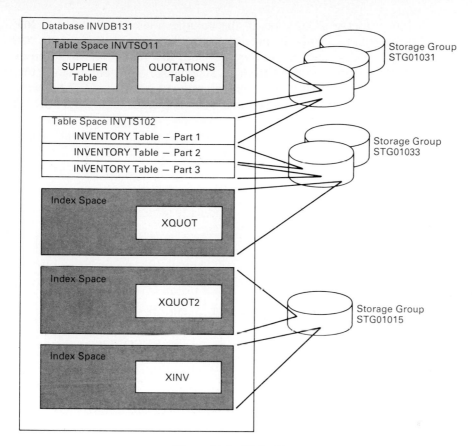

Figure 14.1 DB2 objects.

DEFINING STORAGE GROUPS

A DB2 system administrator creates a storage group by issuing an SQL CREATE statement, typically using an interactive facility, such as SPUFI or QMF. Here is an example of a CREATE statement:

```
CREATE STOGROUP STG01033
    VOLUMES (INV115, INV020, INV021)
    VCAT INVCAT1
    PASSWORD INV077
```

The CREATE statement gives the storage group a name (STG01033) and specifies the volume serial numbers of the DASD volumes that make up the group. The CREATE statement also specifies the name of the VSAM catalog to be used for data sets stored in this storage group (INVCAT1) and specifies the catalog password (INV077).

Up to 133 DASD volumes, all residing on the same type of device, can be included in a storage group, and all the volumes must be available to MVS. A given DASD volume can be included in more than one storage group. When databases, table spaces, and indexes are defined, the storage group to be used for them can be specified in the CREATE statement. A system default storage group, with the name SYSDEFLT, must be assigned when the DB2 software is installed. If no storage group is named in a CREATE statement, the SYSDEFLT storage group is used.

We can modify a storage group by issuing an ALTER statement, like this:

```
ALTER STOGROUP STG01033
    PASSWORD INV077
    REMOVE VOLUMES (INV020)
    ADD VOLUMES (INV012,INV030)
```

We can use ALTER to remove volumes from the storage group or to add new volumes to it. When a volume is removed, any DB2 data on that volume remains intact and available. However, when space is allocated in the future, that volume will not be used.

A storage group can be dropped with a DROP STOGROUP statement. However, a storage group cannot be dropped if any table space or index space is using it, and the system default storage space, SYSDEFLT, can never be dropped.

DEFINING DATABASES

To create a new DB2 database, we must issue a CREATE DATABASE statement:

```
CREATE DATABASE INVDB131
    STOGROUP STG01033
    BUFFERPOOL BP2
```

This CREATE statement gives the database a name (INVDB131). It can also specify the name of the default storage group to be used for table spaces and indexes that do not request a specific storage group. A buffer pool can also be specified for the database; it determines the page size to be used. DB2 pages must be either 4K or 32K in size. A default database named DSNDB04 is defined when the DB2 software is installed; this database is used if a CREATE statement for a table space or indexes does not specify a database name.

A database definition cannot be altered. To change a database definition, it must be dropped using a DROP statement and then re-created with a new CREATE statement. The DROP statement should be used with caution, since dropping a database causes all tables and indexes in the database to be dropped as well, causing the data they contain to be deleted. As we saw in Chapter 3, a database is divided into table spaces and index spaces.

DEFINING TABLE SPACES

A table space is created with a CREATE TABLE-SPACE statement:

```
CREATE TABLESPACE INVTSO11
    IN INVDB131
    USING STOGROUP STG01031
            PRIQTY 20
            SECQTY 10
            ERASE   NO
    LOCKSIZE PAGE
    CLOSE NO
    PCTFREE 10
```

This statement gives the table space a name (INVTSO11). It can specify the name of the database that will contain the table space (INVDB131) and also the storage group to use (STG01031). If no database is specified, the default database DSNDB04 is used. If no storage group is specified, the storage group named in the CREATE DATABASE statement is used. If no storage group was named for the database, the default storage group, SYSDEFLT, is used.

As part of specifying the storage group, primary and secondary allocation values, in kilobytes, can be specified. The ERASE parameter determines whether data is written over when it is dropped. LOCKSIZE specifies whether a page, a table, or an entire table space is the unit of locking. CLOSE determines whether data sets are automatically closed when they are no longer being used. A buffer pool and password specification can be included. The amount of free space to be allocated when a table is loaded or reorganized can be specified using either the PCTFREE or FREEPAGE parameter. A segmented table space can be created by including the SEGSIZE parameter.

A partitioned table space is created by adding a NUMPARTS clause to the CREATE TABLESPACE statement, as shown in the following example:

```
CREATE TABLESPACE INVTSO12
    IN INVDB131
    USING STOGROUP STG01033
            PRIQTY 20
            SECQTY 10
            ERASE   NO
    NUMPARTS 3
        (PART 1 USING STOGROUP STG01031
                        PRIQTY 5
                        SECQTY 5)
    LOCKSIZE PAGE
    CLOSE NO
    PCTFREE 10
```

NUMPARTS specifies the number of partitions to use for the table space. Different storage groups can be specified for each of the partitions if desired. In this example, the first partition uses STG01031, and the other two partitions use the storage group specified for the table space in general, STG01033.

When a table space is created, DB2 defines the necessary VSAM data sets for it. As a data set reaches its maximum size, DB2 automatically creates a new data set. All the data sets that make up a database are contained in the storage group or groups associated with the table space.

A table space can be altered with an ALTER TABLESPACE statement. The storage group, primary quantity, secondary quantity, erase option, buffer pool, lock size, close value, free space, or password can be changed via the ALTER statement. Other changes must be made by dropping the table space and re-creating it. When a table space is dropped, any tables it contains, and their associated indexes, are lost.

DEFINING TABLES

Tables are created with a CREATE TABLE statement. As we have seen in previous examples, the CREATE TABLE statement gives a name to the table. If the name in the CREATE TABLE statement is not qualified with an authorization ID, DB2 qualifies it with the authorization ID of the table's creator. The CREATE table also assigns names to the columns that make up the table. Referential constraints can be defined by specifying a primary key and/or one or more foreign keys, as discussed in Chapter 6. The statement also specifies data type, length, use of nulls, and use of default values for each column. Here is a CREATE TABLE statement that might be used to create the Suppliers table:

```
CREATE TABLE SUPPLIERS
        (SUPSUPP    SMALLINT NOT NULL,
        NAME       CHAR (15),
        ADDRESS    VARCHAR (35),
        CODE       SMALLINT)
        IN DATABASE TABLE1D3
```

The IN clause can be used to specify a database, as shown in the example. In this case, a table space with the same name as the table is created in the specified database. If another table space in the database already uses that name, the table space is given a name that is a modified version of the table name. The IN clause can also specify both a database name and a table space name:

```
IN INVDB.INVSPACE
```

If the CREATE TABLE statement does not include an IN clause, the table space for the database is placed in the default database, DSNDB04.

Exit Routines

A CREATE TABLE statement can specify the use of exit routines. Exit routines can be used to perform validation and editing on table data. Three types of exit routines can be specified in a CREATE TABLE statement: *validation routines, edit routines,* and *field procedures.*

A validation routine applies to the table as a whole and is specified by including a VALIDPROC clause in the CREATE TABLE statement. The specified validation routine is invoked each time a row is to be updated, inserted, or deleted. A validation routine processes an entire row of data and is used to ensure that the data in the row is valid before the update operation is performed. If the validation routine returns a nonzero return code, the insert, update, or delete operation is not performed.

An edit routine also applies to the table as a whole and is specified by including an EDITPROC clause in the CREATE TABLE statement. An edit routine also processes an entire row of data and is used to encode or decode the row in some way. Possible encode-decode functions include data compression and encryption. The encode function is performed when a row is being inserted or updated; the decode function is performed whenever a row is retrieved.

A field procedure applies to an individual column and is specified by including a FIELDPROC clause in the definition of that column. A field procedure is used to perform encoding and decoding on a single data item. A typical use of a field procedure might be to transform a data item value in a way that will alter its sorting sequence, perhaps because the standard sorting sequence will not produce the desired result. Field encoding is performed whenever that data item is inserted or updated, and field decoding is performed whenever the data item is retrieved.

ALTERING AND DROPPING TABLES

A table's definition can be modified by issuing an ALTER TABLE statement. An ALTER statement allows new columns to be added, primary and foreign keys to be added or dropped, and different exit routines to be specified. Any other changes, such as changing the type or length of an existing column, must be made by first dropping the table, re-creating it, and reloading it. When a table is dropped, any data it contains is lost, and any views or indexes defined on the table are also dropped. If a table is in a partitioned table space, the table cannot be dropped. Instead, the table is deleted by issuing a DROP statement for the table space.

Whenever a table is created, altered, or dropped, the entire database containing the table is locked. For this reason, a user that is granted CREATE, ALTER, or DROP table privileges may be given a private database to use so that other users are not adversely affected by these operations.

DEFINING INDEXES

An index is the mechanism used with DB2 to identify the key of a table. With DB2, a key is a column or set of columns on which an index is defined. If the key consists of two or more columns, it is known as a *composite key*. An index contains pointers associated with different key values that are used to retrieve rows, to ensure their uniqueness, or to determine where new rows should be physically stored.

An index is created with a CREATE INDEX statement, as shown in the following example:

```
CREATE INDEX XQUOT
          ON QUOTATIONS (PRICE)
```

This statement gives the index a name (XQUOT), specifies the table on which it is defined (*Quotations*), and specifies the names of the column or columns that make up the key (*Price*). In the example, the XQUOT index does not reference a column that contains unique data item values; there may be several rows in the Quotations table that have the same value for PRICE.

A unique index is defined by including the keyword UNIQUE, as shown in the following example:

```
CREATE UNIQUE INDEX XQUOT2
          ON QUOTATIONS (QUOSUPP, QUOPART)
```

The XQUOT2 index causes DB2 to ensure that there will not be two rows that have the same values for supplier number and part number.

When a table is defined with a primary key, a unique index must be defined for the table using the primary key column or columns as the index key. Although this is not required, IBM recommends that for performance reasons an index should be defined for a foreign key as well. A foreign key may or may not have unique values.

A *cluster index* is used to control where rows are physically stored. When a table has a cluster index, rows are stored as closely as possible in the same physical sequence as the order of their index values whenever the table is loaded or reorganized. A cluster index is specified by including a CLUSTER clause in the CREATE INDEX statement. CLUSTER is also used in creating a partitioned index. A partitioned index specifies how data is to be divided between the various partitions of a partitioned table space. The following is an example of a CREATE statement for a partitioned index.

```
CREATE INDEX XINV1
          ON INVENTORY (INVPART)
          CLUSTER
             (PART 1 VALUES (99),
              PART 2 VALUES (199),
              PART 3 VALUES (999))
```

The value shown for each partition identifies the highest value for *Invpart* that should be stored in that partition.

The CREATE INDEX statement may also specify a storage group to use, primary and secondary allocation quantities, the erase and close options, a buffer pool, a password, and free-space requirements. For a partitioned index, each partition can be assigned to a different storage group. If no storage group is specified, the default storage group for the database is used. The CREATE INDEX can also specify whether the pages of the index are to be subdivided into subpages. An index always uses a page size of 4K. Pages can be subdivided into 2, 4, 8, or 16 subpages. If subpages are specified, a single subpage becomes the unit of locking, thus increasing concurrency. However, using subpages increases storage and processing overhead, so the decisions of whether to use subpages and how big they should be must balance these factors.

When DB2 processes a CREATE INDEX statement, it creates an index space in the database containing the corresponding table. DB2 defines the data sets needed to contain the index space. If the table already contains data, the index itself is also created using the data item values found in the table. From then on, whenever DB2 updates the data item value in a key column, it also automatically updates the corresponding value in the associated index.

The storage group, primary quantity, secondary quantity, erase option, buffer pool, close option, free-space requirements, and password for an index can be modified using an ALTER statement. To change other characteristics of an index, the index must be dropped and recreated. If an index is dropped, any application plans that use the index must be rebound. A partitioned index cannot be dropped directly; instead, the partitioned table space must be dropped, which also drops the associated table.

DEFINING VIEWS

A view is created with a CREATE VIEW statement. Here is the CREATE VIEW statement we looked at in Chapter 6:

```
CREATE VIEW MYDATA
      (SUPPNAME, D17PART, PARTNAME, LEADTIME,
       ONHAND, ONORDER, PRICE, TOTALPRICE)
   AS SELECT NAME, QUOPART, PNAME, TIME, ONHAND,
             ONORD, PRICE, PRICE * ONORD
      FROM INVENTORY, QUOTATIONS, SUPPLIERS
      WHERE INVPART = QUOPART
            AND SUPSUPP = QUOSUPP
            AND PNAME IN ('NUT', 'BOLT')
```

Since a view defines a virtual table using the data in the real tables on which it is based, a CREATE VIEW does not need to specify a database, storage group, or any of the other options associated with a physical table. The ALTER statement cannot be issued for a view; to change a view, it must be dropped and recreated. Dropping a view affects only programs that use the view itself; dropping a view does not affect any of the tables on which the view is based.

THE DB2 SYSTEM CATALOG

The DB2 *system catalog* consists of a set of tables that contain information about all the DB2 objects that are currently defined. The tables that make up the DB2 system catalog store information about all the tables, columns, views, indexes, table spaces, databases, and storage groups that have been defined by the installation. The catalog also contains information about authorizations, application plans, recovery, and linkages that exist between different catalog tables. The various types of DB2 catalog tables are listed in Box 14.1.

The catalog tables have the same characteristics as any other DB2 tables and can be processed with SQL statements. However, data can be retrieved only from catalog tables. SQL statements cannot be used to insert, update, or delete rows from a catalog table, nor can they be used to create, alter, or drop a catalog table.

When DB2 objects, such as databases, views, and indexes, are created, altered, or dropped, DB2 automatically updates the appropriate catalog tables. When an object is created, information about it is stored in the catalog. Cross-reference information about the object's relationships to other objects is also stored in the catalog. For example, in addition to storing information that describes a particular table, information is also stored about all users who have privileges related to that table.

Certain catalog tables are used to maintain information about linkages between the catalog tables. By maintaining this information, along with the standard catalog information about the catalog tables, indexes, and so on, the DB2 catalog is completely self-describing. It both contains all the information needed to describe the catalog itself and describes all the application objects defined to DB2.

BOX 14.1   DB2 system catalog tables

Table	Content
Table and View Catalog Tables	
SYSIBM.SYSCOLUMNS	Information for every column of each table and view, including data type and length
SYSIBM.SYSFIELDS	Information about field procedures associated with columns
SYSIBM.SYSSYNONYMS	Information about each synonym of a table or view

BOX 14.1 *(Continued)*

Table	Content
SYSIBM.SYSTABLES	Information about each table and view, including database and table space
SYSIBM.SYSVIEWDEP	Information about the dependencies of views on tables and other views
SYSIBM.SYSVIEWS	Information about each view, including the authorization ID of the creator
SYSIBM.SYSVLTREE	Remaining part of parse tree representation of views where parse tree does not all fit in SYSIBM.SYSVTREE
SYSIBM.SYSVTREE	Parse tree representation of views

Index Catalog Tables

SYSIBM.SYSINDEXES	Information about each index, including index type and name of table
SYSIBM.SYSINDEXPART	Information about each unpartitioned index and each partition of a partitioned index, including space and storage allocations
SYSIBM.SYSKEYS	Information about each column of an index key, including column name and whether ascending or descending

Application Plan Catalog Tables

SYSIBM.SYSDBRM	Information about each DBRM of each application plan, including authorization ID of plan creator and time and date of precompilation
SYSIBM.SYSPLAN	Information about each application plan, including creation and bind dates and authorization ID of plan creator
SYSIBM.SYSPLANDEP	Information about the dependencies of plans on tables, views, synonyms, table spaces, and indexes
SYSIBM.SYSSTMT	Information about each SQL statement in each DBRM, including the text of the statement

(Continued)

BOX 14.1 *(Continued)*

Table	Content

Database, Table Space, and Storage Group Catalog Tables

Table	Content
SYSIBM.SYSCOPY	Information needed for recovery
SYSIBM.SYSDATABASE	Information about each database, including default storage group and buffer pool to use
SYSIBM.SYSSTOGROUP	Information about each storage group, including the VSAM catalog name and password
SYSIBM.SYSTABLEPART	Information about each unpartitioned table space and each partition of a partitioned table space, including space allocation and free-space values
SYSIBM.SYSTABLESPACE	Information about each table space, including buffer pool, lock size, and erase and close options
SYSIBM.SYSVOLUMES	Information about each volume in a storage group, including the volume serial number

Authorization Catalog Tables

Table	Content
SYSIBM.SYSCOLAUTH	Update privileges held by users on individual columns of a table or view
SYSIBM.SYSDBAUTH	Privileges held by users over databases
SYSIBM.SYSPLANAUTH	Privileges held by users over application plans
SYSIBM.SYSRESAUTH	Privileges held by users over buffer pools, storage groups and table spaces
SYSIBM.SYSTABAUTH	Privileges held by users on tables and views
SYSIBM.SYSUSERAUTH	System privileges held by users

Referential Tables

Table	Content
SYSIBM.SYSFOREIGNKEYS	Information about each column of every foreign key
SYSIBM.SYSRELS	Information about links between tables, including the names of the parent table and dependent table, the delete rule, and the referential constraint name

15 DB2 UTILITIES

A number of DB2 utilities are used for performing various system administration functions, including loading tables, recovering from failures, repairing data, and monitoring and tuning the DB2 system. This chapter examines the functions performed by the various utilities.

DB2 utilities are run as MVS batch jobs, using DB2 services as required; however, they can be invoked using various methods, including the following:

- DB2 utilities can be invoked using the DB2 Utilities panel of DB2I.
- Utilities can be executed via a TSO CLIST named DSNU.
- DB2 includes a JCL procedure named DSNUPROC that can be used to invoke DB2 utilities.
- A user-written set of JCL or a user-written JCL procedure can be used to invoke DB2 utilities.

Box 15.1 introduces the functions of the three major categories of DB2 utilities.

UTILITIES FOR LOADING AND RECOVERING DATA   The first category of DB2 utilities consists of those that are used for loading data into tables and for performing all phases of the database recovery process, including making image and incremental copies, managing the logs, and restoring data.

THE LOAD UTILITY   The LOAD utility is used to load data into tables. The table being loaded can be an empty data table or can already contain rows. The LOAD utility can be used to add new rows to a

BOX 15.1   DB2 utilities

Utilities Associated with Loading and Recovering Data

- **LOAD.** Loads data into tables.
- **COPY.** Makes image copies and incremental copies of table spaces or table space data sets.
- **MERGECOPY.** Merges incremental copies and image copies.
- **RECOVER.** Restores databases to a current state.
- **REPAIR.** Replaces invalid data with valid data.
- **MODIFY.** Removes unwanted image copies.
- **CHECK.** Determines whether indexes are consistent with the data in their corresponding tables.

Utilities Associated with Performance and Tuning

- **RUNSTATS.** Gathers statistics data on DASD space utilization and index efficiency.
- **STOSPACE.** Gathers information about the space allocated to storage groups, table spaces, and indexes.
- **REORG.** Reorganizes table spaces or indexes.

Stand-alone Utilities (invoked only via MVS JCL)

- **Change Log Inventory.** Changes information in the bootstrap data sets.
- **Print Log Map.** Prints out information on all active and archive log data sets.

table and to replace existing rows in the table. The LOAD utility is widely used in most applications by applications personnel as well as by DB2 system administrators. Therefore, we have devoted an entire chapter, Chapter 16, to its use.

The remainder of the DB2 utilities are typically executed only by DB2 system administration staff members. For further information concerning the use of any of the DB2 utilities, the following IBM publications should be consulted:

- SC26-4078 *IBM DATABASE 2 Reference*
- SC26-4077 *IBM DATABASE 2 Data Base Planning and Administration Guide*

DB2 RECOVERY   The general approach to recovery used with DB2 requires that *image copies* be made periodically of DB2 databases. The COPY utility can be used to make image copies of a table space or portion of a table space. As DB2 is processing, it automatically records in a log all changes made to the databases under its control. When a problem occurs with DB2 data, perhaps caused by an I/O error on the storage media or a system failure that generates inconsistent data, the data can be restored using the most recent image copy and using information from the log to reapply all the changes that were made to the database after the image copy was made.

INCREMENTAL COPIES   It is not necessary to copy the entire table space each time an image copy is made. It is possible with COPY to make an incremental copy that includes

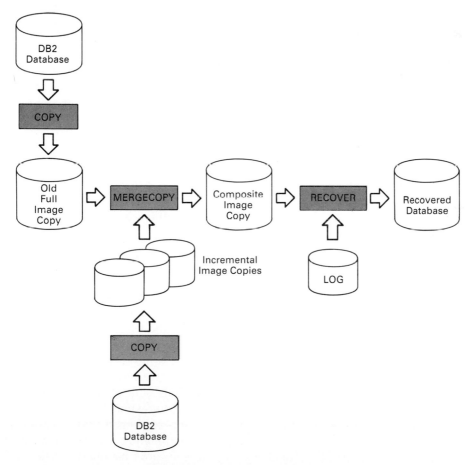

Figure 15.1   DB2 database recovery.

only the portions of the table space that have changed since the last copy. A MERGECOPY utility is available that can be used to merge the last full copy and all incremental copies to create a single copy of the table space. This composite copy can then be used to restore the database using the RECOVER utility. Only changes that were made after the last incremental copy need be applied. The database recovery process is summarized in Fig. 15.1.

TABLE SPACE SETS

There are special recovery considerations for tables that are related by referential constraints. The set of table spaces that contain a group of tables with referential constraints is known as a *table space set*. In Chapter 6, we defined referential constraints for the *Inventory, Quotations,* and *Suppliers* tables. The table spaces used to store these three tables make up a table space set. When recovery is required for a member of the table space set, all the table spaces must be recovered to a point in time when their data are consistent. This point in time is called a *quiesce point*.

The QUIESCE utility is used to generate and record a quiesce point. When the QUIESCE utility is executed, it acquires locks on all the table spaces in the set, which ensures that the data in all the tables is in a consistent state. The utility then records the time of this point in the DB2 catalog. When the table space set needs to be recovered, the REPORT utility can be used to identify quiesce points. The RECOVER utility can then be used to recover the set to a specified quiesce point. When this is done, only the log changes up to that point in time are applied. If the complete table space set is not recovered to a quiesce point, it may be necessary to use the CHECK utility to check for violations of referential constraints. This use of the CHECK utility is discussed further in Chapter 16.

DUAL LOGGING

The DB2 logging system uses two different logs. DB2 uses an *active log* to record changes to databases as they take place. When a data set used for the active log becomes full, the active log is copied to an *archive log*. It is also possible to request DB2 to maintain two copies of each log. This can be done to protect against a log data set becoming unreadable and thus not usable for recovering data.

DB2 maintains a log directory, which contains control information about each active and archive log data set. The directory, known as the *bootstrap data set* (BSDS), indicates when the use of each data set began and ended. This information is used during recovery to determine which log data sets are needed for the recovery process. DB2 dual logging facilities are illustrated in Fig. 15.2.

The various utilities used in the DB2 recovery process are discussed next.

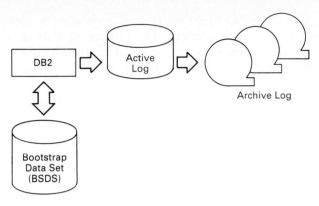

Figure 15.2   DB2 dual logging facilities.

THE COPY UTILITY   The COPY utility is used to make an image copy of a table space or a data set within a table space. The copy can be a full image copy or an incremental copy. A full copy consists of a copy of all the pages in a table space or table space data set. An incremental copy consists only of pages that have been changed since the last time the COPY utility was run against the table space or table space data set.

THE MERGECOPY UTILITY   The MERGECOPY utility is used to merge several incremental copies together to make a single composite incremental copy. It can also be used to merge a full image copy with one or more incremental copies to make a current full image copy.

THE QUIESCE UTILITY   The QUIESCE utility is used to establish a quiesce point, where the data in a set of tables related by referential constraints is in a consistent state. QUIESCE locks out new updates and, when all in-progress updating is completed, records the time in the DB2 catalog.

THE REPORT UTILITY   The REPORT utility can be used to identify all table spaces involved in referential constraints and to identify the location of quiesce points within the DB2 log. This information is used with the RECOVER utility to recover a table space set.

THE RECOVER UTILITY

The RECOVER utility is used to restore a database to a current state. It can be used to recover one or more table spaces, a data set within a table space, a set of pages that are associated with a particular error, or a single page. For a partitioned table space, one or more partitions can be recovered. Data is recovered using the most recent image copy and reapplying changes that have been recorded on the log. The RECOVER utility can also be used to recover indexes. An index is recovered by re-creating it using data from the table to which the table refers.

THE MODIFY UTILITY

The MODIFY utility is used to remove unwanted image copies from the system. MODIFY can remove any image copies of a specific age or can remove image copies that are older than a specified age.

THE CHECK UTILITY

The CHECK utility is used to determine whether indexes are consistent with the data in their corresponding tables. If an inconsistency is found, the RECOVER utility can be used to re-create the index. CHECK is also used to check for referential integrity violations.

THE REPAIR UTILITY

At times, problems with data may occur that are not correctable using the normal recovery process. For example, if log records are damaged as well as the data in a DB2 database, the information required to bring data to a consistent state may not be available. If such a situation occurs, it may be necessary to make corrections to data directly. The REPAIR utility can be used for this purpose. With REPAIR, changes are made to the data directly. Changes can also be made using REPAIR to some types of system data, such as index entries. Obviously, this type of facility must be used with extreme caution, since improper changes could damage the data even further.

UTILITIES FOR MONITORING AND TUNING

DB2 provides three utilities that are helpful in monitoring the activities and performance of the system and providing data that may be needed in order to tune the system's performance: RUNSTATS, STOSPACE, and REORG.

THE RUNSTATS UTILITY

The RUNSTATS utility gathers data on DASD space utilization and index efficiency, which is then used to update statistics stored in the DB2 catalog. These statistics are used in performance analysis that is done as part of path selection in the bind process. Running RUNSTATS periodically ensures that current information is used when DB2 performs path selection. RUNSTATS data can also be useful for identifying performance trends, measuring the impact of changes made to the system, and identifying table spaces or indexes that need to be reorganized.

THE STOSPACE UTILITY

The STOSPACE utility gathers information about the space allocated to storage groups, table spaces, and indexes. This information can be used to determine when DASD space assigned to different DB2 objects needs to be increased or decreased.

THE REORG UTILITY

The REORG utility reorganizes table spaces or indexes. It reestablishes free space and then restores the physical sequence defined by a clustering index. It also reclaims space lost to fragmentation or dropped tables. Reorganizing tables and indexes can improve their access efficiency.

STAND-ALONE UTILITIES

The utilities that we have discussed so far must be invoked while the DB2 system is in operation. They can all be invoked using any of the four methods discussed at the beginning of this chapter. Two additional utility programs are available that run in a stand-alone fashion and do not require that the DB2 system be in operation while they are run.

THE CHANGE LOG INVENTORY UTILITY

The Change Log Inventory utility can be used to change information in the bootstrap data sets (BSDSs). This might be done to add or delete log data sets. This utility cannot be invoked while the DB2 system is in operation; DB2 must be shut down before it can be run.

THE PRINT LOG MAP UTILITY

The Print Log Map utility prints out information on all active and archive log data sets. The information includes the data set name and starting and ending addresses for the data set.

OTHER MONITORING AND TUNING TOOLS There are other tools that can be used to monitor a DB2 system. DB2 provides a trace facility that can be used to record various system data and events. The DB2 trace can record all of the following:

- Statistics data that describes systemwide activities such as I/O activity or frequency of wait conditions
- Accounting information that identifies the activity of individual users and can be used to charge for DB2 usage on an individual basis
- Performance data that describes various subsystem events and is useful for tuning
- Global data that describes entries to and exits from DB2 functions and modules, used for servicing DB2

DB2 commands are used to start a trace, display the trace options in effect, and stop a trace.

DB2 monitoring can also be performed using general tools such as RMF Monitor II, GTF, CICSPARS, IMSPARS, and the IMS/VS monitor.

16 THE LOAD UTILITY

The DB2 LOAD utility is used by both application personnel and DB2 system administrators as an alternative to using custom-written application programs for loading data into tables. This chapter examines various options of the LOAD utility, including loading data into an empty table or one that contains data, loading selected records or fields, loading multiple tables, and loading tables with indexes.

The input to the DB2 LOAD utility must be either a sequential data set or a file produced by unloading one or more SQL/DS tables. The LOAD utility uses the basic sequential access method (BSAM) to process its input, so the records must be unblocked. A common method that is used to produce the input data sets that are processed by the LOAD utility is the *Data Extract* (DXT) product described in Chapter 17.

LOADING AN EMPTY TABLE

The LOAD utility can be used to load data into an empty table, to add rows to a table that already contains data, and to replace existing data in a table. A LOAD utility control statement is used to describe the desired load operation. The following LOAD statement loads data into an empty table named *Suppliers* that was created by the user whose authorization ID is KKC01:

```
LOAD DATA
     INTO TABLE KKC01.SUPPLIERS
```

ADDING OR REPLACING DATA

If the table already contains data and the new data is to be added to the existing data, we include a RESUME YES clause:

```
LOAD DATA
     RESUME YES
     INTO TABLE KKC01.SUPPLIERS
```

To replace existing data with new rows, we include a REPLACE clause:

```
LOAD DATA
     REPLACE
     INTO TABLE KKC01.SUPPLIERS
```

If we attempt to load data into a table that is not empty without specifying either RESUME YES or REPLACE, the utility terminates execution and returns a condition code of 8.

LOAD UTILITY OPTIONS

Here are descriptions of the various processing options the LOAD utility supports:

- Loading selected input records based on specified conditions
- Loading selected fields from the input records
- Loading multiple tables from a single input data set. Different fields from the same input record can be used to create rows for different tables, or different records can be used to create rows for different tables, based on values in the input records.
- Automatically converting data being loaded from one compatible data type to another
- Saving in a discard data set any records that are not loaded by the utility

LOADING SELECTED RECORDS

If only selected input records are to be loaded into the table, we include a WHEN clause in the LOAD statement to specify the condition used to select the records:

```
LOAD DATA
     INTO TABLE KKC01.SUPPLIERS
     WHEN (5:1)='C'
```

In this example, the notation (5:1) defines a field in the input record that starts in position 5 and is 1 position long. This field is then compared to the specified value. In the example, we are selecting only records that contain a C in the fifth position.

SPECIFYING INPUT FIELDS

If the LOAD statement does not specify any input field descriptions, the utility assumes that the field format of the input record matches the column format of the table. The input fields must be in the same relative sequence as the table columns, and the input field lengths and types must be the same as the column lengths and types. Also, the input must specify no null values.

If the format of the input records is different from the column format of the table, we can describe in the LOAD statement the input fields and their correspondence to the table columns:

```
LOAD DATA
    INTO TABLE KKC01.SUPPLIERS
        (SUPSUPP    POSITION (1)   DECIMAL EXTERNAL(4),
         NAME       POSITION (5)   CHAR(15),
         ADDRESS    POSITION (20)  CHAR(30),
         CODE       POSITION (50)  DECIMAL EXTERNAL(2))
```

A POSITION clause specifies the starting position of each field in the input record and is followed by the data type and length of the field.

When the data is loaded, DB2 automatically converts data types where necessary. In the example, the external decimal values in the input are converted to SMALLINT (halfword binary), which is the defined data type for the *Supsupp* and *Code* columns. *Address* values are converted from CHAR to VARCHAR.

For proper execution, the data types of each input field and its associated target column must be compatible. CHAR, VARCHAR, and LONG VARCHAR are considered compatible, and SMALLINT, INTEGER, DECIMAL, and FLOAT are compatible.

LOADING MULTIPLE TABLES

We can load data into multiple tables that reside in the same table space by including multiple INTO TABLE clauses. Each INTO TABLE specification can have its own WHEN clause and input field specifications. This allows selected records and selected input fields to be loaded into each table; for example:

```
LOAD DATA
    INTO KKC01.SUPP20 WHEN (50:2)='20'
    INTO KKC01.SUPP30 WHEN (50:2)='30'
```

With this statement, data is loaded into two tables based on a value contained in the input records.

LOADING PARTITIONED TABLES

We can specify that data be loaded into a particular partition of a partitioned table by including a PART clause:

```
LOAD DATA
    INTO KKC01.INVENTORY
    PART 3
```

With this statement, we are loading data into partition 3 of the *Inventory* table. The selection of records for loading is controlled by values defined in the CREATE INDEX statement for partition 3. Records in the input data set that do not belong in partition 3 are bypassed.

LOADING TABLES WITH UNIQUE INDEXES

The LOAD utility automatically builds all indexes that have been defined for the table being loaded. When a unique index is being built, LOAD checks for any index violations. In earlier versions of DB2, if duplicate key values were detected, an index entry was created for the first occurrence of the key value, but the index was disabled when the second occurrence was detected. This resulted in an index that was incomplete and unusable. DB2 now lists duplicate rows in an error report; they are discarded from the table and are not entered in the index. Optionally, discarded rows can be copied to a discard data set. This approach results in a usable table and index. Discarded data can later be reviewed to determine what should be added to the table.

USING THE CHECK UTILITY TO CHECK INDEXES

To ensure that the indexes that are built by the LOAD utility are consistent with the tables they index, it is a good idea to run the CHECK utility after the LOAD utility run has completed. The following is an example of a control statement for the CHECK utility:

```
CHECK INDEX NAME (KKC01.INVENTORY)
```

The CHECK utility can be run at any time to verify that indexes are consistent with their associated tables. If inconsistencies are found they can often be repaired by running the RECOVER utility with the INDEX option.

LOADING TABLES WITH REFERENTIAL CONSTRAINTS

In addition to checking for unique index violations, the LOAD utility also checks for referential integrity violations. For a table for which a primary key is defined, LOAD will not load data into the table unless the appropriate unique index has also been defined. As part of the load, the unique index is built, ensuring there are no duplicate or null primary key values.

For a dependent table, the LOAD utility optionally checks foreign key values to ensure that they either match a primary key value or are null. If a violation is detected, the row is deleted from the table and listed in an error report. Optionally, the deleted row can be copied to a discard data set. If the option to check referential constraints is not specified as part of the load, the table is marked as being in check pending status. Data in the table cannot be accessed or manipulated until the check pending status is cleared.

USING THE CHECK UTILITY TO CHECK REFERENTIAL CONSTRAINTS

The CHECK utility can be run using the CHECK DATA option to check a table for foreign key values that violate a referential constraint. If a violation is detected, it is listed in an error report. Optionally, the invalid row can be copied to an exception table. As a separate option, the invalid row can be deleted from the table. If CHECK DATA is used on a table in check-pending status, the status is cleared if no violations are detected or if invalid rows are deleted from the table.

The CHECK DATA function is also useful after relational constraints have been added to existing tables. When ALTER is used to define a primary key, the corresponding unique index must already have been created. This ensures that there are no duplicate or null primary key values. When ALTER is used to define a foreign key, the table is placed in check-pending status. CHECK DATA can then be used to check for referential constraint violations, and if necessary, to delete invalid rows, clearing the check-pending status.

17 DATA EXTRACT (DXT)

One method that is often employed for preparing the input data for the DB2 LOAD utility is to use the *Data Extract* (DXT) program product. With DXT, we can extract data from an IMS or DL/I database, from a conventional sequential data set, or from a VSAM data set. DXT formats the data so that it can be used as input to the LOAD utility and also generates the appropriate LOAD statement for the LOAD utility. These outputs can be combined with a predefined set of JCL statements that are needed to execute the LOAD utility, thus generating all the required data, JCL, and utility control statements for loading the extracted data into a DB2 table. DXT provides facilities similar to an SQL SELECT statement and allows selected records and selected fields to be extracted from the input source.

In addition to its use in supporting the DB2 LOAD utility, DXT has many other capabilities. For example, DXT can be used to extract data from DB2 or SQL/DS tables. DXT can produce output in DB2 format, in SQL/DS format, or in a special format called *integration exchange format* (IXF). IXF data has a defined format that can then be processed by an application program for any desired purpose. The extracted data can either be combined with JCL and control statements in order to form a complete MVS job or stored in an output file. We will concentrate here on how to use DXT to prepare data for loading into a DB2 table.

Using DXT to extract data from a nonrelational source, such as a sequential or VSAM data set or an IMS database, requires a three-step process:

1. Describe the source data.
2. Build and submit an extract request.
3. Run the extract request.

DESCRIBING DXT SOURCE DATA

Before running DXT, a description of the data set or database must be prepared and stored in a DXT library. The extract request can then be run any number of times against the specified data set or database. In addition to describing the input, a *DXT view* must be also prepared and stored. A DXT view defines the subset of fields or segments a particular individual has access to. These descriptions, known as *data descriptions*, are of the following types:

- **DXT File Description.** A DXT file description describes a VSAM or sequential data set. It names the fields in the file and may specify record types in the file.

- **DXT PSB Description.** A DXT PSB description is used to describe an IMS database. An IMS/VS program specification block (PSB) consists of a set of program communication blocks (PCBs). Each PCB specifies the database segments an application program has access to and lists a set of program processing options. A DXT PSB description describes the PCBs in a PSB. For each PCB, the PSB description describes the fields of interest, including each field's length, data characteristics, and location in its segment. For each segment, it specifies length, format, and the segment's parent segment.

- **DXT View Description.** A DXT view description defines a subset of fields or segments, based on an existing DXT file or PSB description. This provides selective access to the data, much as an SQL view can be used to restrict access to certain data. A DXT view cannot be created until the underlying DXT file description or PSB description has been created and stored in the DXT library.

BUILDING AND SUBMITTING A DXT EXTRACT REQUEST

Once data descriptions have been prepared and stored in the DXT library, extract requests can be created and run. The extract request provides the information needed to extract the data, including the following:

- The name of each DXT view that defines the data being accessed
- The names of the fields to be extracted
- Conditions that must be met for a record or field to be selected for extraction
- The destination of the output—an output job or an output data set

An extract request can be built online, using DXT facilities, or a request can be submitted in batch mode by coding DXT statements and the appropriate JCL statements. DXT end-user dialogs are menu-driven and do not require the user to learn DXT statement syntax. DXT administrative dialogs can also be used to code DXT statements directly. Once an extract request is created, it is validated and stored in a DXT queue.

An extract request requires two DXT statements: SUBMIT and EX-TRACT. Here is an example of a simple DXT extract request:

```
SUBMIT   EXTID = EXTINV1,
         DBS   = DB2,
         CD    = JCS,
         JCS   = LOADJCL
EXTRACT  INTO INVENTORY (INVPART NOT NULL, PNAME, ONHAND)
         SELECT VIEWPART, VIEWNAME, VIEWONHAND
         FROM INVVIEW
         WHERE VIEWPART BETWEEN 100 AND 200
```

The first operand in the SUBMIT statement (EXTID) assigns an identifier to this request. The DBS = DB2 clause specifies that the extracted data is going to be placed into a DB2 table. This causes DXT to prepare an appropriate LOAD statement for the DB2 LOAD utility in addition to extracting data. The CD = JCS clause specifies where to put this control statement; in this case, we want it placed with the JCL statements used to execute the LOAD utility. The JCS operand specifies the name of a data set that must already contain the JCL statements needed to execute the LOAD utility.

The INTO operand in the EXTRACT statement names the table and the columns that are to be loaded with the extracted data. If a column cannot contain null values, this must be specified with a NOT NULL clause. The SELECT operand identifies the columns in the DXT view for this request that are to be included in the data to be extracted. The FROM operand identifies the DXT view used for the request. Here, the *Viewpart, Viewname,* and *Viewonhand* columns in the *Invview* view are the source of the extracted data. The sequence of the columns in the SELECT operand and the sequence of the columns in the INTO operand determine which value is placed in which column. The data from *Viewpart* goes in *Invpart, Viewname* in *Pname,* and *Viewonhand* in *Onhand.* The WHERE operand specifies any conditions the input records must meet in order to be selected for extraction. Here the part number must be between *100* and *200.*

RUNNING A DXT EXTRACT REQUEST   After being validated and placed in a DXT queue, the DXT request is run. DXT extracts the specified data from the input source and either places it in an output data set or includes it in an output job, as specified in the SUBMIT statement in the request. As discussed earlier, when extracting data that is to be automatically loaded with the DB2 load utility, we must supply a data set that contains the required JCL to execute the LOAD utility. The SUBMIT statement specifies the name of this data set. DXT then creates the LOAD control statement and inserts it into the appropriate place in the LOAD utility JCL. The extracted data can also be combined with the utility JCL, in the form of inline data. If the amount of data being extracted is large, or if we want to keep a copy of the data after the extract run, we can specify that the data be stored in a sequential data set. DXT then puts the name of that data set in the LOAD utility JCL so that the utility will execute using the data set that contains the extracted data.

18 DB2 SECURITY

Given the potential importance of the data that is stored on DB2 databases, providing security mechanisms is a key issue. Access to DB2 resources can be controlled in several ways. This chapter examines DB2's approach to security, including the DB2 authorization system and external facilities such as RACF and VSAM passwords.

As we mentioned in Chapter 6, the approach that DB2 takes to authorization is to require all users to be authorized to perform the functions they request. Privileges must be granted to a user, either explicitly or implicitly, before the user is allowed to use a particular DB2 capability. For example, in order to access DB2 tables and to modify tables or the data they contain, we must have first been granted the proper *authorization* to do so. Authorization applies to processing performed by application programs as well as processing performed interactively using QMF. An application program can be coded, precompiled, and compiled without any privileges having been granted. However, to bind the program and execute it, the proper authorizations must be in effect.

Privileges are typically granted by the person or group responsible for administering DB2 in the installation and are granted on the basis of the *authorization IDs* that are assigned to users. The DB2 system administration staff grants and revokes privileges on the basis of the authorization IDs assigned to DB2 users. The primary authorization ID of a user is supplied to DB2 in various ways when the user connects with DB2. For example, for a user accessing DB2 using foreground TSO, the user's logon ID is the user's primary authorization ID; for a batch program, the USER parameter in the JOB statement supplies the primary authorization ID. A user may also have one or more secondary authorization IDs that identify additional privileges the user has. Secondary IDs can be used to assign privileges to groups of users.

When an application is being developed and tested, privileges are generally granted on the basis of authorization IDs assigned to the appropriate application developers. When an application is transferred from the application developers into production, new privileges must generally be granted using the authorization IDs assigned to production.

Many privileges can be granted, including the right to perform the following functions:

- Selecting data
- Inserting, updating, or deleting data
- Altering a table
- Creating various DB2 objects, including tables, indexes, table spaces, databases, and storage groups
- Using a table space, storage group, or buffer pool
- Binding or executing an application plan
- Executing specific DB2 commands and utilities
- Granting administrative privileges

In general, the privileges that can be granted to an individual user are of five types:

- Tables privileges
- Application plan privileges
- Database privileges
- System resource privileges
- Administration privileges

TABLE PRIVILEGES

In order for one of our application programs to access a table that was created by some other user, we must have been granted the appropriate *table privileges* for that table. Various types of table privileges can be granted to an individual user; they include privileges that allow the user the following functions on the table:

- Select data from the table. This includes the right to retrieve data with SELECT statements, create views based on this table, and use DCLGEN to create a DECLARE statement for the table.
- Insert data into the table.
- Update data in the table.
- Delete data from the table.
- Alter the table structure.
- Create an index for the table.

At a minimum, a user who submits a DB2 application program for execution must have the appropriate table privileges to select data from the application tables and views that the program accesses. In addition to having the privilege of selecting data from tables, some users may also be granted privileges that allow them to insert, update, and delete data from these tables and views. Other users may also be granted privileges that allow them to create their own tables, to use table spaces and storage groups, and to create indexes, table spaces, databases, and storage groups.

APPLICATION PLAN PRIVILEGES

In addition to the normal table privileges that all users require to access DB2 data, application developers and others who submit programs for binding or execution need *application plan privileges*. Programmers do not need either table privileges or application plan privileges to code, precompile, and compile DB2 programs, since these functions do not require access to the DB2 system. However, programmers do require BIND and EXECUTE application plan privileges to bind and execute the programs they develop. Other users who submit application programs for execution must have EXECUTE privileges to execute the programs they submit.

If authorization validity checking is performed at the time binding is done for an application plan, the user performing the bind must have the necessary access authority to access the DB2 data referenced by that application plan. Then when the program is executed, the user invoking the program needs only the authority to execute the plan and does not require individual data access privileges. If validity checking is delayed until the program is executed, the user invoking the program must have all the necessary access privileges.

DATABASE PRIVILEGES

An application may also create tables that it uses. To do this, the user must have specific authorization to create tables in a particular database and also authorization either to use or to create table spaces for the tables created. When a user has authorization to create a table, this implicitly grants certain other authorizations.

Implicit Authorization

Some privileges do not have to be granted explicitly; a user possesses some privileges implicitly as a result of having been granted other privileges. For example, a user who has select privileges on certain tables or views is also allowed to create views based on those tables and views. The user also has the right to generate declarations, using DCLGEN, for those tables and views.

A user who has been granted authorization to create tables is implicitly authorized to perform certain operations on the tables that user creates. For example, the user can alter or drop those tables, create and drop indexes on them, create and drop views based on those tables, generate declarations with DCLGEN, load the tables with data, and select, insert, update, and delete data in the tables. Generally, a user who is able to create a DB2 object is also allowed to access, alter, or drop it.

SYSTEM RESOURCE PRIVILEGES

Some users may require a higher level of authorization than is provided by table privileges, application plan privileges, and database privileges. There is a set of system resource privileges that can be granted that allows a user the ability to use specific buffer pools, storage groups, and table spaces. This means that the user is able to reference those objects in CREATE statements.

ADMINISTRATIVE PRIVILEGES

In addition to individual privileges that are granted to application developers and other users, certain users may be granted *administrative privileges*. Administrative privileges are sets of authorizations that are granted and revoked as a group. DB2 administrative privileges include the following:

- **SYSADM** (system administration). Users with SYSADM authority generally have control over all DB2 resources. They can grant and revoke any of the levels of administrative authority and can grant individual privileges to users. A user with SYSADM authority can alter or drop any DB2 object except the DB2 catalog and certain system databases.

- **DBADM** (database administration). A user with DBADM authority has control over a particular DB2 database and can perform any function on objects in that database. A given user can have DBADM authority over more than one database but does not have authority to create databases unless that authority has specifically been granted.

- **DBCTRL** (database control). A user with DBCTRL authority has all the capabilities of DBADM, except that access to data in the database is not allowed unless it has been specifically granted as an individual authority.

- **DBMAINT** (database maintenance). A user with DBMAINT authority has the same privileges as a user with the DBCTRL authority, except that he or she cannot modify any DB2 object. This level of authority allows a user to perform such tasks as making image copies and obtaining statistics.

- **SYSOPR** (system operation). A user with SYSOPR authority is allowed to issue DB2 commands to display, recover, start, and stop various DB2 objects. This does not include the authority to access data in DB2 databases.

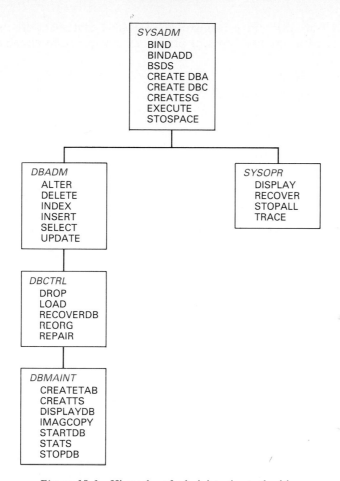

Figure 18.1　Hierarchy of administrative authorities.

Administrative privileges are hierarchical; a user with a higher-level authority also possesses privileges associated with lower level authorities. Figure 18.1 illustrates the hierarchy and the individual privileges associated with each position. So, for example, the DBCTRL authority includes the privileges listed for DBMAINT, as well as all the privileges listed in its box.

The different levels of administrative privileges can be used to divide system administration responsibilities among various users. Different groups can be given the authority needed to manage a given database or group of databases without affecting any other databases.

GRANTING PRIVILEGES

A user or system administration staff member grants privileges to other users by issuing SQL GRANT statements, typically by using an interactive facility such as SPUFI or QMF. Five forms of the GRANT statement are used to grant privileges related to the five types of privileges that we have already discussed:

- Table privileges
- Application plan privileges
- Database privileges
- System resource privileges
- Administrative privileges

Box 18.1 describes the different types of privileges that can be granted with GRANT statements.

BOX 18.1   GRANT privileges

Table Privileges

GRANT SELECT ON TABLE	Retrieve data from a table or view.
GRANT INSERT ON TABLE	Insert data into a table or view.
GRANT UPDATE ON TABLE	Modify data in a table or view.
GRANT DELETE ON TABLE	Delete data from a table or view.
GRANT INDEX ON TABLE	Define an index on a table.
GRANT ALTER ON TABLE	Alter a table.
GRANT ALL ON TABLE	Grant all of the above table privileges.

Application Plan Privileges

GRANT BIND ON PLAN	Bind, rebind, replace, free, or change ownership of an application plan.
GRANT EXECUTE ON PLAN	Run a program associated with an application plan.

BOX 18.1 *(Continued)*

Database Privileges

GRANT CREATETAB ON DATABASE	Create tables.
GRANT CREATETS ON DATABASE	Create table spaces.
GRANT DROP ON DATABASE	Drop a database.
GRANT DBADM, DBCTRL, DBMAINT ON DATABASE	Have DBADM, DBCTRL, or DBMAINT authority.
GRANT STARTDB, STOPDB, DISPLAYDB ON DATABASE	Use operator commands to start, stop, or display a database.
GRANT IMAGCOPY, LOAD, REORG, RECOVERDB, REPAIR, STATST ON DATABASE	Use specified DB2 utilities.

System Resource Privileges

GRANT USE OF BUFFERPOOL	Use a buffer pool.
GRANT USE OF STOGROUP	Use a storage group.
GRANT USE OF TABLESPACE	Use a table space.

System Privileges

GRANT CREATEDBA	Create databases with DBADM authority over them.
GRANT CREATEDBC	Create databases with DBCTRL authority over them.
GRANT CREATESG	Create storage groups.
GRANT BINDADD	Create new application plans.
GRANT SYSADM, SYSOPR	Have SYSADM or SYSOPR authority.
GRANT STOSPACE	Use the STOSPACE utility.
GRANT DISPLAY, RECOVER, BSDS, TRACE, STOPALL	Issue operator commands to display a database or thread, to recover databases, to start or stop a trace, or to stop DB2.

GRANT OPTIONS   Each of the forms of the GRANT statement uses a TO clause to specify the user or users receiving the privileges named in the statement. The clause can list one or more authorization IDs or can use the keyword PUBLIC to grant the privileges to all users.

A GRANT statement can include a WITH GRANT OPTION clause. If this clause is included, the specified user or users receive the right to grant to other users the privileges specified in the GRANT statement. The WITH GRANT OPTION cannot be included in a GRANT statement that specifies PUBLIC in the TO clause.

For example, we might grant a particular table privilege by issuing the following GRANT statement:

```
GRANT SELECT
      ON MFG03.INVENTORY
      TO KKC01, RGT02
```

This statement allows the users assigned the authorization IDs KKC01 and RGT02 to select data from the *Inventory* table that was created by the user whose authorization ID is MFG03. A GRANT statement can be executed by an application program, but GRANT statements are more typically executed interactively, using QMF or SPUFI, by staff members who administer the DB2 system.

Here is an example of a GRANT statement that is used to grant plan privileges to a user:

```
GRANT BIND
      ON PLAN QUOTUPDT
      TO JAL01
```

REVOKING PRIVILEGES   Privileges are revoked using a REVOKE statement. There are five forms of the REVOKE statement, corresponding to the five forms of GRANT. When a privilege is revoked for a user, any privileges directly or indirectly dependent on that privilege are also revoked. For example, if the authority to access a table is revoked, the authority to use views defined on that table is also revoked. If the user has granted another user the privilege being revoked, the second user's privilege is also revoked.

AUTHORIZATION INFORMATION IN THE DB2 CATALOG   The DB2 catalog includes tables that contain authorization information. Box 18.2 lists these tables and the information they contain. This information can be helpful in determining what privileges have been granted and which users will be affected if a change is made to a DB2 object.

For example, SYSIBM.SYSTABAUTH could be used to display a list of

BOX 18.2   Authorization catalog tables

SYSIBM.SYSTABAUTH	Information about privileges held by users over tables and views
SYSIBM.SYSCOLAUTH	Information about update privileges held by users over specific columns of a table or view
SYSIBM.SYSPLANAUTH	Information about privileges held by users over application plans
SYSIBM.SYSUSERAUTH	Information about system privileges held by users
SYSIBM.SYSDBAUTH	Information about privileges held by users over databases
SYSIBM.SYSRESAUTH	Information about privileges held by users over buffer pools, storage groups, and table spaces

all users who are authorized to access a particular table or view or to identify all the tables and views a particular user can access. SYSIBM.SYSUSERAUTH could be used to obtain a list of all the users with a particular system privilege, such as creating storage groups.

OTHER SECURITY MECHANISMS

In addition to the DB2 authorization system discussed in this chapter, other security mechanisms that can be used with DB2 include *views,* the facilities provided by the *Resource Access Control Facility* (RACF), and *VSAM passwords.*

DB2 Views

Views can be used to control access to sensitive data. For example, we might define a view in such a way that users of the view are restricted to accessing only selected columns or selected rows of the underlying tables. For example, one view might allow users to access general personnel information but not salaries. Another view might allow a department manager to access salary information for one department but not for others.

RACF

The *Resource Access Control Facility* (RACF) can be used to prevent unauthorized users or applications from accessing the DB2 system or specific DB2 resources. RACF can be used to protect specific data sets, DASD volumes, or other system resources that have been defined to RACF. RACF cannot be used, however, to protect resources defined only within the DB2 system, such as DB2 tables and views.

VSAM Passwords

VSAM passwords can be used to protect the underlying VSAM data sets that contain DB2 data. Passwords can be used either as an alternative or as a supplement to a security subsystem like RACF. VSAM passwords can be used to protect system data sets and DB2 catalog data sets as well as data sets containing application data.

19 LOCKING FACILITIES

DB2 is designed to allow concurrent access to DB2 data by multiple users. In order to ensure that concurrent access to data does not lead to inconsistent results, DB2 uses a system of *resource locks*. The use of resource locks ensures that data can be restored to a consistent state when recovering from a program or system failure. We begin this chapter by examining the problems that are associated with concurrent access to DB2 data and seeing how locks are used to avoid these problems. We then examine the nature of the locking system used by DB2.

UNREPEATABLE READS

One potential problem with concurrent access is that of *unrepeatable reads*. A program may need to read a row from a database table and then at a later point read that same row again and find the same data item values that the row contained previously. If another program has accessed the row in the meantime, it may have changed data item values in that row. An example of an unrepeatable read is shown in Box 19.1. An unrepeatable read is an example of a *loss of read integrity* in accessing the database.

ACCESS TO UNCOMMITTED DATA

Another way in which loss of read integrity can occur is by allowing a program to access uncommitted data. This involves a program reading a data item value after it has been updated by a second program and before the second program causes the data to be rolled back to its original value because of a failure. An example of access to uncommitted data is illustrated in Box 19.2.

BOX 19.1   Unrepeatable read

1. Program B retrieves a row from a database table.

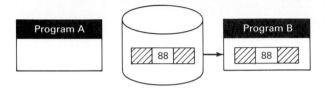

2. Program A retrieves the same row.

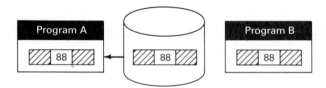

3. Program A updates the ON-HAND-QUANTITY data item in the row and writes the new version of the row back into the database.

4. Program B reads the same row a second time. The value for ON-HAND-QUANTITY is now different from when Program B first accessed the table.

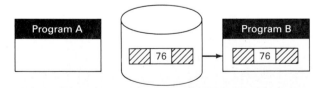

BOX 19.2   Access to uncommitted data

1. Program A reads a table row.

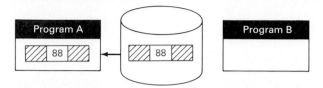

2. Program A updates a data item value in the row and stores the new version of the row into the table.

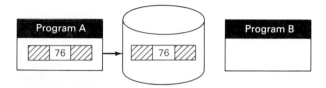

3. Program B reads the updated row and uses it for its processing.

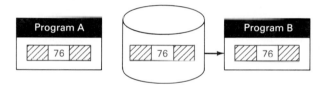

4. Program A then determines that the changes to the row should be rolled back, thus restoring the data item values in the row to their original values.

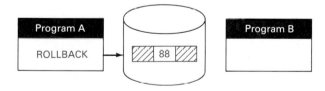

5. Program B's processing is now based on the wrong data. If program B reads the row a second time, the value for ON-HAND-QUANTITY will be different from when it first accessed the table.

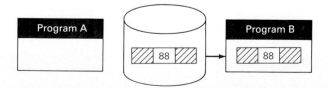

BOX 19.3 Lost update

1. Program A retrieves a row that has the value 88 in the ON-HAND-QUANTITY data item.

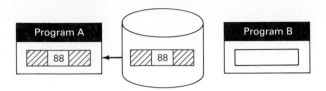

2. Program B retrieves the same row.

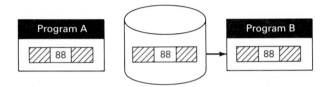

3. Program A updates the ON-HAND-QUANTITY data item by deducting 10 from it and writing a new version of the row into the database. At this point the value of ON-HAND-QUANTITY is 78.

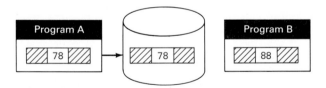

4. Program B updates the same row by deducting 5 from the value 88 and then writes the row back into the database. The value of ON-HAND-QUANTITY in the database is now 83. The correct value for ON-HAND-QUANTITY is 73, which reflects both updates.

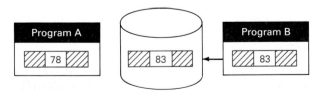

LOST UPDATES   Another potential problem with concurrency is that of *lost updates*. Box 19.3 shows how an update can be lost when two concurrently executing programs are both allowed to update the same table row. When two concurrently executing programs both simultaneously update data item values in a row, the results of the first program's update can be nullified by the second program, resulting in an incorrect value being stored in the table. A lost update is an example of a *loss of write integrity* in accessing the database.

DB2 RESOURCE LOCKS   In order to avoid the problems associated with loss of data integrity, DB2 implements a system of locks. When DB2 places a lock on a DB2 resource, the lock controls whether some other user can access the locked resource and, if so, in what way. The basic principle DB2 follows is that no program is allowed to access data that another program has changed but has not yet committed. The way the principle is implemented is by having DB2 place locks on resources that are affected by a change whenever a program performs an activity that involves the updating of data. The locks are released when the program reaches a commit point, and the changes are either committed or backed out.

DB2 automatically places locks on resources and removes them as required to protect the integrity of the data in the database. Generally, an application program is not concerned with the acquiring and releasing of locks. However, application program processing that is related to recovery can affect the length of time during which locks are held, so a general understanding of the DB2 approach to locking can be helpful to the application programmer.

LOCK SIZE   DB2 uses three types of resource locks in controlling data integrity. With the first type of lock, DB2 locks an entire table space. When this is done, all tables and indexes in the table space are controlled by the lock. With the second type of lock, DB2 locks a single table in a segmented table space. With the third type of lock, DB2 locks a single page within a table space. The page might be one that stores part of a table or one that stores part of an index. Only the data in that particular page is affected by a lock on a page. Other pages in the table space can be accessed by other users and might be subject to other locks.

Options can be specified at the time that a table space is defined that control whether DB2 locks the entire table space, a single table, or individual pages. Alternatively, DB2 can determine which type of lock is used. The application program can also issue a LOCK TABLE SQL statement to explicitly request a table lock.

LOCK DURATION The length of time a lock is held depends on several factors, including whether it is a table space lock or a page lock. For table space locks, the lock is acquired:

- for a dynamic SQL statement that modifies data, at the time the statement is about to be executed.
- for a normal, or static, SQL statement that modifies data, either when the statement is about to be executed or when the application plan is allocated. The ACQUIRE option on the BIND or REBIND statement, used as part of the bind process, specifies which approach is used for a given program.

For table space locks, the lock is released:

- for dynamic SQL statements, when a commit point is reached.
- for static SQL statements, either when a commit point is reached or when the application plan is deallocated. The RELEASE option in the BIND or REBIND command specifies which approach is used.

In general, page locks are acquired when the page is first accessed and released at the next commit point.

The application program can control the length of time that a lock remains in effect by controlling the duration of each unit of recovery. If the program does not explicitly define commit points, locks remain in effect for the resources the program accesses until the program terminates. If the program does explicitly define commit points, DB2 releases all currently held locks at each commit point. Following the commit point, DB2 may lock additional resources, which are then held until the next commit point or until the program's execution terminates.

LOCK MODES A lock's mode indicates the type of access to the locked object that is permitted to other concurrent users. The basic modes are as follows:

- **SHARE (S).** A share mode lock allows the lock owner and any concurrent users to read the locked data but not to change it. Other users can also acquire a share mode or update mode lock on the data.
- **UPDATE (U).** An update mode lock allows the lock owner to read the locked data with an intent to change it. When the owner finally does change the data, the lock is changed to exclusive. Other users can acquire share locks and read the data while the lock remains an update mode lock.
- **EXCLUSIVE (X).** An exclusive lock allows the lock owner to read and change the locked data. No other user can access this data or acquire a lock on it while the exclusive lock is in effect.

DB2 typically places a share mode lock on data when an application executes SQL statements that only retrieve table data, such as the SELECT statement. DB2 typically places update mode locks on data when an application executes SQL statements that cause changes to data and table structures, including CREATE, ALTER, DROP, INSERT, UPDATE, DELETE, UPDATE WHERE CURRENT OF, and DELETE WHERE CURRENT OF. As mentioned, an update mode lock is changed to an exclusive lock as soon as data is actually modified.

When an application program executes an SQL statement, DB2 automatically locks the appropriate resources before performing the processing specified by the SQL statement. If the required resources have already been locked, the application program waits until those locks have been released.

CONTROLLING LOCKS

A number of processing options affect locking. The ACQUIRE and RELEASE options on the BIND and REBIND commands affect the duration of locks. The LOCKSIZE clause on a CREATE TABLESPACE or ALTER TABLESPACE statement can be used to control the size of locks. LOCKSIZE TABLESPACE specifies that all locks are table space locks. LOCKSIZE PAGE specifies that page locks should be acquired whenever possible. LOCKSIZE ANY leaves the choice of lock size to DB2, which generally chooses page locks.

The LOCK TABLE statement can be used to lock a table space and to specify whether the lock is share mode or exclusive mode. With LOCK TABLE, the lock is acquired when the statement is executed. It is released when a commit point is reached or when the application plan is deallocated, depending on the RELEASE option specified.

The ISOLATION parameter on the BIND or REBIND command affects page locks when a cursor is used. If cursor stability is specified, the page lock is held only while the cursor is positioned on that page. When it moves to a new page, the lock is released, provided that no data on the previous page has been changed. (If data has been changed, the lock must be held until the data is committed.) If repeatable read is specified, page locks are held until the next commit point is reached. With this option, if the program returns to the same page and reads the same row, the values will not have been changed by another program.

There are trade-offs involved in the different lock options. Since a lock held by one program can prevent another program from accessing data, page locks generally allow more concurrency than table space locks. However, storage and processing time are required to manage locks, so overall processing efficiency may be better with table space locks. These considerations have to be balanced when making decisions about lock specifications.

SUMMARY OF PART V

A DB2 database consists of a set of tables, with their associated indexes, that can be referred to as a group in an operation. A table space is an area of a database containing one or more tables. A partitioned table space is divided into partitions, and each partition contains part of a table. An index is a set of pointers to the rows in a table and can be used to provide faster access to data. A unique index ensures that no two rows contain the same key values. A cluster index controls the physical sequence in which table rows are stored and can be used to specify how rows are divided between partitions in a partitioned table space. Table spaces and index spaces are assigned to sets of DASD volumes called storage groups. DB2 objects are created with the SQL CREATE statement. There are separate forms of the CREATE statement for storage groups, databases, table spaces, tables, indexes, and views. The DB2 system catalog is a set of tables containing information about all DB2 objects.

DB2 utilities are available to assist with loading tables, recovering and repairing data, and performance monitoring and tuning. DB2 recovery is based on image copies of table spaces and logs that record all changes made to DB2 data. Either full or incremental copies can be made. DB2 maintains an active log and archival logs. Optionally, two copies of each log can be maintained. DB2 utilities assist with making image copies, managing logs, and restoring data. DB2 utilities also gather statistics on space utilization, index efficiency, and space allocation. Utilities are available for performing database reorganizations. A trace facility can also be used to record system data and information about events that occur.

Data can be loaded into a DB2 table using an SQL INSERT statement. Depending on the form of the statement, either individual rows or multiple rows can be inserted. The LOAD utility can be used to load data into a DB2 table from a sequential input source or from an SQL/DS table. Data can be loaded into an empty table, added to existing data in a table, or used to replace existing data. Loading can be limited to selected records or fields in the input data. Multiple tables can be loaded from a single input data set. Data being loaded is automatically converted to the appropriate data type. Indexes are automatically constructed as part of LOAD utility processing.

The Data Extract (DXT) facility can be used to prepare data for processing by the LOAD utility. Data can be extracted from a physical sequential data set, a VSAM data set, or an IMS/VS database. The source data must be described using a DXT file description or PSB description and a DXT view description. The extract request is then constructed and run. The extracted data and a LOAD statement are then available to be used with the LOAD utility.

DB2 security facilities are provided through the use of DB2 views, a security subsystem such as RACF, VSAM passwords, and DB2 authorization facilities. DB2 privileges can be granted explicitly or implicitly. Administrative authorities are sets of privileges granted or revoked as a group. Administrative authorities include system administration, database administration, database control, database maintenance, and system operation. Authorities are granted with a GRANT statement and revoked with a REVOKE statement. There are different forms of the GRANT and REVOKE statements for privileges associated with a table or view, an application plan, a database, the use of system resources, and system privileges. The DB2 catalog includes tables containing information on all authorizations that have been granted.

DB2 supports concurrent access to data through a system of resource locks that DB2 automatically acquires and releases. DB2 can place a lock on an entire table space or on one or more pages within a table space. Locks are held until a commit point is reached. A lock can be shared, allowing other users to access the locked data, or it can be exclusive. Various processing options affect lock size and duration.

PART **VI** IBM APPLICATION DEVELOPMENT
PRODUCTS

In this chapter and in Chapter 21, we describe two application development products complementary to DB2 that IBM has identified as strategic in its line of software products: Application System (AS) and Cross System Product (CSP). Application System is a fourth-generation language (4GL) that is intended for use by end users for query-and-reporting applications. Cross System Product is a 4GL that is intended primarily for use by professional application developers to develop traditional types of information system applications.

20 APPLICATION SYSTEM (AS)

Application System is a tool that many DB2 installations use to allow end users to enter queries and produce reports. The operation of AS is controlled by entering easy-to-use, English-like commands at a terminal. Many end users find AS easier to use than either the SQL or QBE capabilities of QMF. The ability to combine the powerful commands that AS supports in a variety of ways allows the end user to address a wide range of applications. The inexperienced user can interact with the system in a conversational manner to build up command sequences that can then be executed. AS provides the end user with the following facilities:

- Data management
- Query processing
- Report generation
- Business communications
- Project control
- Financial analysis
- Business planning
- Business graphics

The user communicates with AS by using a terminal to enter commands and to request screen displays. The information presented by AS in response to commands can take the form of a simple listing, a graphical display, or a formal report with a complex format. Color terminals are supported, and AS makes good use of color in formatting displays when this feature is available.

AS APPLICATIONS   The AS software provides the user with a variety of commands, such as SELECT (not the same as the SQL SELECT statement), SEQUENCE, and REPORT. The user can also enter DB2 queries using SQL statements as an alternative to the command language that AS itself supports. AS operations can be combined in various ways to develop query-and-reporting applications. A group of AS operations is known as a *procedure*. Procedures that are run regularly, perhaps by many different users, can be built up in advance, stored, and then initiated by a single terminal command whenever needed. AS also allows the end user to modify a stored procedure before running it. For example, a particular user may want to change a file or table name in the procedure, or some of the detailed processing steps may require modification for a particular application. AS allows these types of changes to be made without affecting other people's use of the procedure.

INTERACTIVE PROCESSING   In addition to working with predefined procedures, end users can also work with AS in an interactive manner to perform ad hoc query-and-reporting functions. In some cases a user may need to perform operations that will not be repeated, such as examining the contents of a unique file or table or producing a simple one-time report. In other cases a user might specify a process that cannot be rigidly defined in advance because the steps that must be performed are dependent on the results of the previous operations.

USING AS   After signing on to the system, AS responds with a sign-on message and requests our user code, as shown in Fig. 20.1. The user code is employed by AS to relate files of data to a particular user or project. The user code provides a basic level of security, since no one can gain access to an AS file without first knowing the user code of the person who created it.

When the user code is accepted, AS prompts us for further commands by displaying a question mark in the lower left-hand corner of the screen. The area following the question mark is called the *command area* and is generally the place where AS commands are entered. There are many times, however, when AS allows the entire screen to be used for data or commands.

OPERATING ENVIRONMENT   Versions of the AS product are available that operate in the MVS environment in conjunction with TSO and in the VM/CMS environment. Both versions of AS have their own file systems that allow AS files to be created, maintained,

252

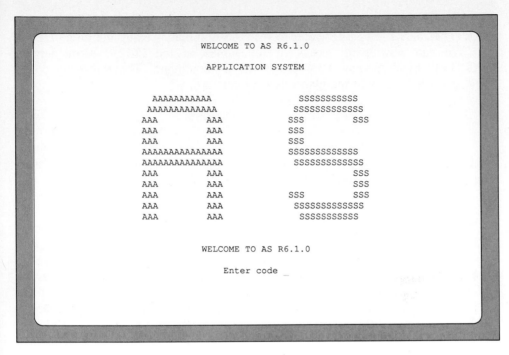

```
                    WELCOME TO AS R6.1.0

                    APPLICATION SYSTEM


        AAAAAAAAAAA                SSSSSSSSSSS
        AAAAAAAAAAAA               SSSSSSSSSSSSS
        AAA        AAA             SSS          SSS
        AAA        AAA             SSS
        AAA        AAA             SSS
        AAAAAAAAAAAAAA             SSSSSSSSSSSSS
        AAAAAAAAAAAAAA             SSSSSSSSSSSSS
        AAA        AAA                          SSS
        AAA        AAA                          SSS
        AAA        AAA             SSS          SSS
        AAA        AAA             SSSSSSSSSSSSS
        AAA        AAA             SSSSSSSSSSS


                    WELCOME TO AS R6.1.0

                       Enter code _
```

Figure 20.1   AS signon message.

and displayed. Both versions also allow VSAM and sequential files to be accessed. What is of more interest to us, however, is that the MVS version of AS allows access to DB2 tables and the VM version of AS allows access to SQL/DS tables as alternatives to other types of AS file access.

ACCESSING FILES AND TABLES

The IN command is used to identify the AS file or DB2 table we would like to access. The following IN command gives us access to an AS file named ASSETS:

```
IN ASSETS
```

To use AS to display and manipulate the information contained in DB2 tables, we must first issue an ATTACH command that gives AS access to the DB2 software. Here is an example of such an ATTACH statement:

```
ATTACH DB2,SYSTEM(MARTDB2)
```

This ATTACH command attaches AS to the DB2 system named MARTDB2 and allows us to refer to it in AS commands using the name DB2.

We can now gain access to the tables in the DB2 system named MARTDB2 by issuing an appropriate AS IN command. The following command gives us access to the *Quotations* table:

```
IN (DB2) QUOTATIONS
```

After executing the command, any subsequent commands that we enter will be applied against the *Quotations* table until we execute a command that creates an output file or table. We will have more to say about output later.

ENTERING SQL STATEMENTS

Once AS has been attached to a DB2 system, we can use SQL statements to formulate queries and to manipulate the data in DB2 tables. However, there is little advantage to an end user's employing AS for this purpose. In most cases, end users employ AS because its own command syntax is easier to learn than the syntax of SQL (although also less powerful). In the remainder of this chapter we will concentrate on the unique command language of AS.

THE AS COMMAND LANGUAGE

AS commands begin with keywords that have particular meanings to AS. AS allows us to use these same keywords in other contexts, such as for table or column names. In general, AS command keywords are straightforward and are easily remembered. Examples of a few AS command keywords are VIEW, SEQUENCE, and REPORT. As a shortcut, we can enter commands using only their first three characters, such as VIE, SEQ, and REP. The command examples in this chapter, however, show the command keywords spelled out.

Items that follow the command keyword, such as file names, table names, and column names, are separated from the command keyword and from one another using *separator* characters. An unusual characteristic of AS is that blanks do not constitute separator characters; the comma is used as the main separator character instead. This feature allows names to have blanks embedded in them for increased readability.

Numeric data is entered without using commas. For example, the number 99,999 must be entered as 99999. However, AS can display numeric information with the commas inserted in the appropriate places. Negative numbers are indicated with a preceding minus sign, and decimal values can be entered using a decimal point in the appropriate position. Alphanumeric data can consist of any of the characters that can be entered at the keyboard.

When AS detects an error, an appropriate error message is displayed on the terminal, and the cursor is placed at the point on the screen where the error was detected. This enables users to locate mistakes quickly and correct them. Most AS error messages are self-explanatory, but a full explanation of any message can be obtained by entering the ERROR command.

THE VIEW COMMAND

With the VIEW command, we can display any or all of the columns of a table in any desired order. For example, the following three commands request a complete display of the information contained in the *Quotations* table:

```
ATTACH DB2,SYSTEM(MARTDB2)
IN (DB2) QUOTATIONS
VIEW
```

As shown in Fig. 20.2, every row in the table is displayed, with its columns listed in the order in which they appear in the table. When the display fills more than one screen, we can browse backward and forward through the display by using the PF7 and PF8 keys.

In some cases we might need to restrict a display to specific columns, or we might want to change the order in which the columns are displayed. The

```
VIEW          QUOTATIONS                                   2 May 89 13:54
QUOSUPP  QUOPART   PRICE      TIME     ONORD
    51      124    1.25          5       400
    51      125    0.55          5         0
    51      134    0.40          5       500
    51      135    0.39          5      1000
    51      221    0.30         10     10000
    51      231    0.10         10      5000
    52      105    7.50         10       200
    52      205    0.15         20         0
    52      206    0.15         20         0
    53      124    1.35          3       500
    53      125    0.58          3       200
    53      134    0.38          3       200
    53      135    0.42          3      1000
    53      222    0.25         15     10000
    53      232      -          15         0
    53      241    0.08         15      6000




?  _
```

Figure 20.2   VIEW command display.

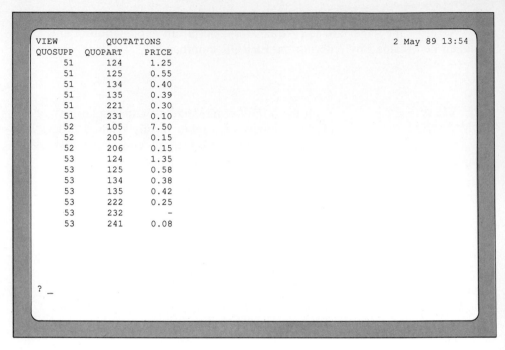

```
VIEW        QUOTATIONS                                    2 May 89 13:54
QUOSUPP   QUOPART     PRICE
      51      124      1.25
      51      125      0.55
      51      134      0.40
      51      135      0.39
      51      221      0.30
      51      231      0.10
      52      105      7.50
      52      205      0.15
      52      206      0.15
      53      124      1.35
      53      125      0.58
      53      134      0.38
      53      135      0.42
      53      222      0.25
      53      232        -
      53      241      0.08




  ? _
```

Figure 20.3   Viewing selected columns.

following command restricts the display to the three specified *Quotation* table columns:

```
VIEW QUOSUPP,QUOPART,PRICE
```

The display produced by this command is shown in Fig. 20.3. To display a number of consecutive columns, we need not list all their names; instead, we can specify the first and last columns in a *range* of columns. By separating these names with a colon, we indicate to AS that we want all columns between two specified columns to be displayed, as in the following example:

```
VIEW QUOSUPP:TIME
```

ARITHMETIC   We can also request that the results of calculations be
EXPRESSIONS   displayed. For example, we might want to multiply
                        the *Price* and *Onord* data items to produce a total.
This can be done using the following command:

```
VIEW QUOSUPP,QUOPART,PRICE,ONORD,PRICE*ONORD
```

Arithmetic expressions can be as complex as necessary and can be combined with requests for the display of individual data item contents. Box 20.1

BOX 20.1   Arithmetic expression operators

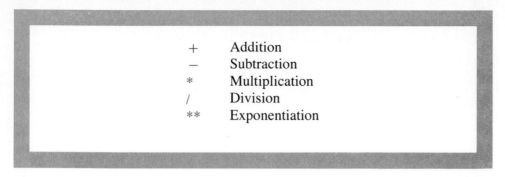

+	Addition
−	Subtraction
*	Multiplication
/	Division
**	Exponentiation

shows the operators that can be used in created arithmetic expressions. Operations are carried out from left to right in the ordinary order of exponentiation, followed by multiplication and division, followed by addition and subtraction. Parentheses can be included in arithmetic expressions to clarify the expression or to change the order in which calculations are to be carried out.

STATEMENT CONTINUATION

The following command shows how the previous VIEW command can be specified using two lines rather than one:

```
VIEW QUOSUPP,QUOPART,PRICE,ONORD,;
     PRICE*ONORD
```

An AS command can occupy as many lines as desired. A semicolon is entered at the end of a line to indicate that the next line is a continuation of the same command.

REPORT GENERATION

The listings produced by the VIEW command provide quick and easy access to file and table contents. However, more formal reports can also be requested that use specially formatted detail lines and include totals and subtotals. The AS REPORT language is used to request formal reports. The AS REPORT language provides a conversational facility that leads the user through the report specification process. Figure 20.4 shows an example of the screen displayed during a report generation session. This session generates a *REPORT language specification* that when executed produces the desired report. The language specification is stored in a system-generated file, known as a *REPORT language file*, which can be kept for future use if required. Figure 20.5 shows an example of the screen displayed by this REPORT language file.

```
APPLICATION SYSTEM                                        27 Apr 89   09:15

AS Conversational Report

Enter display title.
Value of Capital Assets
Which fields do you want displayed?
department,description,purchase cost,purchase date,replacement cost,
date(purchase date+expected life*10000)
Which field(s) should control sub-totaling ?
department
Enter the column heading for date(purchase date+expected life*10000)
Date
Do you want subtotals only ?
no
Generating specifications.

OUT    38  Lines   - Lang File #BATC001



? RUN 1
Press ENTER to execute specifications, or give next command.
```

Figure 20.4   Conversational report generation.

```
Page     1                 VALUE OF CAPITAL ASSETS            27 May 89   13:56

                           Purchase  Purchase Replacement Expected
         Dept  Asset           Cost      Date      Cost     Life

          21  CALCULATOR      $23.75  1 Jun 85    $15.00     1
              TYPEWRITER     $674.00 31 Oct 84   $811.00     3
              CALCULATOR     $115.75  1 Jul 85    $99.55     1
                            ----------           -----------
          21                 $813.50             $925.55

          22  CALCULATOR   $7,358.18 14 Sep 84 $9,750.00     3
              TYPEWRITER     $612.73  6 Oct 85   $712.45     3
              COMPANY CAR  $2,974.55 14 Sep 83 $3,790.00     3
              CALCULATOR     $127.32  1 Jun 84    $95.00     1
              DICTATING UNIT $116.00 16 Sep 85   $203.00     1
                            ----------           -----------
          22              $11,188.78           $14,550.45

                            ==========           ===========
                         $12,002.28           $15,476.00
                            ==========           ===========
```

Figure 20.5   A typical AS report.

VIEWING SELECTED ROWS

AS allows us to use the SELECT command (again, this is not the same as the SQL SELECT statement) followed by VIEW to select a subset of the rows in a table. Suppose that we were interested only in the rows for supplier *51* in the *Quotations* table. The following commands would allow us to view only the specified columns for the supplier *51* rows:

```
IN (DB2) QUOTATIONS
SELECT QUOSUPP=51
VIEW QUOSUPP,QUOPART,PRICE,ONORD
```

As in this example, the selection criteria specified in a SELECT command take the form of a *logical expression* that defines a test to be applied against the contents of each row in the active table.

LOGICAL EXPRESSIONS

Logical expressions are used to compare two values. Either value can be a constant, the contents of a data item, or the results of an arithmetic expression. The allowable logical expression operators are listed in Box 20.2. The semicolon and colon separators can be used in logical expressions to specify a *series* or *range* of values. For example, semicolons can be used to define a series of values on the right side of a logical expression. The following SELECT command selects all rows whose part numbers are *124, 125,* or *134*:

```
SELECT QUOPART=124;125;134
```

Similarly, we can use a colon to specify a range of values. The following SELECT command selects rows whose part numbers are between *124* and *134* (including part numbers *124* and *134*):

```
SELECT QUOPART=124:134
```

As shown in Box 20.2, the allowable operators in logical expressions include the & (and) and │ (or) operators, which can be used to create complex expressions. The following SELECT command selects rows for part numbers that are less than *124* and greater than *205:*

```
SELECT QUOPART < 124 | QUOPART > 205
```

The featured SELECT commands all use numeric literals; logical expressions can also specify alphanumeric literals. Alphanumeric literals consist of

BOX 20.2.   Logical expression operators

=	Equal to
<>	Not equal to
>	Greater than
<	Less than
>=	Greater than or equal to
<=	Less than or equal to
&	AND
|	OR

character strings enclosed in single quotation marks. Here are three examples of SELECT commands that use alphanumeric literals:

```
SELECT NAME='SMITH JOHN'
SELECT DEPT='PURCHASING'
SELECT PART='PQO NO>10256/431/K'
```

Alphanumeric literals can contain any of the characters that can be generated by the terminal and can be up to 250 characters in length.

CANCELING A SELECTION

Once we issue a SELECT command, the selection criterion specified in that command remains in effect for subsequent retrieval commands, such as VIEW or PLOT. We can change the selection criterion whenever we like by issuing a new SELECT command, or we can cancel the effect of the previous SELECT command by issuing the CANCEL command, as follows:

```
CANCEL SELECT
```

AS OUTPUT FILES AND TABLES

Many AS processes, such as VIEW and PLOT, simply retrieve information from the input file or table named in an IN command without changing the data in that file or table. Other AS processes operate on the data and change it in some way. An example is the SEQUENCE command, which sorts rows into a different sequence. In most cases an AS process that changes the data in an input file or table does not modify the data contained in the input file or table. Instead, AS creates an output file that contains a copy of the input modified in the specified way. We can give an explicit name to an AS output file in a similar manner to the way we name an input file. For example, the following command specifies that the name of the output file for subsequent processes is an AS file named OUTFILE:

```
OUT OUTFILE
```

An output file explicitly created with an OUT command is considered a *permanent* file and is kept after the session ends. Output files created in this way are kept until we explicitly delete them (subject, of course, to individual installation cleanup procedures). We can delete an output file that we create by issuing a PURGE command, as in the following example:

```
PURGE OUTFILE
```

Instead of placing output into an AS file, output can be placed into a new DB2 table if desired. The table name is specified in an OUT command that also references the name we assigned to the DB2 system in a previous ATTACH command:

```
OUT (DB2) NEWTABLE
```

If we issue an AS command that requires an output file and we have not explicitly created one using an OUT command, AS automatically creates a *system-generated file*. System-generated files are temporary and are automatically deleted at the end of the AS session. Each system-generated file is given a name constructed from our AS user code and a unique three-digit number. This name is displayed at the time the system-generated file is created, and we can refer to a system-generated file by its full name or by its serial number alone. For example, if our user code is MART, the first system-generated file in a session will be named MART001. We can refer to it either by the name MART001 or simply as 1.

When we issue a command that invokes a process that does not require an output file, the current input file or table remains the input for any subsequent commands. If, however, a command creates an output file, that output file automatically becomes the input file for any subsequent process. If we then create yet another output file, that file becomes the input to the next process, and so on. The automatic creation of output files can be illustrated by the SEQUENCE command.

SORTING

In earlier examples, we viewed rows in the order in which they are stored in the table. To change the order in which rows are retrieved from a table, we can issue the SEQUENCE command. For example, the following set of commands displays the selected rows in sequence by part number:

```
IN (DB2) QUOTATIONS
SELECT PRICE<.30
SEQUENCE QUOPART
VIEW QUOSUPP,QUOPART,PRICE
```

Since we did not issue an OUT command, the SEQUENCE command in this example causes a system-generated file to be created. It contains the rows selected from the *Quotations* table based on the selection criterion specified in the SELECT command. The selected rows are sorted into ascending sequence based on *Quopart* values. Now, unless we issue a new IN command, all subsequent commands that are issued will apply to the system-generated file that contains the result of the selection and sequencing operation.

A SEQUENCE command can request that a file or table be sorted on more than one column. If multiple columns are specified, the first column is considered the major sort field, and the last the minor one. In the following example, rows are sorted first by supplier number and then by part number within supplier number:

```
SEQUENCE QUOSUPP,QUOPART
```

Sorting is performed in ascending sequence unless otherwise specified. To sort on a column in descending sequence, the column name is preceded by a minus sign. In the following example, rows are sorted in ascending sequence by part number and in descending sequence by price within part number:

```
SEQUENCE QUOPART,-PRICE
```

BUSINESS GRAPHICS

As mentioned earlier, the data contained in AS files or DB2 tables can also be displayed using graphical techniques. AS provides particularly powerful facilities for producing charts and graphs of various types using the data contained in DB2 tables or AS files. AS implements two approaches to obtaining graphical displays. First, there are a number of commands, such as PLOT and HISTOGRAM, that produce graphs automatically. The scaling and labeling of axes and titles are all prepared automatically. The second approach is to use the GRAPH language to produce a customized plot. We will show examples of the PLOT and HISTOGRAM commands using a sales table.

THE PLOT COMMAND

With the PLOT command, we can request that one or more sets of data item values be plotted against another set of data item values. Each set of values can be derived from a data item in a table or from an arithmetic expression. The following is a simple example of a PLOT command sequence:

```
IN (DB2) SALES
PLOT SALES,MONTH
```

Figure 20.6 shows an example of the display produced by this PLOT command. The first columns specified in the PLOT command occupy the vertical axis, and the last column listed occupies the horizontal axis. If a color terminal is being used, appropriate colors are automatically added to enhance the displayed chart.

The next example plots both *Sales* and *Expsales* data item values against *Month*.

```
PLOT SALES;EXPSALES,MONTH
```

In this command, the semicolon is used as a separator character to indicate that a *series* of multiple items is to be plotted against *Month*.

The next example plots the result of the values obtained for the *Sales*Price* arithmetic expression against the set of values for *Month·*

```
PLOT SALES*PRICE,MONTH
```

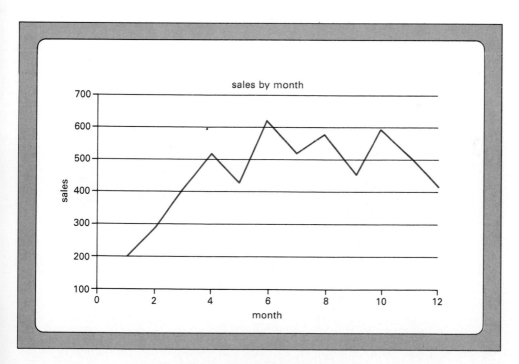

Figure 20.6   Output of PLOT command.

THE HISTOGRAM COMMAND

The HISTOGRAM command can be used to produce a bar chart. A column is displayed for each different value of the horizontal-axis variable, provided that there are few enough to fit across the screen. If not, each column covers a range of values for the horizontal variable. The height of a column represents the *total* of all values of the horizontal variable that qualify for that column. We can alternatively request that the *average* value be displayed. Using the *Sales* table, we could plot the sales for each month as a separate column. If any month had more than one sales figure, the column would reflect the *total* sales value for that month. This is the command to produce the required bar chart:

HISTOGRAM SALES,MONTH

Figure 20.7 shows an example of the output produced by this HISTO-GRAM command. Again, color is automatically used, if it is available on the terminal, to increase readability and attractiveness.

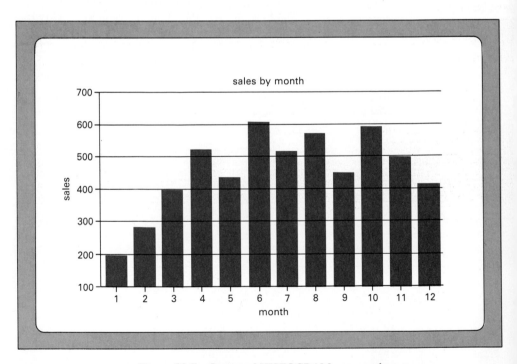

Figure 20.7 Output of HISTOGRAM command.

Examples of other types of charts that can be produced using AS are shown in Figs. 20.8 through 20.11. AS can produce the following types of charts and graphs:

- Tower charts that display data in the form of towers that appear to be three-dimensional
- Maps that are colored and shaded to compare values
- Radar charts
- Pie charts
- Bar charts
- Scatter diagrams
- Surface charts that show data in the form of overlapping surfaces
- Histograms that can include overlapping bars
- PERT charts
- Mixed charts that might include curves and bars on a single screen

AS LANGUAGES

As AS commands are entered and executed, AS stores them in a system-defined *log file* that is given a name consisting of the # character, followed by our AS user code, followed by the characters AS. An example might be #MARTAS. Each time we log on to the system, this file is rewritten and any commands entered into the language

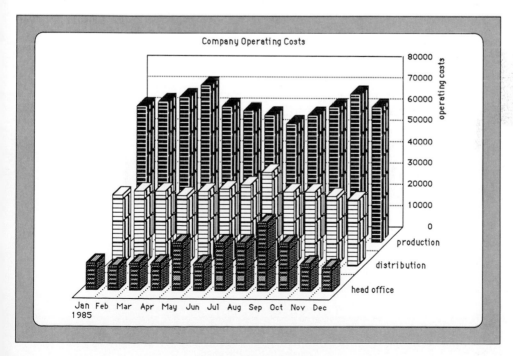

Figure 20.8   Tower chart.

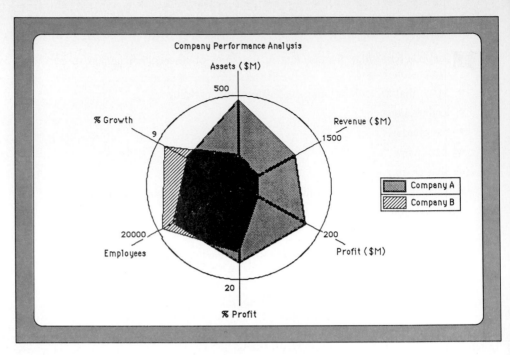

Figure 20.9   Radar chart.

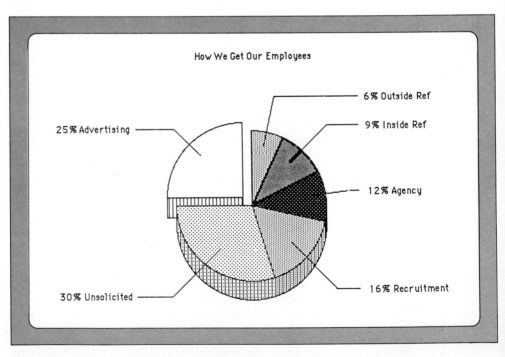

Figure 20.10   Pie chart.

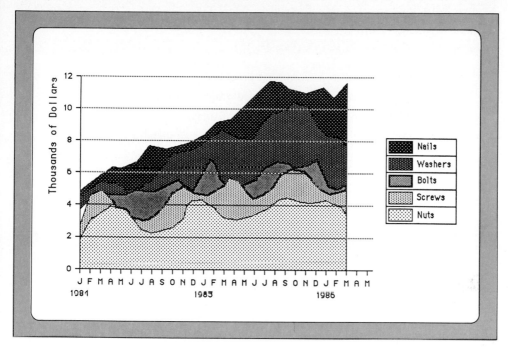

Figure 20.11   Surface chart.

file previously are lost. If we want to retain the contents of the language file that AS automatically creates, we can do so by copying them into an output file that we define. The log file is an example of an AS *language file*. AS provides a variety of languages that can be used to create language files to be executed. We have already briefly introduced the REPORT and GRAPH languages. Box 20.3 lists some of the available AS languages.

The statements of all AS languages are stored in language files that are similar to the log file just discussed. Each statement in a language file has a number that is unique within the file. Figure 20.12 shows an example of a procedure built using the PROCEDURE language. AS provides many facilities that can be used to work with language files and to perform such functions as deleting, copying, and moving statements within the file. After storing a series of commands in a language file, we can either execute the commands immediately or execute the statements at a later time. To gain access to a particular language processor, we enter the language name. For example, to access the PROCEDURE language, we enter the PROCEDURE command.

All AS languages have a *syntax checker* that examines each statement as it is entered to ensure that the statement conforms to the syntax rules of that language. If any syntax rules are violated, appropriate error messages are displayed, and the statement is rejected.

BOX 20.3 AS languages

- **COMPOSE.** Used to perform text processing functions.
- **GRAPH.** Used to produce customized graphical displays.
- **IMAGE.** Used to create custom screen displays.
- **MODEL.** Used for creating business planning applications.
- **PROCEDURE.** Used to build up sets of AS commands called *procedures* that are executed as a unit to perform unified AS applications.
- **REPORT.** Used to generate all types of tabular reports.
- **TABULATE.** Used to create data analysis applications.

```
_PROCEDURE repproc,repproc        Origin 1000        15 Lines in range 1000:1140
screen lower                                                             01000
terminal newline(_)                                                      01010
in machine                                                               01020
run machrep                                                              01030
in parts,movements                                                       01040
match                                                                    01050
run partrep                                                              01060
cancel                                                                   01070
run option                                                               01080
run optrep                                                               01090
in optprice                                                              01110
run trend                                                                01120
in assets                                                                01130
select department=22;23                                                  01140
run assrep                                                               01150
                                                                         01160
—                                                                        01170
                                                                         01180
                                                                         01190
                                                                         01200
                                                                         01210
                                                                         01220

P?
```

Figure 20.12 PROCEDURE language statements.

A comprehensive set of maintenance commands is provided for working with the statements in any type of language file that enable us to examine and change statements. Among these are the following:

ALTER	EXTRACT	LIST
DELETE	FIND	MOVE
DUPLICATE	GET	RENUMBER

When using AS, a special screen layout is provided for the entry of language statements. Line numbers are automatically displayed down the right side, and the rest of the display is available for the entry of statements. *Local commands* are available for operation on the statements during language entry. The scope of their effect is usually limited to statements currently being displayed. Local commands allow us to delete, insert, and move language statements in any desired way.

If we want to display an existing language file to list its contents or to make changes to it, we can include its name on the command that invokes the language used to create the language file, as in the following example:

```
PROCEDURE ACCOUNTS
```

If we then make changes to our language specifications, AS allocates a system-generated file to hold the new version of the language file. If we want the new file to be placed in a file of our own, we give the new name as well as the existing name, as in the following example:

```
PROCEDURE ACCOUNTS,NEWACCT
```

We can cause AS to replace the old version of the language file with the new version by using the same name in both places, as follows:

```
PROCEDURE ACCOUNTS,ACCOUNTS
```

To create a new language file, we can code an asterisk in place of the input file name, as in the following example:

```
PROCEDURE *,ACCOUNTS
```

After we have finished working with a language file, we can enter the END command to request AS to store the file for future use. Before we enter the END command, however, we can enter RUN to cause AS to execute the commands in the active language file. To execute the commands in a language file that has been previously stored, we include the name of the language file on the RUN command, as in the following example:

```
RUN ACCOUNTS
```

THE PROCEDURE LANGUAGE As we mentioned earlier, procedures are sets of any of the commands that can be entered at the terminal during a normal AS session. These include commands such as IN, SEQUENCE, SELECT, and VIEW. AS procedures cannot contain language statements for other AS languages, such as the REPORT or MODEL languages. However, a procedure can contain statements that execute complete language specifications written in any of the AS languages, including other procedures written using the PROCEDURE language.

The POINT parameter of the RUN command allows us to request that a procedure be executed from a line other than the first or that only a block of selected lines from within the procedure be executed. For example, the following command executes statements 1035 through 1078 in a language file called DEPTS:

```
RUN DEPTS,POINT=1035:1078
```

REFERENCES

1. Application System Introduction, User Guide, Order Number SC34-2209, IBM Corporation, P.O. Box 30021, Tampa, FL 33630.

2. Application System, General Reference Manual, Order Number SC34-2210, IBM Corporation, P.O. Box 30021, Tampa, FL 33630.

21 CROSS SYSTEM PRODUCT (CSP)

IBM's *Cross System Product Set* is a family of products, designed for use by professional application developers, that supports application definition, testing, generation, and execution across a variety of computing system and operating system environments. Figure 21.1 illustrates the various components of the Cross System Product set. The following are brief descriptions of each of the individual modules that make up the CSP family of products:

- **CSP/Application Development (CSP/AD).** CSP/AD is an interactive application generator that runs on IBM and IBM-compatible mainframes in the CICS/VS, SSX/VSE, VM/SP CMS, and MVS/TSO environments. CSP/AD can be used to build applications for IBM and IBM-compatible mainframes, for IBM and IBM-compatible personal computers, and for the 8100 line of computing systems. A version of CSP/AD is also available that runs on the 8100 under the control of DPPX/SP and builds applications for the 8100. CSP/AD can be used to create applications that access DB2 databases.

- **CSP/Application Execution (CSP/AE).** CSP/AE controls the execution of applications developed using CSP/AD. Applications developed in one environment can be run in another environment under the control of CSP/AE. For example, an application developer could create applications in the MVS/TSO environment for execution in the CICS/VS, SSX/VSE, or VM/SP CMS environments. A version of CSP/AE is available that takes applications developed using CSP/AD on either a mainframe or an 8100 and runs them on the 8100.

- **CSP/Query.** CSP/Query supports online access to VSAM and CMS files using IBM's Structured Query Language (SQL). CSP/Query cannot be used to access DB2 tables. File access is provided using file definitions from CSP/AD. The results of a query can be displayed or reported in the form of tables or graphs. CSP/Query runs in the CICS/VS, SSX/VSE, and VM/SP CMS environments.

- **CSP/EZ-PREP and CSP/EZ-RUN.** These modules are used to prepare and run on an IBM or IBM-compatible personal computer applications defined using CSP/AD.

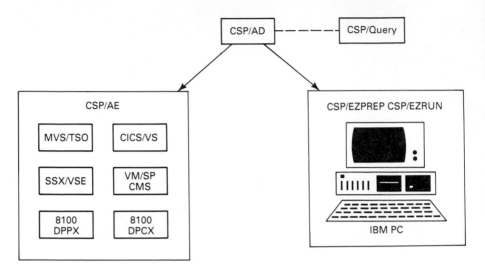

Figure 21.1   CSP components.

CSP/AD

CSP/AD is a single tool that combines the functions of an editor, design aid, data dictionary, screen definition facility, high-level language processor, prototyping tool, and online debugging facility. Since this is the CSP module that application developers use in creating and maintaining CSP applications that access DB2 databases, CSP/AD is the subject of most of this chapter.

CSP/AD supports interactive application development at a display terminal. The CSP/AD menus encourage the application developer to think of the application in terms of the following:

- Maps
- Records
- Processes

MAPS

Maps define the screen or printer formats that the user of the application interfaces with. CSP/AD allows the application developer to enter maps that define screen and report formats exactly as they will appear in the production environment. The application developer is able to select validation and edit checks using a simple fill-in-the-blanks technique. CSP/AD supports a wide variety of terminal types, including color terminals, and provides control over all terminal attributes.

RECORDS

Records store the data created or accessed by the application. A record definition for describing DB2 data consists of column definitions from one or more DB2 tables. Data definitions can be entered quickly and easily using menus and prompts. Once a record is defined, it can be used in any CSP application without requiring redefinition. Records can be stored in either file or database form using the following data management systems:

- Sequential access method
- VSAM
- CMS
- DL/I
- DB2
- SQL/DS

PROCESSES

CSP applications are designed around nine building blocks called *processes* that define the logic steps that display maps and access records. The flow of control between processes is specified using a high-level procedural language that supports data movement, calculations, conditional processing, loops, and calls.

The following is a list of available CSP/AD processes; the functions of the nine processes are described later in this chapter.

- ADD
- DELETE
- INQUIRY
- UPDATE
- REPLACE
- SCAN
- DISPLAY
- CONVERSE
- EXECUTE

A CSP application is divided into sections, each of which executes a single task or input/output operation.

EASE OF USE A CSP/AD application developer defines applications at a display terminal by selecting options and filling in requested information in formatted fields. Default data is often assumed for many fields and options. Definitions are syntax-checked when entered, and definitions are not accepted by CSP/AD unless they are in the correct format. The application developer uses the terminal's PF keys to obtain help screens that describe the current menu or message. CSP/AD automatically performs many functions that the application developer would have to supply program code for if using a conventional programming language, such as COBOL.

ONLINE PROTOTYPING AND TESTING CSP/AD includes a *test* facility that executes an application directly from the source definition without waiting for a separate compilation or application generation run. A test can be initiated at any time, even before the application is completely defined. The test terminates with an error message the first time an error is detected. The application developer can also request that the validity of an application definition be checked before starting a test.

Online testing makes CSP/AD a powerful prototyping tool. Maps can be defined and displayed to end users before the detailed logic of the application is in place. Maps can be changed online and redisplayed to the user without waiting for batch compilations.

Once application definition is complete, online testing is a powerful productivity tool. Test runs can be executed quickly and fixes applied immediately. Online tracing facilities are also available that shorten the time required to debug an application.

USING CSP We will next show how CSP/AD can be used by an application developer to develop a CSP/AD application. In using CSP/AD, the application developer uses the CSP/AD *definition* facility to define objects called *members* in a CSP/AD file called the *Member Specification Library* (MSL).

When an application and its associated members have been defined, the application developer uses the CSP/AD test facility to test the application or to demonstrate it to an end user. When the application works correctly, the application developer puts the completed application through the CSP/AD *generation* facility to prepare the application for use in a production environment under the control of CSP/AE. CSP/AD also provides the application developer with the following facilities that help to increase application development productivity:

- **List Processor.** Used to maintain the members in the MSL.
- **Utilities.** Perform a variety of operations on the members in the MSL.
- **File Maintenance Facility.** Used to initialize VSAM files for testing.
- **Tutorial Facility.** Used for training by beginning CSP/AD application developers.

CSP/AD MENUS

Figure 21.2 shows an example of a CSP/AD menu. All CSP/AD menus have a similar format. At the top of the menu is a title line, a message line, a command line, one or more information lines, and an input area. The input area is formatted in either of two ways, depending on the functions supported by the menu:

- As a prompt area, with one or more fields to be filled in.
- As a line-edit area in which the application developer enters information in the form of lines in a table. The first field in each line is a command field; the remaining fields in a line vary with the function being performed.

```
EZEM23                         MAP DEFINITION

==>
          ENTER = Edit changes (or go to next field)    PF3 = Exit
                      Map Name = TEST MAP
   NORMAL,DARK,BRIGHT      => BRIGHT     NODETECT,DETECT           => NODETECT
   UNPROTECT,PROTECT,ASKIP => UNPROTECT  NOHILITE,BLINK,
   ALPHA,NUMERIC           => NUMERIC    RVIDEO,USCORE             => USCORE
   NOCURSOR,CURSOR         => CURSOR     NOMDT,MDT                 => NOMDT
   NOENTER,ENTER           => NOENTER    MONO,BLUE,RED,TURQUOISE,
   NOFILL,FILL             => NOFILL     PINK,GREEN,YELLOW,WHITE   => TURQUOISE

Total Positions 080                              Positions 001 to 080
Total Lines     024 .................................... Lines    001 to 017


                     Part Number = > *****

                     Supplier    = >
```

Figure 21.2   Map Definition menu.

TERMINAL PF KEYS

Program function (PF) keys on the terminal provide standard functions that can be invoked with a single keystroke. The following are commonly used PF key functions:

- **ENTER.** Used to process current inputs.
- **PF1.** Invokes a help function.
- **PF3.** Used to exit the current function.
- **PF7.** Used to scroll back in the line-edit area.
- **PF8.** Used to scroll forward in the line-edit area.
- **PA2.** Used to cancel the current function.

Pressing the help key (PF1) displays a screen that describes the function of the current menu. If a message is currently displayed in the message line, the help screen provides further descriptive information about the message rather than information about the menu.

All CSP/AD menus display a command line that can be used for the entry of mnemonic commands. However, in actual practice, the menu command line is rarely used. Most menu commands duplicate functions that can be performed by using terminal PF keys.

Line-edit commands entered in the line command field let the application developer insert, repeat, copy, move, or delete lines in the line-edit area of a menu.

APPLICATION DEFINITION FACILITY

As mentioned earlier, the CSP/AD application developer thinks in terms of *maps* that describe the screens and printouts seen by the end user of the application, *records* (or rows of DB2 tables) in which the application data is stored, and application logic that uses *processes* to display maps and process records.

The application definition facility lets the application developer define members in the MSL that describe the screens, records, and processing logic in an application. The functions performed by MSL members can be divided into three categories. Each category of function is supported by multiple MSL member types. Here is a summary of the MSL member functions:

- **Data Definition.** Supported by the MSL member types *Record, Table, Data Item,* and *DL/I Program Specification Blocks* (PSBs).
- **Map Definition.** Supported by the MSL member types *Map* and *Map Group.*
- **Application Definition.** Supported by the MSL member types *Application, Process,* and *Statement Group.*

DATA DEFINITION   Data definition is normally done directly by the CSP/ AD application developer. However, in the database environment, data definition is often performed by the database administration (DBA) group. Data definition begins by displaying a Definition menu, an example of which is shown in Fig. 21.3. In the Definition menu, we enter the name of the record we wish to define, in this case PART, and select the Record option. This causes the Record Definition menu to be displayed, as shown in Fig. 21.4. To define a record that describes one or more DB2 tables, we list the DB2 table or tables from which the *Part* record should be derived, in this case from the *Inventory* and *Quotations* tables. We then select the SQL Row option. This causes the SQL Row Definition menu to be displayed next (See Fig. 21.5). Notice that all the columns from the *Inventory* and *Quotations* tables are displayed in this menu. We can now edit information in the SQL Row Definition menu. For example, the names under the *Name* column are initially set to the same values as their corresponding table column names; we can change these if we like. In this case, we have changed the *Invpart* column name to *Partnum*. Also, we can enter the "d" line editor command in the first position of each line that we do not want included in the record definition. In the example, we are deleting the *Onhand, Quopart,* and *Onord* columns from the *Part* record.

```
 EZEM10                        DEFINITION

 ==>
                    ENTER = Continue   PF3 = Exit

 .................... DEFINITION SELECTION ...........................


         Enter name to define or review  => PART

         Enter number of new member type => 1

                  1  Record
                  2  Table
                  3  Map (Mapgroup Mapname)
                  4  Data Item
                  5  Application
                  6  Process
                  7  Statement Group
                  8  PSB (DL/I Program Specification Block)
```

Figure 21.3 Definition menu.

```
EZEM11                     RECORD DEFINITION
EZE00087I New definition being created
==>
               PF3 = Exit  (or continue if new definition)
                        Record Name = PART
.................... RECORD SPECIFICATION .............................

  Organization  => 7
   1  Indexed
   2  Relative
   3  Serial                Default Key Item        =>
   4  Working Storage
   5  Redefined Record
   6  DL/I Segment
   7  SQL Row               Alternate Specification for =>

 ....Total Lines 00003  ..SQL Table Name(s)..................................
    CREATOR ID:       TABLE NAME      TABLE LABEL:
 ***                  TOP OF LIST
 001 martin           inventory       T1
 002 martin           quotations      T2
 ***                  END OF LIST
```

Figure 21.4 Record Definition menu.

```
EZEM15                        SQL ROW DEFINITION

==>
   PF3 = Exit   PF4 = SQL Compare   PF10 = Scroll Left   PF11 = Scroll Right
                        Record Name = PART
 Total lines 0008 ........ DATA ITEM DEFINITION ..............................

 *** NAME       TYPE   LENGTH DEC BYTES  READ SQL COLUMN NAME
 ***                                     ONLY
 ***                       TOP OF LIST
 001 PARTNUM    BIN    00004      00002  YES  T1.INVPART
 002 PNAME      CHA    00015      00015  YES  T1.PNAME
 d03 ONHAND     BIN    00004      00002  YES  T1.ONHAND
 004 QUOSUPP    BIN    00004      00002  YES  T2.QUOSUPP
 d05 QUOPART    BIN    00004      00002  YES  T2.QUOPART
 006 PRICE      BIN    00004      00002  YES  T2.PRICE
 007 TIME       BIN    00004      00002  YES  T2.TIME
 d08 ONORD      BIN    00004      00002  YES  T2.ONORD
 ***                       END OF LIST
```

Figure 21.5 SQL Row Definition menu.

```
EZEM16                 SQL ROW RECORD DEFINITION
EZE006421 SQL syntax check has completed successfully
==>
 PF3 = File and exit PF4 = Reset to default statement PF5 = SQL syntax check
 Record Name = PART
                                        Modified clause = YES
Total lines 0009 .... DEFAULT SELECTION CONDITIONS DEFINITION ...............

 ***                    TOP OF LIST
 *** SELECT
 ***    T1.INVPART, T1.PNAME,
 ***    T2.QUOSUPP, T2.PRICE, T2.TIME
 *** FROM
 ***    martin.inventory T1,
 ***    martin.quotations T2
 *** WHERE
 010    t1.invpart = t2.quopart
 ***                    END OF LIST
```

Figure 21.6   SQL Row Record Definition menu.

The next step is to define the SQL SELECT statement that CSP will use in deriving the *Part* record from the *Inventory* and *Quotations* tables. This is done using the SQL Row Record Definition menu, as shown in Fig. 21.6, which is displayed next. CSP/AD generates a suggested SELECT statement for us. In this case, CSP/AD supplied the appropriate SELECT and FROM clauses for us. We must supply the WHERE clause, however, since we will be joining the *Inventory* and *Quotations* tables on part number values to construct the *Part* record.

MAP DEFINITION

The maps in an application are defined in an MSL member set called a *map group*. The application developer "paints" each map directly on the terminal screen by entering the layout of map as it should appear to the end user. The application developer designates the beginning and end of each variable field on the screen using character codes. (A variable field is a field on the screen into which the terminal operator enters a value after the map is displayed.)

Once the map is laid out, CSP/AD uses menus to prompt the application developer for the following:

- Information about the types of devices on which the map will be displayed
- Names of the record fields that will be displayed in the various variable fields in the map
- Descriptions of editing characteristics for each variable field
- Display attributes for each variable field, including input protection, highlighting, and color

The editing characteristics can include tests to be applied to the data entered in each variable field. When the terminal operator running the application enters invalid data (data that does not pass the tests defined for the field), CSP/AE redisplays the map with an appropriate error message and prompts the user to correct the input.

Editing characteristics that can be specified for a variable field include these:

- Data type (character or numeric)
- Justification (left, right, or none)
- Fill character
- Upper-case translation
- Required input field
- Minimum input length

Additional editing characteristics that can be specified for numeric fields include these:

- Decimal places
- Sign (leading, trailing, or none)
- Display of leading zeros
- Numeric separator
- Currency symbol
- Date format
- Minimum value
- Maximum value

If the edit tests that CSP/AD makes available are not sufficient, the application developer can define an edit table or edit subroutine to perform additional

checking. An edit table contains lists or ranges of valid values. An edit subroutine consists of a set of statements coded in the CSP/AD high-level procedural
language that makes the additional checks required for the field.

APPLICATION DEFINITION

As mentioned earlier, during application definition,
the application developer defines *applications, processes,* and *statement groups.* An application consists
of a set of processes along with statements that define the flow of control between processes. The Application Definition menu, shown in Fig. 21.7, illustrates the set of processes defined for a sample application.

As mentioned earlier, a CSP/AD application consists of a set of processes.
A process generally performs a single basic input or output operation. The Application Process List menu is used to define the following for each process:

- **Process Name.** The name assigned to the process.
- **Process Option.** The function performed by the process.
- **Process Object.** The map or record accessed by the process.

```
 EZEM12                    APPLICATION DEFINITION

 ==>
             ENTER = File and continue    PF3 = File and exit
            PF4 = Display application structure
                        Application Name = NEWORDER
 Select definition:   S = P+F+L   P = Processing    F = Flow    E = Edit Object
                      O = Object Selection          L = Structure list

 Total Lines 0005 ...... APPLICATION PROCESS LIST ...........................

 SEL  PROCESS    OPTION      OBJECT      ERROR      DESCRIPTION
 ***                  TOP OF LIST
 001  NEOORD10   CONVERSE    MORDER      EZERTN     User enters order info
 002  NEOORD20   UPDATE      PRODUCT     NEIOER     Read product record
 003  NEOORD30   REPLACE     PRODUCT     NEIOER     Write back change record
 003  NEOORD40   ADD         ORDER       NEIOER     Write new order record
 003  NEOORD50   CONVERSE    MORDER      EZERTN     Display order updated msg
 ***                  END OF LIST
```

Figure 21.7 Application Definition menu.

- **Error Routine.** A subroutine called when an error occurs in accessing the process object.
- **Process Description.** A description of the function performed by the process.

CSP/AE modules use standard parameter list linkage conventions when an application is invoked or when it calls another application. This means that CSP/AD applications can be linked together with programs written in conventional languages, such as COBOL, PL/I, or Assembler.

PROCESS TYPES

As indicated earlier, nine different processes can be used in a CSP/AD application. The ADD, DELETE, INQUIRY, UPDATE, REPLACE, and SCAN processes have records as their objects; the DISPLAY and CONVERSE processes have maps as their objects; and the EXECUTE process has no object. Here are brief descriptions of the functions performed by each of the nine process types:

- **ADD.** Used to create a new record occurrence in a file or database.
- **DELETE.** Used to erase a record.
- **INQUIRY.** Used to read a record.
- **UPDATE.** Used to read a record for subsequent updating.
- **REPLACE.** Used to write out a new version of an existing record.
- **SCAN.** Used to read the next sequential record during sequential retrieval.
- **DISPLAY.** Used to display a map on a terminal or printer. The DISPLAY process does not wait for input from the terminal operator.
- **CONVERSE.** Also used to display a map on a screen. After displaying the map, the CONVERSE process waits for input and then reads and verifies the data entered by the terminal operator.
- **EXECUTE.** Used to execute a set of statements coded in the CSP/AD high-level procedural language.

For each process, the application developer can use a menu to specify CSP/AD processing statements to be executed before or after the process is executed. The CSP/AD programming language supports data movement, calculations, conditional processing, loops, calls to other statement groups (subroutines), and calls to programs written in conventional programming languages.

Each process definition is stored with its processing statements as a member in the MSL. The application developer can reuse a process defined in another application by entering the process name in the application process list.

The application developer uses another menu to enter flow statements that define the branching logic to be executed after a process completes. The flow statements determine the order in which the processes are executed. The default flow is to proceed sequentially to the next process on the process list.

STATEMENT GROUPS

A statement group is a sequence of CSP/AD processing statements to be executed as a subroutine. A statement group can be

- Invoked directly
- Named as an input edit routine for a map field
- Named as an error exit for a process

A statement group is an MSL member and can be used by any number of CSP/AD applications.

TEST FACILITY

As introduced earlier, CSP/AD supports a comprehensive test facility that can be used in debugging and to support fast prototyping of applications. The CSP/AD test facility can be used in three ways:

- **Preprocessor Run.** Can be used to check all definitions used with an application for completeness, correctness, and compatibility. The preprocessor creates a list of messages that describe any problems it discovers.
- **Test/debug without Options Run.** Can be used to execute an application interpretively from the definition of the application in the MSL. The test terminates with a message if a problem is discovered.
- **Test/debug with Options Run.** Can be used to add tracing to the test execution of the application. The trace results can be written to the terminal or to a file. Options supported by the trace facility include the following:

    Label tracing
    I/O tracing
    Statement tracing
    Data modification tracing
    Call tracing

All functions supported by the test facility are invoked online from menus. The test/debug functions display the application maps and access files and databases just as if CSP/AE were running a production version of the application.

APPLICATION GENERATION   The application generation facility takes the application definition from the MSL and builds a production version of the application. The production version consists of a set of application load modules that are constructed by the application generator from the application definition. The load modules are stored in a file called the *application load file* (ALF). The load modules do not consist of executable machine code; instead, each contains a set of tables designed for efficient interpretive execution by CSP/AE.

An application generation run is invoked online at the terminal. The application developer can optionally specify the system on which the application is to run, as shown in the sample application generator menu in Fig. 21.8. The default target system is the same as the development system.

Application generation calls a preprocessor to check the application definition before actually building the load modules. Application generation performs additional checks to ensure that all the functions used in the application are supported on the system on which the application will run.

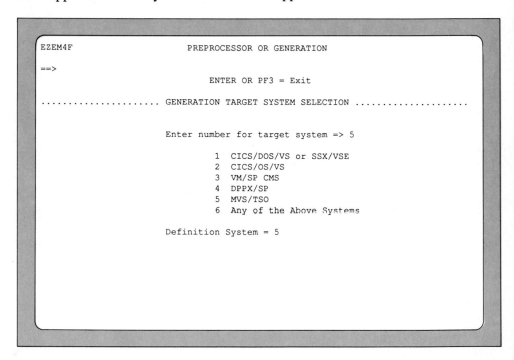

```
 EZEM4F                          PREPROCESSOR OR GENERATION

 ==>
                                   ENTER OR PF3 = Exit

 ..................... GENERATION TARGET SYSTEM SELECTION .....................


                        Enter number for target system => 5


                               1  CICS/DOS/VS or SSX/VSE
                               2  CICS/OS/VS
                               3  VM/SP CMS
                               4  DPPX/SP
                               5  MVS/TSO
                               6  Any of the Above Systems

                        Definition System = 5
```

Figure 21.8   Selecting a target system.

LIST PROCESSOR, UTILITIES, AND FILE MAINTENANCE   The CSP/AD list processor and utilities support the following functions for MSL members:

- Listing member contents
- Printing, including cross-reference reports
- Exporting and importing data
- Copying members
- Renaming members
- Deleting members

The file maintenance facility allows the application developer to view or modify the contents of a test VSAM file.

Two other utility programs are also provided with CSP/AD. These utilities are implemented as CSP/AD applications.

- **ALF Utility.** Supports the following functions for application load files (ALFs):

    Listing file contents
    Exporting and importing data
    Copying files
    Renaming files
    Deleting files

- **Message Utility.** Lets an application developer define messages to be stored in a message file. An application can issue the message by moving the message number to a special variable name (EZEMNO).

APPLICATION EXECUTION

The CSP/AE products each execute applications generated by CSP/AD in a specific operating environment. CSP/AE has a minimal direct user interface consisting simply of the command that starts an application and the error messages that CSP/AE writes in case of abnormal application termination. If the application was generated with the *reference file* option, one of the messages displays the failing statement and identifies the location of the statement in an application print listing.

PART VII APPENDIXES

■ NORMALIZATION

A theory known as *normalization theory,* first described by E. F. Codd, has been used to aid in the design of all types of databases. Normalization is a design technique that is widely used in designing all types of databases; its use is not limited to relational database structures.

Normalization theory, like the relational data model itself discussed in Chapter 2, can be described in rigorous mathematical terms. However, its underlying ideas are simple and have much to do with ordinary common sense. We will take the same approach with normalization that we took with the relational data model in Chapter 2. We will rely on simple explanations and examples to show how the normalization process can be used to help stabilize the design of relational databases.

The overall goals of the normalization process are as follows:

- To arrange data so that it can be represented in tables where each row-column position contains a single data item (no repeating groups)
- To ensure that data items are associated with the correct keys and thereby minimize data redundancy

Normalization involves a series of steps that change the column structure of the various tables that make up a relational database by placing the data into a series of different forms called *first normal form, second normal form,* and so on.

FIRST NORMAL FORM

The first step of the normalization process is to place the data into *first normal form*. This involves the removal of repeating groups. In Chapter 2, we learned that the process of removing repeating groups in order to store data in tabular form produces a *normalized structure*. If we already have our data in the form of tables, it is already in first normal form. Any DB2 table is automatically in first normal form, since each element in a DB2 table must be a single data item.

As we saw in Chapter 2, we remove repeating groups by simply creating a separate row for each of the elements in the repeating group. Suppose we begin with the following employee data:

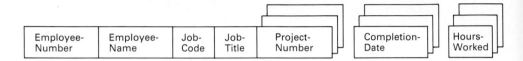

Employee-Number	Employee-Name	Job-Code	Job-Title	Project-Number	Completion-Date	Hours-Worked

Here a given record stores information about a number of different projects that a particular employee has worked on. To represent this data in tabular form, we generate a row for each project an employee has worked on by repeating the employee information in each row:

EMPLOYEE

EMPLOYEE-NUMBER	EMPLOYEE-NAME	JOB-CODE	JOB-TITLE	PROJECT-NUMBER	COMPLETION-DATE	HOURS-WORKED
120	JONES	1	PROGRAMMER	01	7/17	37
120	JONES	1	PROGRAMMER	08	1/12	12
121	HARPO	1	PROGRAMMER	01	7/17	45
121	HARPO	1	PROGRAMMER	08	1/12	21
121	HARPO	1	PROGRAMMER	12	3/21	107
270	GARFUNKEL	2	ANALYST	08	1/12	10
270	GARFUNKEL	2	ANALYST	12	3/21	78
273	SELSI	3	DESIGNER	01	7/17	22
274	ABRAHMS	2	ANALYST	12	3/21	41
279	HIGGINS	1	PROGRAMMER	01	7/17	27
279	HIGGINS	1	PROGRAMMER	08	1/12	20
279	HIGGINS	1	PROGRAMMER	12	3/21	51
301	FLANNEL	1	PROGRAMMER	01	7/17	16
301	FLANNEL	1	PROGRAMMER	12	3/21	85
306	MCGRAW	3	DESIGNER	12	3/21	67

In Chapter 2, we learned that the relational data model requires that we define a primary key for each table, and we will assume that we are following this principle in defining DB2 tables. In this case, we must use both the *Employee-Number* and *Project-Number* columns to uniquely identify each row:

EMPLOYEE

EMPLOYEE-NUMBER	PROJECT-NUMBER	EMPLOYEE-NAME	JOB-CODE	JOB-TITLE	COMPLETION-DATE	HOURS-WORKED
120	01	JONES	1	PROGRAMMER	7/17	37
120	08	JONES	1	PROGRAMMER	1/12	12
121	01	HARPO	1	PROGRAMMER	7/17	45
121	08	HARPO	1	PROGRAMMER	1/12	21
121	12	HARPO	1	PROGRAMMER	3/21	107
270	08	GARFUNKEL	2	ANALYST	1/12	10
270	12	GARFUNKEL	2	ANALYST	3/21	78
273	01	SELSI	3	DESIGNER	7/17	22
274	12	ABRAHMS	2	ANALYST	3/21	41
279	01	HIGGINS	1	PROGRAMMER	7/17	27
279	08	HIGGINS	1	PROGRAMMER	1/12	20
279	12	HIGGINS	1	PROGRAMMER	3/21	51
301	01	FLANNEL	1	PROGRAMMER	7/17	16
301	12	FLANNEL	1	PROGRAMMER	3/21	85
306	12	MCGRAW	3	DESIGNER	3/21	67

We have said that one of the goals of the normalization process is to reduce data redundancy. At this point, it appears that we are actually increasing data redundancy by placing the data into first normal form; *Job-Code* and *Job-Title* data item values are repeated many times, and the same *Completion-Date* values are stored several times as well. This increase in data redundancy is an important argument for why further normalization steps are required in order to produce a stable design. A table that is in first normal form only may have many undesirable characteristics, of which data redundancy is only one. We will see how subsequent steps in the normalization process will reduce the redundancy that we have introduced by placing the data into first normal form and how additional normalization steps improve our data structure in other important ways as well.

SECOND NORMAL FORM

The second step in the normalization process places our data into *second normal form*. Second normal form involves the idea of *functional dependence*.

Functional Dependency

In general, a given column, say, column *B*, is functionally dependent on some other column, say, column *A*, if for any given value of column *A* there is a single value of column *B* associated with it. Saying that column *B* is functionally dependent on column *A* is equivalent to saying that column *A* *identifies* column *B*. Notice in our table that there are three rows that have an *Employee-Number* value of *121*, but in each of those rows, the *Employee-Name* data item value is the same—*Harpo:*

EMPLOYEE

EMPLOYEE-NUMBER	PROJECT-NUMBER	EMPLOYEE-NAME	JOB-CODE	JOB-TITLE	COMPLETION-DATE	HOURS-WORKED
120	01	JONES	1	PROGRAMMER	7/17	37
120	08	JONES	1	PROGRAMMER	1/12	12
121	01	HARPO	1	PROGRAMMER	7/17	45
121	08	HARPO	1	PROGRAMMER	1/12	21
121	12	HARPO	1	PROGRAMMER	3/21	107
270	08	GARFUNKEL	2	ANALYST	1/12	10
270	12	GARFUNKEL	2	ANALYST	3/21	78
273	01	SELSI	3	DESIGNER	7/17	22
274	12	ABRAHMS	2	ANALYST	3/21	41
279	01	HIGGINS	1	PROGRAMMER	7/17	27
279	08	HIGGINS	1	PROGRAMMER	1/12	20
279	12	HIGGINS	1	PROGRAMMER	3/21	51
301	01	FLANNEL	1	PROGRAMMER	7/17	16
301	12	FLANNEL	1	PROGRAMMER	3/21	85
306	12	MCGRAW	3	DESIGNER	3/21	67

A similar relationship exists between the *Employee-Number* and *Employee-Name* columns in the other rows that have the same *Employee-Number* value. Therefore, we can assume that as long as no two employees can have the same employee number, *Employee-Name* is functionally dependent on *Employee-*

Number. We can use the same argument to show that *Job-Code* and *Job-Title* are also functionally dependent on *Employee-Number*.

Full Functional Dependency

In some cases, a column will not be functionally dependent on a single column but will be functionally dependent on a *group* of columns. For example, *Hours-Worked* is functionally dependent on the combination of *Employee-Number* and *Project-Number*. This leads to the idea of *full functional dependency*. A column can be said to be fully functionally dependent on some collection of other columns when it is functionally dependent on the entire set but not on any subset of that collection. *Hours-Worked* is fully functionally dependent on *Employee-Number* and *Project-Number*. However, *Completion-Date* is not fully functionally dependent on *Employee-Number* and *Project-Number*, since *Completion-Date* is functionally dependent on *Project-Number* alone.

To place into second normal form a group of columns that are in first normal form, we identify all the full functional dependencies that exist and create a separate table for each set of these. We begin by identifying a likely key—in this case, *Employee-Number*—and determining which other columns are fully functionally dependent on that key. *Employee-Name, Job-Code,* and *Job-Title* are functionally dependent on *Employee-Number*, so we leave them in the *Employee* table, which has *Employee-Number* as its primary key:

EMPLOYEE

EMPLOYEE-NUMBER	EMPLOYEE-NAME	JOB-CODE	JOB-TITLE
120	JONES	1	PROGRAMMER
121	HARPO	1	PROGRAMMER
270	GARFUNKEL	2	ANALYST
273	SELSI	3	DESIGNER
274	ABRAHMS	2	ANALYST
279	HIGGINS	1	PROGRAMMER
301	FLANNEL	1	PROGRAMMER
306	MCGRAW	3	DESIGNER

Of the remaining columns, *Completion-Date* is dependent on *Project-Number*, so we move the *Project-Number* and *Completion-Date* columns to a separate *Project* table that has *Project-Number* as the primary key:

PROJECT

PROJECT-NUMBER	COMPLETION-DATE
01	7/17
08	1/12
12	3/21

This leaves the *Hours-Worked* column. *Hours-Worked* is fully functionally dependent on the concatenated key that consists of *Employee-Number* and *Project-*

Number. So we create a third table called *Hours* that consists of *Employee-Number*, *Project-Number,* and *Hours-Worked.* The key of the *Hours* table consists of *Employee-Number* and *Project-Number*:

HOURS

EMPLOYEE-NUMBER	PROJECT-NUMBER	HOURS-WORKED
120	01	37
120	08	12
121	01	45
121	08	21
121	12	107
270	08	10
270	12	78
273	01	22
274	12	41
279	01	27
279	08	20
279	12	51
301	01	16
301	12	85
306	12	67

We can now say that our set of columns is in second normal form because they are in first normal form and every nonkey column is fully functionally dependent on the primary key of its table.

Notice that we have repeated the *Employee-Number* column in two of the tables and that we have repeated the *Project-Number* column in two of the tables:

EMPLOYEE

EMPLOYEE-NUMBER	EMPLOYEE-NAME	JOB-CODE	JOB-TITLE
120	JONES	1	PROGRAMMER
121	HARPO	1	PROGRAMMER
270	GARFUNKEL	2	ANALYST
273	SELSI	3	DESIGNER
274	ABRAHMS	2	ANALYST
279	HIGGINS	1	PROGRAMMER
301	FLANNEL	1	PROGRAMMER
306	MCGRAW	3	DESIGNER

PROJECT

PROJECT-NUMBER	COMPLETION-DATE
01	7/17
08	1/12
12	3/21

HOURS

EMPLOYEE-NUMBER	PROJECT-NUMBER	HOURS-WORKED
120	01	37
120	08	12
121	01	45
121	08	21
121	12	107
270	08	10
270	12	78
273	01	22
274	12	41
279	01	27
279	08	20
279	12	51
301	01	16
301	12	85
306	12	67

Duplicating columns is perfectly valid and often occurs when converting a group of columns to second normal form. By duplicating columns in multiple tables, we are able to use a relational operator to combine the tables in various ways to extract the data we need from them.

Notice that placing the data into second normal form has reduced much of the value redundancy that existed in the original table. *Job-Code* and *Job-Title* data item values now appear only once per employee, and *Completion-Date* data item values appear only once per project. Now that we have our data in second normal form, we can point out another undesirable characteristic of a table that is first normal form only.

When our data was in first normal form only, we had a single table whose primary key consisted of *Employee-Number* and *Project-Number*. Because of the entity integrity constraint, we need to have valid values for both *Employee-Number* and *Project-Number* in order to create a new row. This means that we would be unable to store a row for an employee who is currently not assigned to a project (null *Project-Number* value). Similarly, we would be prevented from storing a row for a project that currently has no employees assigned to it (null *Employee-Number* value).

With our columns in second normal form, we can add a new employee by adding a row to the *Employee* table without having to change either of the other two tables. After the new employee has been assigned to a project and has logged some time on that project, we can add a row to the *Hours* table to describe the project assignment and the number of hours logged. In a similar manner, we can add a row to the *Project* table to describe a new project without changing either the *Employee* or *Hours* tables. Both of these functions would be impossible if our tables were not in second normal form.

THIRD NORMAL FORM

The third step in the normalization process involves the idea of *transitive dependency*. Suppose we have a table with columns *A*, *B*, and *C:*

A	B	C

If column *C* is functionally dependent on column *B* and column *B* is functionally dependent on column *A*, then column *C* is functionally dependent on column *A*. We can show this by drawing links between columns:

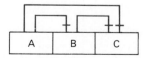

The bar at the end of each link indicates a *one cardinality*. In other words, for each value of A there is one and only one value of B, for each value of A there is one and only one value of C, and for each value of B there is one and only one value of C.

In most cases, similar dependencies exist in the opposite direction as well. A is functionally dependent on B, and B is functionally dependent on C:

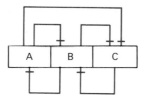

If similar dependencies are *not* true in the opposite direction (i.e., column A is *not* functionally dependent on column B or column B is *not* functionally dependent on column C), then column C is said to be transitively dependent on column A, as in this example:

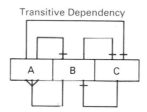

In this diagram, the link with the *crow's foot* symbol from B to A indicates that for each value of B there can be many values of A associated with it.

We said earlier that *Job-Code* and *Job-Title* were functionally dependent on *Employee-Number* (we are omitting the *Employee-Name* data item for clarity):

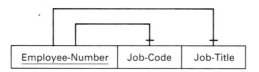

Assuming there is only one job title associated with a given job code, *Job-Title* is functionally dependent on *Job-Code:*

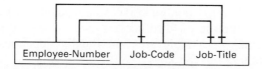

In the reverse direction, *Job-Code* is functionally dependent on *Job-Title* as long as a given job title is associated with only one job code. However, many employees may have the same job code. So *Employee-Number* is not functionally dependent on *Job-Code*. This means that *Job-Title* is transitively dependent on *Employee-Number*:

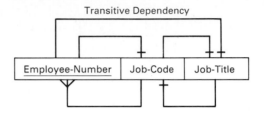

To place our data into third normal form, we must remove transitive dependencies. This is done by placing the *Job-Title* column in a separate table called *Jobs* with *Job-Code* as primary key. The third normal form of the data is as follows:

EMPLOYEE

EMPLOYEE-NUMBER	EMPLOYEE-NAME	JOB-CODE
120	JONES	1
121	HARPO	1
270	GARFUNKEL	2
273	SELSI	3
274	ABRAHMS	2
279	HIGGINS	1
301	FLANNEL	1
306	MCGRAW	3

JOBS

JOB-CODE	JOB-TITLE
1	PROGRAMMER
2	ANALYST
3	DESIGNER

PROJECT

PROJECT-NUMBER	COMPLETION-DATE
01	7/17
08	1/12
12	3/21

HOURS

EMPLOYEE-NUMBER	PROJECT-NUMBER	HOURS-WORKED
120	01	37
120	08	12
121	01	45
121	08	21
121	12	107
270	08	10
270	12	78
273	01	22
274	12	41
279	01	27
279	08	20
279	12	51
301	01	16
301	12	85
306	12	67

A table is said to be in third normal form if it is in second normal form and every nonkey column is nontransitively dependent on the primary key. We can give a simpler definition of third normal form by saying that in third normal form, all the columns of a table are functionally dependent on the key, the whole key, and nothing but the key.

Placing data into third normal form eliminates more potentially undesirable characteristics of data that is in only first or second normal form. Our set of tables shows that a job title associated with a given job code now appears in only one place rather than for each employee who has that job code. This makes it easier to change a job title, since the change has to be made in only one place. Also, we can now add a new job code with its associated job title even though no employee has yet been assigned that job code. And we will not lose the job title if we temporarily have no employees assigned a given job code.

FOURTH NORMAL FORM

In the great majority of cases, placing data into third normal form provides a sufficient level of normalization. Higher levels of normalization are possible, however, and it is occasionally beneficial to place data into *fourth normal form*.

Suppose that an employee can be assigned to several projects concurrently. Also suppose that an employee can possess a series of skills. If we record this information in a single table, we need to use all three columns as the key, since no other column grouping produces unique row identification:

EMPLOYEE-PROJECT-SKILL

EMPLOYEE-NUMBER	PROJECT-NUMBER	SKILL
120	01	DESIGN
120	01	PROGRAM
120	01	DOCUMENT
120	08	DESIGN
120	08	PROGRAM
120	08	DOCUMENT

Using a single table like this is not desirable because values have to be repeated, which could cause consistency problems when updating. However, since there are no columns in this table that are not part of the key, the table is in third normal form. We can represent the relationships in this table in a simpler manner if we split them into the following two separate all-key tables:

EMPLOYEE-PROJECT

EMPLOYEE-NUMBER	PROJECT-NUMBER
120	01
120	08

EMPLOYEE-SKILL

EMPLOYEE-NUMBER	SKILL
120	DESIGN
120	PROGRAM
120	DOCUMENT

These tables are in fourth normal form. Fourth normal form involves the idea of *multivalued dependencies,* in which a given value for a single column identifies multiple values of another column. A multivalued dependency is defined in terms of the set of values from one column that is associated with a given pair of values from two other columns. Look again at our original three-column table:

EMPLOYEE-PROJECT-SKILL

EMPLOYEE-NUMBER	PROJECT-NUMBER	SKILL
120	01	DESIGN
120	01	PROGRAM
120	01	DOCUMENT
120	08	DESIGN
120	08	PROGRAM
120	08	DOCUMENT

The relationship between *Employee-Number* and *Project-Number* is a multivalued dependency because for each pair of *Employee-Number/Skill* values in the table, the associated set of *Project-Number* values is determined only by *Employee-Number* and is independent of *Skill*. Similarly, the relationship between *Employee-Number* and *Skill* is a multivalued dependency, since the set of *Skill* values for an *Employee-Number/Project-Number* pair is independent of *Project-Number*. It can be shown that multivalued dependencies in all-key tables always occur in pairs, as in this example. Conversion to fourth normal form involves decomposing the original table into multiple tables so that the multivalued dependencies are eliminated.

Notice that the two individual tables better represent the true relationships between the columns because there is no real relationship between projects and skills. Also, there is less redundant data in the two separate tables, and the update behavior of the two separate tables is better as well. For example, if an employee acquires a new skill, we simply add a new row to the *Employee-Skill* table. With the single table, we would have to add multiple rows, one for each of the projects the employee is assigned to.

Another way of looking at fourth normal form is as multiple repeating groups. We could view the original set of data in the following manner, where *Project-Number* and *Skill* each takes the form of a repeating group:

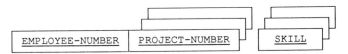

Placing the data into fourth normal form simply eliminates the repeating groups by placing each of them into a separate table. In actual practice, the earlier steps of normalization often identify such repeating groups and removes them, thus producing third-normal-form tables that are already also in fourth normal form.

FIFTH NORMAL FORM

In all of the normalization steps we have discussed so far, we have been able to split a table into two of its projections while still retaining all the data contained in the original table. In other words, we can perform a *join* operation on the two constituent tables to re-create the original table. There exist, however, some tables, in fourth normal form, that cannot be split into two projections without changing the original data in some way. Consider the following table:

EMPLOYEE-PROJECT-SKILL

EMPLOYEE-NUMBER	PROJECT-NUMBER	SKILL
120	01	DESIGN
120	08	PROGRAM
120	01	PROGRAM
205	01	PROGRAM

An employee is assigned to one or more projects and uses one or more skills on each project. In this case, though, the particular combination of data item values that occur in the table imply that there is a relationship not only between employees and skills (an employee has a particular skill) but also between projects and skills (certain skills are employed by each project). We can interpret these relationships to mean that an employee *uses* a skill that he or she possesses on a project only if the skill is *employed* by that project. This means that employees may *have* skills that are not *used* on projects to which they are assigned.

At first glance, the table seems to have the same characteristics as the table in the previous example. Suppose we decompose the new table into two of its projections as we did earlier:

EMPLOYEE-PROJECT

EMPLOYEE-NUMBER	PROJECT-NUMBER
120	01
120	08
205	01

EMPLOYEE-SKILL

EMPLOYEE-NUMBER	SKILL
120	DESIGN
120	PROGRAM
205	PROGRAM

If we now perform a *join* operation on these two tables, we get the following result:

EMPLOYEE-PROJECT-SKILL

EMPLOYEE-NUMBER	PROJECT-NUMBER	SKILL
120	01	DESIGN
120	08	DESIGN
120	01	PROGRAM
120	08	PROGRAM
205	01	PROGRAM

Notice that the table has an extra row that the original table did not have (the second row). Project *08* now appears to use design skills when the original data shows no employee performing design for that project. The reason this occurs is that the two projections that we created from the original table do not accurately represent the associations inherent in the original table. In this case, there *does* exist a relationship between projects and skills; each project uses only certain types of skills. This relationship is lost when we decompose the table into the two projections shown here.

Note that the original table does not contain multivalued dependencies and thus is already in fourth normal form. The set of *Project-Number* values associated with each *Employee-Number/Skill* pair is dependent on both *Employee-Number* and *Skill* and not just on *Employee-Number*. Similarly, *Skill* value sets are dependent on both *Employee-Number* and *Project-Number*. Thus we cannot separate the table into two projections as we did before. The table can, however, be further normalized by placing it into *fifth normal form*. This involves decomposing the table into *three* of its projections, thus retaining the true relationships among the various columns:

EMPLOYEE-PROJECT

EMPLOYEE-NUMBER	PROJECT NUMBER
120	01
120	08
205	01

EMPLOYEE-SKILL

EMPLOYEE-NUMBER	SKILL
120	DESIGN
120	PROGRAM
205	PROGRAM

PROJECT-SKILL

PROJECT-NUMBER	SKILL
01	DESIGN
08	PROGRAM
01	PROGRAM

We can now join the first two tables to form the combined table having the spurious row as we did previously. This intermediate table corresponds to all the skills that *might* be used on projects. The third table specifies that skills that each project *actually* uses. When we then join the intermediate table with the third table, using both the *Project-Number* and *Skill* columns for the join, we eliminate the spurious row and get a result that is identical to our original table:

EMPLOYEE-PROJECT-SKILL

EMPLOYEE-NUMBER	PROJECT-NUMBER	SKILL
120	01	DESIGN
120	08	PROGRAM
120	01	PROGRAM
205	01	PROGRAM

The three tables shown, which *can* be rejoined to produce the original relation, are in fifth normal form. This constraint on which projections can be validly rejoined is called a *join dependency*. The join dependency in the original table causes that table to have somewhat bizarre update behavior. Consider the following table, in which an employee uses *Design* skills on one project and *Programming* skills on a different project:

EMPLOYEE-PROJECT-SKILL

EMPLOYEE-NUMBER	PROJECT-NUMBER	SKILL
120	01	DESIGN
120	08	PROGRAM

Suppose we added to the table a new employee, who uses *Programming* skills on project *01:*

EMPLOYEE-PROJECT-SKILL

EMPLOYEE	PROJECT	SKILL
120	01	DESIGN
120	08	PROGRAM
205	01	PROGRAM

The addition of that one row to the table on first glance seems to be valid. But let us now again decompose the table into three of its projections:

EMPLOYEE-PROJECT

EMPLOYEE-NUMBER	PROJECT NUMBER
120	01
120	08
205	01

EMPLOYEE-SKILL

EMPLOYEE-NUMBER	SKILL
120	DESIGN
120	PROGRAM
205	PROGRAM

PROJECT-SKILL

PROJECT-NUMBER	SKILL
01	DESIGN
08	PROGRAM
01	PROGRAM

We now rejoin the three tables, producing the following result:

EMPLOYEE-PROJECT-SKILL

EMPLOYEE-NUMBER	PROJECT-NUMBER	SKILL
120	01	DESIGN
120	08	PROGRAM
120	01	PROGRAM
205	01	PROGRAM

Notice that this table has one row more than the table we began with. This result at first seems intuitively wrong. Does this mean that the three projections are not in fifth normal form? No, it means that it is not valid to add only that one row to the non-fifth-normal-form table. By adding the one new row to the non-fifth-normal-form table, we are actually stating three facts:

1. Employee *205* has been assigned to project *01*.
2. Employee *205* has *Programming* skills.
3. Project *01* now uses *Programming* skills.

By analyzing the content of the original table together with these facts, we can see that when we add the new row for employee *205*, project *01*, and the *Programming* skill, we must also add a new row for employee *120*, project *01*, and the *Programming* skill. This is because employee *120* already had the programming skill and was already assigned to project *01*; thus employee *120's Programming* skill is now available to project *01*.

By using the three projections rather than the composite table, we can be sure that all three facts are reflected properly and completely in the table data.

The join dependencies that exist in the single table that is not in fifth normal form create constraints on the updating of the table. If the table is left in fourth normal form, we must sometimes add two rows to the table at a time instead of only one. There can be similar problems with deletions. It is often quite difficult to determine when these updating anomalies occur. By placing the data into fifth normal form, we can add the employee *205* data in a straightforward manner by simply adding a new row to each of the three individual tables. The two new rows will then automatically appear in the result if we rejoin the three fifth-normal-form individual tables.

Placing the data into fifth normal form also allows us to add data that couldn't be added to the composite table. For example, we can show an employee having a particular skill, even though no project currently uses that skill, by adding a row only to the *Employee-Skill* table. This information cannot be added to the composite table, since it would require a null *Project-Number* value. Null values are not allowed in columns that make up the key of a table.

Research is continuing on normalization, and even higher forms of normalization have been identified. However, it can be shown that fifth normal form is the highest form of normalization that is possible with respect to the relational operations of projection and join. Thus fifth normal form is the highest form of normalization that is generally required in practice.

∎ DATA TYPES AND EXPRESSIONS

The various data types supported by DB2 can be grouped into three categories: numeric data, string data, and date and time data. Numeric data includes the data types INTEGER, SMALLINT, DECIMAL, and FLOAT. String data includes the various forms of character and graphic data. Date and time data includes the data types DATE, TIME, and TIMESTAMP. Each of these categories has operators and functions available that can be used with the data types to construct expressions, which can then be used in SQL clauses such as SELECT, WHERE, and HAVING.

NUMERIC DATA

Numeric data can be combined with arithmetic operators to form numeric expressions. Numeric data can also be used with appropriate conversion functions to change the format of the data. The arithmetic operators include +, −, *, and /. An example of an expression with arithmetic operators would be

```
PRICE * ONORD
```

A number of conversion functions are available that convert numeric data from one format to another, including these:

- **DECIMAL.** Converts a numeric value to decimal representation.
- **DIGITS.** Converts a numeric value to character string representation.
- **FLOAT.** Converts a numeric value to floating-point representation.
- **HEX.** Converts a numeric value to a character string that is the internal hexadecimal representation of the value (two hex digits per numeric digit).
- **INTEGER.** Converts a number to integer representation.

Assuming ONORD has been defined as an INTEGER field, specifying DECI-MAL (ONORD, 7, 2) would cause a retrieved value to be converted to decimal format with seven decimal digits and two digits to the right of the decimal point.

STRING DATA

There are also operators and functions that can be used with character and graphic data, including these:

- **Concatenation.** The concatenation operator (||) can be used to combine two strings of the same type. The following is an example of an expression that uses concatenation operators:

```
CITY||', '||STATE
```

This example concatenates the string contained in the data item named CITY, a literal consisting of a comma followed by a blank, and the string contained in the data item named STATE.

- **HEX.** The HEX function can be used to convert string data to a character string that is the internal hexadecimal representation of the string value (two hex characters per byte of string data).

- **VARGRAPHIC.** The VARGRAPHIC function can be used to convert a character string into a graphic string.

- **LENGTH.** The LENGTH function returns a numeric value that is the length of a string in bytes or, for graphic data, in double bytes. This is particularly useful with variable-length strings.

- **SUBSTR.** The SUBSTR function can be used to define a substring within a character or graphic string. For example, SUBSTR(SUPPNAME, 1, 5) defines a substring that consists of the first five characters of SUPPNAME.

In addition to operators and functions used with string data, there is a special register named USER that returns a character data value. The keyword USER in an SQL statement will contain the user's authorization ID when the SQL statement executes.

DATE AND TIME DATA

A number of processing facilities are associated with date and time data, including special registers, conversion functions, and methods of handling duration.

Special Registers

These are the special registers that return date and time values:

- **CURRENT DATE.** Returns the current date.
- **CURRENT TIME.** Returns the current time.
- **CURRENT TIMESTAMP.** Returns a concatenated value for current date and current time.
- **CURRENT TIMEZONE.** Returns a value that represents the difference between Greenwich Mean Time and the local time zone. This value is used to adjust the reading of the CPU clock so that the values returned by the other registers represent local time and date.

The CURRENT DATE, CURRENT TIME, and CURRENT TIMESTAMP registers are used to provide default values for DATE, TIME, and TIMESTAMP columns, respectively, when the column is defined NOT NULL WITH DEFAULT. These registers can also be used to allow an SQL statement to access current time and date values.

Specifying Dates and Times
as Constants

Just as constants can be used to represent numeric values (3, −5.2) and character values ('BOLT'), constants can be used to represent date and time values. However, with data and time, a formatted character string is used to represent the value. Several formats are supported, including U.S. style, European style, International Standards Organization style, Japanese Industrial Standard Christian Era style, and installation-defined. In U.S. style, the formats are as follows:

- **DATE:** 'mm/dd/yyyy'. For example, '10/28/1950' or '1/1/2001'.
- **TIME:** 'hh:mm AM' or 'hh:mm PM'. For example, '9:00 AM' or '11:07 PM'. Note that time values do not include seconds. In the U.S. style, seconds are not specified in a constant that specifies a time value, although a seconds value is stored internally.
- **TIMESTAMP:** 'yyyy-mm-dd-hh.mm.ss.nnnnnn'. For example, '2010-5-21-23.30.00.000000'. Trailing zeros in the microseconds portion can be omitted: '2010-5-21-23.30.00'.

Constants specified in this way are converted to the appropriate internal format for comparison or storage. For example, if START_DATE has been defined as data type DATE and START_TIME is data type TIME, the SQL statement

```
INSERT INTO PERS (START_DATE, START_TIME)
VALUES ('10/28/1950', '1:00 PM')
```

will result in the following column values being stored:

```
START_DATE — 195001028
START_TIME — 130000
```

Duration

DATE and TIME data types are associated with the notion of duration. For example, if a time value of 113000 is increased by a duration of 45 minutes, the result is a time value of 121500. A duration value can be represented using a decimal number. A date duration is in the format *yyyymmdd,* and a time duration is *hhmmss.* For example, as a date duration, 00000014 is 14 days, and as a time duration, 004500 is 45 minutes.

Duration values can also be represented as a labeled duration, where a keyword indicates the units involved. The following keywords may be used for labeled durations:

- YEAR(S)
- MONTH(S)
- DAY(S)
- HOUR(S)
- MINUTE(S)
- SECOND(S)
- MICROSECOND(S)

Examples of labeled durations are 4 HOURS or 7 DAYS.

Various types of expressions can be constructed involving durations. A date value can be increased or decreased by a particular duration. Assuming that ORDER_DATE has been defined as the data type DATE, the following expressions could be used:

```
ORDER_DATE + 00000010
          or
ORDER_DATE - 5 DAYS
```

One date value can also be subtracted from another date value, with the result being a decimal duration value:

```
WHERE SHIP_DATE - ORDER_DATE > 14 DAYS
```

Similarly, a time value can be increased or decreased by a time duration, or one time value can be subtracted from another to give a time duration as the result. A timestamp value can be increased or decreased by a date or time duration, but one timestamp value cannot be subtracted from another to give a duration.

Conversions

Several conversion functions are available. These functions allow an SQL statement to extract portions of a time or date or to change the form of representation. The following functions can be used to extract a portion of a time or date value:

- **YEAR, MONTH, DAY.** Select the specified portion of a date value and convert it to a binary integer. The value can be part of a DATE field, a TIMESTAMP field, or a date duration. For example, suppose we have the following values:

  ```
  — START_DATE   —  20010315
  — SHIP_DATE    —  19900425
  — ORDER_DATE   —  19900410
  ```

  The expression MONTH(START_DATE) returns the value 03, and the expression DAY(SHIP_DATE − ORDER_DATE) gives the value 15.

- **HOUR, MINUTE, SECOND.** Select the specified portion of a time value and convert it to a binary integer. The value can be part of a TIME field, a TIMESTAMP field, or a time duration. For example, HOUR(DEPART) or MINUTE(END_PERIOD).

- **MICROSECOND.** Selects the microseconds portion of a timestamp and converts it to a binary integer. For example, MICROSECOND (FIRST_STAMP).

The form of representation can be converted using the following functions:

- **DATE, TIME, TIMESTAMP.** Convert a numeric or character string value into a date, time, or timestamp value. For a timestamp, two values can be specified, representing the date and time. For example, TIME(’2:30 PM’) gives the value 143000.

- **CHAR.** Convert a date or time value to its character string representation. The format to be used, such as U.S. style or European style, can be specified as part of the function, or the local default format can be used. For example, if ORDER_DATE has a value of 19501028, CHAR (ORDER_DATE) will be ’10/28/1950’ (assuming U.S. style format).

- **DAYS.** Converts a date or timestamp value to a binary integer that is the number of days between this date and December 31, 1 B.C. For example, DAYS(BIRTH_DATE).

REFERENTIAL INTEGRITY: HIERARCHIES AND CYCLES

As discussed in Chapter 6, a referential integrity relationship links two tables— a parent table and a dependent table. However, it is possible for more than two tables to be linked by referential constraints, thus forming more complex structures. There may be special considerations related to a complex referential structure, particularly in the area of delete rules.

HIERARCHIES   Suppose that we have defined the following referential constraints:

Table	Primary Key	Foreign Key
DEPT	DEPTNO	—
EMPLOYEE	EMPNO	DEPTNO referencing DEPT
PROJECT	PROJNO	LEADER referencing EMPLOYEE

The *Employee* table is a dependent table, since it contains a foreign key. The *Dept* table is the parent table for this relationship. However, *Employee* is also a parent table, since the *Project* table contains a foreign key that relates to *Employee*. We can represent the dependency relationship between the tables as follows:

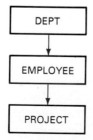

This type of structure is called a *hierarchy*. The table immediately below a parent table is called a dependent table. Thus *Employee* is a dependent of *Dept,* and *Project* is a dependent of *Employee*. Any table below a parent table, at any level in a hierarchy, is called a *descendant*. *Employee* and *Project* are both descendants of *Dept*. A parent table may have more than one dependent, and a dependent table, by having multiple foreign keys defined, may have more than one parent. This can lead to hierarchies with quite complex structures, such as this one:

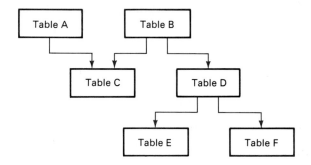

CYCLES

A *cycle* is a structure in which a table is a descendant of itself. Suppose that we had defined the following referential constraints:

Table	Primary Key	Foreign Key
DEPT	DEPTNO	EMPNO referencing EMPLOYEE
EMPLOYEE	EMPNO	DEPTNO referencing DEPT

We can represent these relationships as follows:

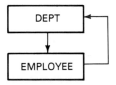

Here *Dept* is a dependent of *Employee* and *Employee* is a dependent of *Dept,* so *Dept* is a descendant of itself, thus constituting a cycle.

A cycle can involve more than two levels of tables, as in the following example:

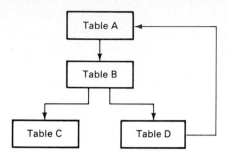

A table may also have a foreign key that references itself. For example, the *Employee* table may contain a *Manager* column that defines an employee's manager, who is also an employee:

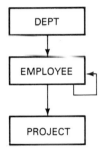

This referential constraint ensures that the *Manager* column contains only values that are also valid employee numbers (or are null). This is known as a *self-referencing cycle*.

DELETE CONSIDERATIONS

When a DELETE statement is used to delete a row in a parent table, the DELETE request may also affect tables that are referentially related to it. As discussed in Chapter 6, the delete rule that is specified for a foreign key defines the way DELETE requests are handled for rows in a parent table. For example, consider this structure:

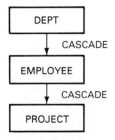

With this structure, if a department is deleted from the *Dept* table, dependent rows for that department are deleted from the *Employee* table. The rows deleted from the *Employee* table may in turn cause dependent rows to be deleted from the *Project* table.

The term *delete-connected* is used to designate all dependent tables plus any other descendant tables that are under a dependent table that has CASCADE as its delete rule. Delete-connected tables are tables that can have rows automatically deleted when a deletion occurs in a parent table.

Multiple Paths

There are restrictions in the delete rules that can be chosen when a descendant table is delete-connected to a single parent table by multiple paths. Two possible structures for this type of situation are as follows:

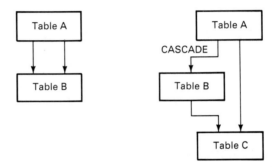

When such relationships occur, both paths must use the same delete rule for the descendant table, and both must be either CASCADE or RESTRICT. Here are possible choices for the structures just shown:

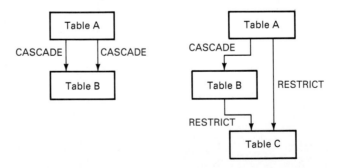

The two paths cannot use SET NULL, since this may cause incorrect results under certain circumstances.

Deletion Based on a Subquery

If a delete-connected table is referenced in a subquery as part of a DELETE request, the table referenced in the subquery must not itself be affected by the DELETE request. This means that RESTRICT must be specified at some point along the delete path to the table referenced in the subquery. For example:

```
DELETE FROM TABLEA
WHERE .....(SELECT ...
            FROM TABLEC...)
```

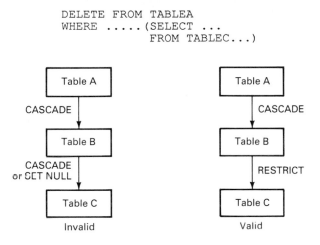

Cycles

Another restriction on deletions is that a table must not be delete-connected to itself. This means that in a cycle, there must be at least two delete rules that are RESTRICT or SET NULL. For example:

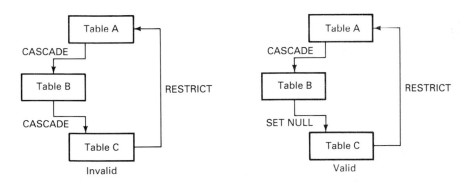

For a self-referencing cycle, the delete rule must be CASCADE. Also, deletions cannot be made using a cursor.

DB2 does check for invalid delete rules when a table is being created and will not allow an invalid situation to be defined. An error message is returned that identifies that problem.

LOAD CONSIDERATIONS   Special processing is required when the tables in a cycle are being loaded, since the first table loaded will not have a parent table available for checking foreign key values. Suppose that we have defined the following tables:

Table	Primary Key	Foreign Key
DEPT	DEPTNO	EMPNO referencing EMPLOYEE
EMPLOYEE	EMPNO	DEPTNO referencing DEPT

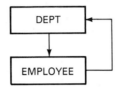

If we load *Dept* before loading *Employee,* the foreign key values in *Employee* cannot be checked. If we load *Employee* before *Dept,* the foreign key values in *Dept* cannot be checked.

Several methods can be used to handle this situation. In the first method, one table is created and loaded without specifying its foreign key. After the second table is loaded, the foreign key is added to the first table via an ALTER statement. This places the first table in check-pending status. The CHECK DATA function of the CHECK utility can then be used to check for referential constraint violations and to clear the check-pending status. The sequence of operations is as follows:

1. CREATE DEPT (no foreign key)
2. CREATE UNIQUE INDEX on DEPT
3. LOAD DEPT

4. CREATE EMPLOYEE (with foreign key)
5. CREATE UNIQUE INDEX on EMPLOYEE
6. LOAD EMPLOYEE (with ENFORCE = YES)

7. ALTER DEPT (add foreign key)
8. CHECK DATA in DEPT

The second method involves loading a table without specifying the EN-FORCE option to check for referential integrity violations. After both tables are loaded, CHECK DATA is used to check for referential integrity violations. Here the sequence of operations is as follows:

1. CREATE DEPT (with foreign key)
2. CREATE UNIQUE INDEX on DEPT
3. LOAD DEPT (with ENFORCE = NO)

4. CREATE EMPLOYEE (with foreign key)
5. CREATE UNIQUE INDEX on EMPLOYEE
6. LOAD EMPLOYEE (with ENFORCE = YES)

7. CHECK DATA in DEPT

A third method can be used if there is a small number of rows in one of the tables. Here we insert rows in one of the tables with null values for the foreign key. After the second table is loaded, we update the first table to add actual foreign key values. The sequence of operations is as follows:

1. CREATE DEPT (with foreign key)
2. CREATE UNIQUE INDEX on DEPT
3. INSERT rows into DEPT (with null values for EMPNO)

4. CREATE EMPLOYEE (with foreign key)
5. CREATE UNIQUE INDEX on EMPLOYEE
6. LOAD EMPLOYEE (with ENFORCE = YES)

7. UPDATE rows in DEPT (with actual values for EMPNO)

A final method that can be used is to load both tables into a single table space in a single execution of the LOAD utility. For this, the sequence of operations is as follows:

1. CREATE DEPT (with foreign key)
2. CREATE UNIQUE INDEX on DEPT

3. CREATE EMPLOYEE (with foreign key)
4. CREATE UNIQUE INDEX on EMPLOYEE

5. LOAD DEPT and EMPLOYEE (with ENFORCE = YES)

INDEX

A

Active log, 214
Administrative privileges, 232–33
All-key table, 14
Alternate keys, 15
ALTER statement, SQL, 202, 207
ALTER TABLESPACE statement,
    SQL, 204
ALTER TABLE statement, SQL,
    97, 205
ANSI/SPARC architecture, 36–37
Application Development Facility
    (ADF), 4
Application plan catalog tables, 209
Application plan privileges, 231.
    234
Application System (AS), 4, 251–70
    accessing files and tables, 253–54
    applications, 252
    arithmetic expressions, 256–57
    business graphics, 262
    cancelling a selection, 260
    command language, 254–55
    entering SQL statements, 254
    HISTOGRAM command, 264–65
    interactive processing, 252
    languages, 265–69

    logical expressions, 258–59
    operating environment, 253
    output files and tables, 260–61
    PLOT command, 262–63
    PROCEDURE language, 267, 270
    report generation, 257–58
    sorting, 260–61
    statement continuation, 257
    VIEW command, 255–56
    viewing selected rows, 259–60
Archive log, 214
Assembler language, 154–55
Atomic data item, 12
ATTACH statement, AS, 253–54
Attribute, 11–12
Authorization, 9, 170–71, 229
Authorization catalog tables, 210,
    236–37

B

Base table, 37
Basic sequential access method
    (BSAM), 219
Binding, 169–70
Bootstrap data set (BSDS), 214,
    217

The Conceptual Prism of
Information Systems:

THE JAMES MARTIN BO

Information Systems Management and Strategy

- AN INFORMATION SYSTEMS MANIFESTO
- INFORMATION ENGINEERING (Volume I: Introduction and Principles)
- INFORMATION ENGINEERING (Volume II: Strategy and Analysis)
- STRATEGIC INFORMATION PLANNING METHODOLOGIES (second edition)
- SOFTWARE MAINTENANCE: THE PROBLEM AND ITS SOLUTIONS
- DESIGN AND STRATEGY FOR DISTRIBUTED DATA PROCESSING
- CORPORATE COMMUNICATIONS STRATEGY

Expert Systems

- BUILDING EXPERT SYSTEMS: A TUTORIAL
- KNOWLEDGE ACQUISITION FOR EXPERT SYSTEMS

Methodologies for Building Systems

- STRATEGIC INFORMATION PLANNING METHODOLOGIES (second edition)
- INFORMATION ENGINEERING (Volume I: Introduction and Principles)
- INFORMATION ENGINEERING (Volume II: Strategy and Analysis)
- INFORMATION ENGINEERING (Volume III: Design and Construction)
- STRUCTURED TECHNIQUES: THE BASIS FOR CASE (revised edition)

Diagramming Techniques

- DIAGRAMMING TECHNIQUES FOR ANALYSTS AND PROGRAMMERS
- RECOMMENDED DIAGRAMMING STANDARDS FOR ANALYSTS AND PROGRAMMERS
- DIAGRAMMING STANDARDS FOR CASE
- ACTION DIAGRAMS: CLEARLY STRUCTURED SPECIFICATIONS, PROGRAMS, AND PROCEDURES (second edition)

Analysis and Design

- STRUCTURED TECHNIQUES: THE BASIS FOR CASE (revised edition)
- DATABASE ANALYSIS AND DESIGN
- DESIGN OF MAN-COMPUTER DIALOGUES
- DESIGN OF REAL-TIME COMPUTER SYSTEMS
- DATA COMMUNICATIONS DESIGN TECHNIQUES
- DESIGN AND STRATEGY FOR DISTRIBUTED DATA PROCESSING
- SOFTWARE MAINTENANCE: THE PROBLEM AND ITS SOLUTIONS
- SYSTEM DESIGN FROM PROVABLY CORRECT CONSTRUCTS
- INFORMATION ENGINEERING (Volume II: Strategy and Analysis)
- INFORMATION ENGINEERING (Volume III: Design and Construction)
- SAA: IBM's SYSTEMS APPLICATION ARCHITECTURE

CAS

- STRUCTURED T THE BASIS F (revised ed
- DIAGRAMMING FOR C
- INFORMATION E (Volume I: In and Princ

Languages and F

- APPLICATION DE WITHOUT PROG
- FOURTH-GEN LANGUA (Volume I: P
- FOURTH-GEN LANGUA (Volume II: Repres
- FOURTH-GEN LANGUA (Volume III: 4G
- ACTION DIAGRAM STRUCTURED SPE PROGRAMS, AND (second e